THE ROUTLEDGE INTRODUCTION TO NATIVE AMERICAN LITERATURE

This *Introduction* makes available for student, instructor, and aficionado a refined set of tools for decolonizing our approaches prior to entering the unfamiliar landscape of Native American literatures. This book will introduce indigenous perspectives and traditions as articulated by indigenous authors whose voices have been a vital, if often overlooked, component of the American dialogue for more than 400 years. Paramount to this consideration of Native-centered reading is the understanding that literature was not something bestowed upon Native peoples by the settler culture, either through benevolent interventions or violent programs of forced assimilation. Native literature precedes colonization, and Native stories and traditions have their roots in both the precolonized and the decolonizing worlds. As this far-reaching survey of Native literary contributions will demonstrate, almost without fail, when indigenous writers elected to enter into the world of western *letters*, they did so with the intention of maintaining indigenous culture and community. Writing was and always remains a strategy for survival.

Drew Lopenzina is Associate Professor at Old Dominion University and teaches in the intersections of Early American and Native American literatures. His 2017 book, *Through an Indian's Looking Glass* (University of Massachusetts Press), is a cultural biography of nineteenth-century Pequot activist and minister William Apess. Lopenzina is also the author of *Red Ink: Native Americans Picking up the Pen in the Colonial Period* (SUNY Press 2012). The journal *American Studies* has called *Red Ink* "an impressively thorough and often compelling study" that "extends the bounds and enriches our understanding of Native American Literary history." Lopenzina's essays appear in the journals *Early American Literature, Native American and Indigenous Studies, American Literature, American Quarterly, Studies in American Indian Literature, American Indian Quarterly,* and others.

"Offering a historical context from which students can understand the participation of Native American writers in literacy practices from the start, Lopienza challenges readers to rethink what he calls the 'rhetorical firewall between modern perceptions of oral and literate cultures,' that has led to an underappreciation of the complex legacy of the Native American literary canon. A valuable tool for students and teachers alike."

—**Vanessa Holford Diana**, Westfield State University

ROUTLEDGE INTRODUCTIONS TO AMERICAN LITERATURE

Series Editors: D. Quentin Miller and Wendy Martin

Routledge Introductions to American Literature provide critical introductions to the most important topics in American Literature, outlining the key literary, historical, cultural, and intellectual contexts. Providing students with an analysis of the most up-to-date trends and debates in the area, they also highlight exciting new directions within the field and open the way for further study.

Volumes examine the ways in which both canonical and lesser known writers from diverse class and cultural backgrounds have shaped American literary traditions, addressing key contemporary and theoretical debates, and giving attention to a range of voices and experiences as a vital part of American life. These comprehensive volumes offer readable, cohesive narratives of the development of American Literature and provide ideal introductions for students.

Available in this series:

The Routledge Introduction to African American Literature
D. Quentin Miller

The Routledge Introduction to American Modernism
Linda Wagner-Martin

The Routledge Introduction to American Women Writers
Wendy Martin, Sharone Williams

The Routledge Introduction to American War Literature
Jennifer Haytock

The Routledge Introduction to American Postmodernism
Linda Wagner-Martin

The Routledge Introduction to Native American Literature
Drew Lopenzina

THE ROUTLEDGE INTRODUCTION TO NATIVE AMERICAN LITERATURE

Drew Lopenzina

NEW YORK AND LONDON

First published 2020
by Routledge
52 Vanderbilt Avenue, New York, NY 10017

and by Routledge
2 Park Square, Milton Park, Abingdon, Oxon OX14 4RN

Routledge is an imprint of the Taylor & Francis Group, an informa business

© 2020 Taylor & Francis

The right of Drew Lopenzina to be identified as author of this work has been asserted by him in accordance with sections 77 and 78 of the Copyright, Designs and Patents Act 1988.

All rights reserved. No part of this book may be reprinted or reproduced or utilised in any form or by any electronic, mechanical, or other means, now known or hereafter invented, including photocopying and recording, or in any information storage or retrieval system, without permission in writing from the publishers.

Trademark notice: Product or corporate names may be trademarks or registered trademarks, and are used only for identification and explanation without intent to infringe.

Library of Congress Cataloging-in-Publication Data
A catalog record for this title has been requested

ISBN: 978-1-138-29125-6 (hbk)
ISBN: 978-1-138-63024-6 (pbk)
ISBN: 978-1-315-20972-2 (ebk)

Typeset in Bembo
by Taylor & Francis Books

CONTENTS

List of figures   *viii*
Acknowledgments   *x*

Introduction to the Introduction: Entering Native Space   1

1   Oral Encounters: Moving the Forest and Rocks by Song   18

2   "Still the Same Unbelieving Indian": Native Voices in the Emerging Republic   41

3   Red Progressives and Indian "Pass-Words"   65

4   Sunset, Sunrise: The American Indian Novel and the Dawning of the Native American Literary Renaissance   88

5   "Many of Our Songs Are Maps": Poetry in the Native American Literary Renaissance and Beyond   113

6   "Every One of Those Stars Has a Story": Narrative and Nationhood   134

7   Teaching Louise Erdrich's *Tracks*: A Case Study   158

Conclusion: Greetings from Standing Rock   184

Appendix: Sample Syllabus for Native American Literature   *190*
Index   *195*

FIGURES

I.1 Frontispiece to the 1738 *A Sermon Preached on the Occasion of the Execution of Katherine Garret, an Indian Servant*, Courtesy American Antiquarian Society   3
I.2 Engraving of Pocohontas. Unidentified artist, copy after Simon van de Passe. Publisher William Richardson/ Engraving on paper, 1793/ National Portrait Gallery, Smithsonian Institution   7
1.1 Interpretation of Caleb Cheeshateaumauk commissioned by the Harvard Foundation Portraiture Project and on display at Harvard University's Annenberg Hall. Image used with permission of the artist, Stephen Coit. All rights reserved   22
1.2 Artist's rendition of Cahokia by Lloyd K. Townsend. Courtesy of Cahokia Mounds State Historic Site   32
1.3 The Great Council Belt of the Five Nations as depicted in Arthur Parker's *Seneca Myths & Folktales*. Courtesy American Antiquarian Society   34
1.4 Commemoration Belts of the Five Nations recording events and alliances, from "The Constitution of the Five Nations," *Parker on the Iroquois*. Courtesy American Antiquarian Society   35
2.1 Felix Octavius Carr Darley, "John Eliot Preaching to the Indians," Drawings: 1999.368.2, Metropolitan Museum of Art   44
2.2 John White, "Village of Secoton," Watercolor, circa 1685, British Museum, London   45

2.3	Engraving from William Apess's 1831 *A Son of the Forest*. Courtesy American Antiquarian Society	52
3.1	"An Omaha Dance given by the prisoners on the solicitation and to please their new friends in St. Augustine as well as to amuse themselves." Courtesy Beinecke Rare Book and Manuscript Library, Yale University	76
4.1	Rand McNally and Company 1892 *Map of the Indian and Oklahoma Territories*. [Smithsonian Institute, 1892] Map. www.loc.gov/item/98687110/. Courtesy Library of Congress, Geography and Map Division	89
7.1	Illustration of "The Woman Who Loved a Serpent Who Lived in a Lake" by Passamaquoddy artist Joseph Tomah. *The Algonquin Legends of New England or Myths and Folk Lore of the Micmac, Passamaquoddy, and Penobscot Tribes* by Charles G. Leland (1884). Courtesy of the Maine historical Society	168
C.1	November 2016 view of the Oceti Sakowin campsite and the Missouri River at Standing Rock (author's photo)	185

ACKNOWLEDGMENTS

While writing this book I attempted to draw from my years of experience teaching classes in Native American Literature, but I was reminded every step of the way of the debt owed my own teachers, both in and out of the classroom, who helped shape this journey. I have endless appreciation for Siobhan Senier, John Ernest, Brigitte Bailey, and all my other professors at the University of New Hampshire for their ethical guidance, wisdom, and expertise. They demonstrated that being a teacher and a mentor involves more than just time spent in the classroom, and my career would have been much more improbable without the time they graciously extended beyond the classroom to help me develop ideas and enter upon my own path of scholarship. It is a practice, a way of being, that I have always tried to emulate and extend to my own students when possible.

I am also indebted to the great network of indigenous friends and scholars who have guided me along the way. They include, but are certainly not limited to, Lisa Brooks, Margaret Bruchac, Melissa Tantaquidgeon Zobel, Rae Gould, Jace and Laura Weaver, Joyce Rain Anderson, Ron Welburn, Cheryl Savageau, Rhonda Anderson, Donna Moody, Karenne Wood, and others. They have proven to be a community of sharp-witted, poetic, activist scholars and thinkers whose example, commitment, generosity, and passion have fortified me at various stages of writing this book.

It would also be impossible to map out the endless ways that my students, over the years, either creatively pushed back, added something new, or afforded me opportunity to look at certain materials in a different light, transforming the entire constellation of connections and meanings around which a semester coheres. Although I could not name them all here, I am endlessly grateful to those students who, through their willingness to learn and engage at a high level, made the study of indigenous literatures a truly collaborative venture. Some of them, I am both happy and proud to say, are teachers now themselves, and their work continues to inspire and energize me.

And, as always, I am grateful to my family for all their patience and love.

I may as well also acknowledge that Native American Literature is difficult to teach. To do it properly requires so much more than simple good will or a love of diverse literatures. There is no real comfort zone here. Regardless of who you are, it will be incumbent upon you to teach materials pertaining to an identity or culture other than your own, and there is a responsibility to get it right—to not contribute to the endless layers of misrepresentation and falsehood that have resulted in so much cultural, physical, and spiritual struggle for America's indigenous peoples. There is a great deal to celebrate in Native literature, both past and present, but there is also a great deal of painful terrain to be charted that must not be swept under the rug, and it can test the capacities of teachers and students. But it can also lift us all up and bring out what is best in us. Particularly in trying times, it is sometimes all we can do to lean in the direction of hope and, with patient determination, tell the story in a good way, in a manner that, in accordance with Haudenosaunee tradition, imagines the richest possible future for those yet seven generations separated from ourselves.

INTRODUCTION TO THE INTRODUCTION

Entering Native Space

In 2012 Anishinaabe author Louise Erdrich received the National Book Award for her novel *The Round House*, a story told from the perspective of Joe Coutts, a 13-year-old boy whose life is upended when his mother is brutally raped on (or near) the Indian reservation on which they live. Although the award was certainly deserved, it might easily be viewed as belated acknowledgment for a long, unparalleled career of astonishing work by an American author who also just happens to be Native American. Included in Erdrich's oeuvre of 17 novels, three books of poetry, seven children's books, numerous short stories, and multiple works of non-fiction can be found some of the most richly drawn characters and landscapes in contemporary American letters. The world Erdrich has summoned in prose (mostly centered in and around the fictional Little No Horse reservation in North Dakota) is one of layered human complexity, poetic beauty, historical breadth, bawdy humor, and *tragic wisdom* that, while immersing us in the rich emotional worlds of her protagonists, also presents a lucid and often biting perspective on what it means to claim a Native identity in America today.

Erdrich is often celebrated for her poetic prose and the intricate layers of interwoven narrative voices that inform her work—a style that, in its intimate attention to place and identity has been compared to that of William Faulkner. *The Round House*, however, offered a stylistic departure for Erdrich in regards to its polemic directness and consistent first-person perspective. This more pared-down style suggests a deliberate effort on Erdrich's part to reach a wider audience and to get America to focus its limited attention span on issues of sexual violence and outright predation that persist to this day on Indian reservations and First Nation reserves across the North American continent. That predation has been the direct result of lax law enforcement and ambiguous legal frameworks regarding jurisdiction that appear almost deliberately designed to invite abuse. As

Erdrich noted in the brief afterword to her novel, the international watchdog group Amnesty International has gone so far as to declare the ongoing legacy of sexual assaults upon Native women in the United States (86% of which are perpetrated by non-Native men) an ongoing humanitarian crisis.[1]

Erdrich stands alongside Spokane Indian author Sherman Alexie (whose *Absolutely True Diary of a Part-Time Indian* has recently made an indelible mark on the YAL scene) and Muskogee Creek poet Joy Harjo, named U.S. Poet Laureate in 2019, as one of the few highly visible writers of Native American literature today. Her novels often make national best-seller lists, she has won widespread acclaim, and she has been the recipient of some of America's highest literary honors. This *Introduction to Native American Literature* will examine the contributions of Erdrich, Alexie, and Harjo to the literary scene and the many questions provoked by their works. But it is also important to recognize that these authors are only three strands in a large and ever-expanding network of Native American literary accomplishments. In fact, Native Americans have been picking up the pen and recording their experiences on paper for far longer than most readers suspect. And contemporary Native writers often construct their narratives upon a profound understanding and appreciation of this web of oral and literary traditions that remains unrealized by most non-Native audiences.

This *Introduction to Native American Literature* is designed to serve as an aid to those who wish to read, study, teach, or simply enjoy Native American literature. Literature, of course, is written to be encountered and appreciated without necessitating the added burden of supplemental reading. But the very purpose of literary studies has ever been to open up the world of textual encounter in ways that are not always immediately evident in one's isolated engagement with a particular book or author. Acquiring a deeper understanding of an author's life, craft, influences, and the complicated cultural contexts that inform any given work of literature will often generate new awarenesses, new meanings, and new connections that help to inform and enrich one's life. One of the reasons audiences turn to Native literature is in hopes of learning more about Native lifeways and perspectives. But many, upon entering the world of Native literature, can feel themselves on uncertain ground. Reading about a culture of which so little is generally known can be a disorienting experience, rendering readers as tourists without a guidebook, unable to speak the local language and uncertain as to what exactly is being witnessed and why it should matter. There is always the risk that, in the end, we leave the experience with an imperfect understanding of what was actually encountered. The revealed daily exterior of a particular environment cannot readily offer up the rich complex composition of stories, histories, traditions, victories, losses, and overall resiliencies that mark the inner life of the community.

Which brings us back to Louise Erdrich. It is helpful to consider that, even as Erdrich's *The Round House* offers an approachable narrative vehicle by which readers may enter into the extremely difficult and painful topic of sexual violence endemic to Indian reservations, the issue takes on an even more layered urgency when we understand that the earliest example of an indigenous authored narrative text to appear in print in North America was written in 1737 by a Native woman of the Pequot tribe named Katherine Garret. Garret, known in the Connecticut colony where she lived as "Indian Kate," found herself embroiled in a legal battle of her own over the violation and control of her body in Puritan New England. She was ultimately hanged for the crime of infanticide. Although in court she stridently maintained her innocence, in the 1738 publication of her "Confession" (assembled by the Puritan reverend, Eliphalet Adams), she was made to pronounce her own guilt to the local magistrates, "left under her own hand," as she was (to the great surprise of many), a *writing* Indian schooled in western forms of literacy.[2]

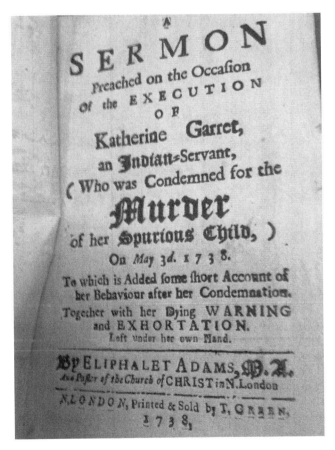

FIGURE I.1 Frontispiece to the 1738 *A Sermon Preached on the Occasion of the Execution of Katherine Garret, an Indian Servant*, Courtesy American Antiquarian Society

Then, as now, the legal system was not engineered to protect and promote the rights of Natives. Rather, it was designed to maintain the propriety and power of the dominant white class. No one, throughout Katherine Garret's trial, thought to enquire as to who the father of the child might be or under what circumstances her pregnancy occurred. No one in eighteenth-century New England either cared or bothered to ask whether her sexual liaison was coerced or consensual, an act of violence or an act of passion. The actual circumstances of her "crime" are something that we, today, can never truly know. But one thing we do know is that Native women were among the most unprotected and vulnerable class of humans in colonial New England and, as such, were constantly exposed to unwanted advances and abuses. The matter of Garret's confession was never in doubt. She ultimately had no agency to defy the will of the colonial power structure that accused and sentenced her. "Indian Kate" was forced, on the day of her execution, to march from the jailhouse to the gallows, following the horse-drawn cart that carried her coffin, with the rope by which she would be hanged already fastened around her neck. According to the Reverend Adams, who in the account given of these events comes across as deeply affected by her composure in the face of death, "she past [sic] out of life, in the posture of one praying."[3]

Worth noting, then, is that, when Louise Erdrich takes on the issue of sexual violation in Native space in her literature, she is not speaking to a concern specific to our own time or to the Anishinaabe alone, but rather to a pattern of violations that have been repeated and exacerbated over the course of some 400 or more years, invoking cycles of *generational trauma* that are a direct result of the unequal protections afforded by a *settler-colonial* power structure. Today, at the time of this writing, according to statistics gathered from the Department of Justice, it is conservatively estimated that one in three indigenous women in America will be raped in their lifetimes, a rate 2.5 times higher than the national average. If you were to teach *The Round House*, it would be helpful to have your students read some or all of Amnesty International's investigative report, *Maze of Injustice: The Failure to Protect Indigenous Women from Sexual Violence in the USA*, which details the labyrinthine cultural and legal structures that allow for this reprehensible abuse to continue in our country, unabated and largely in media silence.[4] But you might also wish to visit Kathrine Garret's short narrative, because, in a sense, the writings of Garret and Erdrich form literary bookends between which the systemic abuses we see occurring today trace directly back to a colonial past and to the good Puritan fathers from whom the U.S. claims so much of its national identity. The key to ending the cycles of trauma engendered by such a history may very well lie in creating an audience of listeners (readers) who comprehend, are in sympathy with, and openly acknowledge the strands of violence that connect Garret's coerced confession to Erdrich's powerful testimonial of contemporary indigenous *survivance*.

Begin Where You Are

Perhaps when you decided, or were asked, to teach Native American literature, generational cycles of sexual violence were not what you had in mind. But the question remains, once you know about it, can it be ignored? Still, you might want to wade into these waters more cautiously. It is always a good idea, when teaching Native literature, to begin where you are. Ask your students to look around and seek signs of indigenous presence in their surroundings. How is the space in which you are currently located also what Abenaki scholar Lisa Brooks would call "Native space"? Lisa King, who is Lenape, has written that, if she could go back in time to when she was a graduate student first teaching Native literature classes, she would remind herself to

> start small and local, to remember the land, the place, and the first peoples there ... to do my work well means that each time I am in a new place, by default, I must read up on the history, build relationships with the Native community there, and make use of the resources available (Internet! Libraries! Native American organizations on campus!).[5]

None of these things will fall immediately into place on your first or second go round, but they are important standards to keep in mind and will help ground your discourse in the Native space you occupy.

For me, that space just happens to be Eastern Virginia, not far from First Landing State Park and Historic Jamestown, ground zero in regards to English settlement on this continent. As such, it is no coincidence that the geography of my community is mapped out in street names such as Pocahontas Street, Powhatan Ave, Matoaka Ave, Orapax, Omohundro—names taken directly from documents of Virginia's early colonization. There's a lot to work with there, and also ample reason to interrogate why our geography is plotted out with these namesakes despite the fact that there is little else here to visibly suggest how Native people have survived the seventeenth century. My students are often surprised to learn that there are today 13 different state-recognized tribes in Virginia, 7 of which are now recognized on the federal level as well.

But perhaps you live in Utah, Illinois, or Massachusetts. Where did these state names come from? What is the history behind them? And, perhaps more importantly, where are those people now, and how do they continue to define themselves as a culture? Most tribes today have official websites, and you can learn a lot by going to these pages and finding out what are their activities, projects, and concerns. A good first-day exercise is to get students thinking about both the practical and symbolic meanings of local indigenous presence and use this as a springboard for further course planning and discussion. Once you have delved deeply into the indigenous history of your region, as informed by indigenous authors and scholars, you will find the knowledge you gain will resonate in useful ways as you discuss other regions and writings.

For me, living on the intersection of Pocahontas Ave and John Smith Boulevard, there is obviously a great deal to talk about, and the story of Pocahontas can be a good place to begin a semester. It is an essential American myth that most students know something about, having watched the Disney movie as children. Students are typically invested in this narrative and yet curiously willing to participate in its deconstruction—up to a point. There is a great deal of colorful source material to which educators can turn, a wealth of nineteenth-century paintings depicting the "rescue" of John Smith, a plethora of children's books, the 1870s-era statue in my local museum which portrays Pocahontas as an ivory-white child saint contemplating the cross, or the Simon van de Passe engraving of Pocahontas which she actually sat for during her 1616–17 visit to England. Students will be puzzled why the name "Matoaka als Rebecca" appears under her likeness in the portrait. They are also often genuinely surprised to learn that Pocahontas died in England, at a place called Gravesend along the River Thames, having grown ill aboard ship while waiting to return home. She was, in fact, buried in this place, and, because the church burned down in the nineteenth century, her remains can never be located or fully repatriated. But it is also useful to remind students of the unreliable nature of colonial history-keeping in general, and how the romantic myths that have been built up and endlessly perpetuated around the actual historical figure of Pocahontas provide a surprisingly effective historical smoke screen that works to conceal much of the underlying violence of colonialism.[6]

For instance, we can admit, at last, that Pocahontas probably never rescued John Smith from death at the hands of her father, or, if she did, it was not because she had fallen head over heels for this belligerent white stranger who was unapologetically there to strip her people of land and resources. Some have suggested that the famous "rescue" scene, if we can credit it at all, was in fact a ceremony designed to incorporate Smith into the kinship networks of the Powhatan confederacy in an attempt to situate him within tribally recognized hierarchies.[7] From an indigenous perspective, such a ceremony may have been a timeworn strategy for making peace with uncooperative new neighbors. Then again, it is worth noting that the story of his rescue was one Smith himself had neglected to communicate to seventeenth-century audiences until well over a decade after the fact, when Pocahontas was being welcomed as a royal dignitary and minor celebrity during her 1616 tour of England. The western world was curious about this exotic "FILLA POTENTISS: PRINC: POWHATANI IMP: VIRGINIA," and Smith may have elaborated on a number of old folk tales to concoct a crowd-pleasing yarn that effectively drew attention to himself by exploiting public interest in this seemingly exotic young woman. And let's face it. He completely nailed it. We've been telling the story ever since.

This should not distract us from the fact that the early Jamestown settlers, Smith included, were nothing less than brutal in their dealings with the local Virginia Natives of Tsenacomocah (the indigenous name for what we now call Eastern Virginia). Their settlement was poorly planned and ill prepared to survive

FIGURE I.2 Engraving of Pocohontas. Unidentified artist, copy after Simon van de Passe. Publisher William Richardson/Engraving on paper, 1793/ National Portrait Gallery, Smithsonian Institution

in a land of which the would-be-planters knew virtually nothing. The English were almost constantly on the brink of starvation, and it was only through the agricultural surplus of Native peoples that they managed to survive at all. This is important to emphasize, because, yes, the Natives of Virginia were agricultural people, not hunter gatherers. They lived in villages, not in dense forests, they had intricate laws, traditions, and religious customs, and they had cultivated a practical and spiritual relationship with the region rooted in thousands of years of occupancy. When the Natives' initial attempts at customary hospitality wore out and the Jamestown settlers could no longer strike an acceptable bargain to trade for food (Powhatan quickly determined that he preferred guns over useless trinkets), the settlers resorted to violence. It's all there in the narratives that the settlers themselves wrote. Check out George Percy's report, for instance, in which he describes in detail the horrific 1610 slaughter of the local Paspehegh village, the burning of their temples, the drowning of innocent children, and the rape and murder of the local "queen." Pocahontas herself was kidnapped by Samuel Argall in 1612, and it was only under this coercive pressure, as captive and witness to atrocities against her people, that she finally agreed to adopt the Christian faith and marry John Rolfe in an effort to establish peace. She played the role of diplomat in time of war. According to the oral tradition of the Mattaponi (the direct descendants of Pocahontas' indigenous community), Pocahontas was raped and impregnated during her captivity by none other than the governor of the colony, Thomas Dale, and it was because of this indelicacy that Rolfe, a handy vassal of the settlement, was called upon to marry her. Rolfe himself was working to develop a new strain of marketable Virginia tobacco. His efforts, most likely enabled by his newly established kinship relations with local Natives, led to the first commercially successful Virginia tobacco crop and cleared a path for the financial success of the colony. It also opened the door to African slavery in the region, and Rolfe, himself, was among the first group of planters to procure slave labor for the colony in 1619.

See what happens to our innocuous cultural romances when you wander off the beaten path and attempt to see things from a *decolonizing* perspective? Save for the Mattaponi tradition that Pocahontas was raped, everything I just related can be pulled directly from primary documents—the "interesting" and "true" narrative reports of the colonists themselves. You just have to learn to strip away the exceptionalist veneer, the forced Christian pieties, the insistence in all of this troubled literature that the "savage" indigenes brought their ill-fortunes upon themselves because they were a primitive and backward people who refused to play along with the demands of their God-ordained superiors. And this is where students, and so many others, can start to get uncomfortable. Because, when we begin to tell indigenous history, using indigenous strategies and stories, employing decolonized perspectives, we quickly find ourselves in a space that challenges most of our basic assumptions about what it means to be American. This is Native space.[8]

To Be of a Place

Of course, Native writers today are interested in much more than simply addressing and redressing historic wounds. Though the U.S. has been long enamored of narratives of Indian vanishing (best exemplified, perhaps, by James Fenimore Cooper's quintessential 1826 frontier novel *Last of the Mohicans*), in many parts of the U.S. tribal enrollments are on the rise as more and more people of indigenous descent rediscover and reclaim their heritages. The U.S. for a long time actively sought to discourage Native people from acknowledging their traditional identities and even created elaborate legal processes to disinherit Native peoples, whether through forced removal, federally funded boarding school programs, census practices that categorized Native peoples as "black" or "colored," or through government initiatives that simply attempted to "terminate" Indianness as a legal identity. Despite all of these daunting efforts, Native peoples are still here on "Turtle Island" (the name many indigenous people give to the North American continent). They are still claiming their traditional identities, still claiming sovereign title to their lands through treaty rights and original title claims, still holding onto their languages and spiritual traditions, and, perhaps most importantly, they are still telling their stories. In some ways, the ravages of living in a colonial world have even compelled Native writers to adopt more poignant and innovative strategies for storytelling, which often makes Native American literature some of the most compelling, creative, and exciting literature on the market today.

But just as when, for instance, we teach *The Scarlet Letter* in our classrooms and assume the need for at least a partial understanding of the history stretching from Puritan New England to the more progressive period of American Romanticism in which Hawthorne wrote, we need to do better at creating cultural and historical contexts for understanding Native American literatures. Hester Prynne's peculiar punishment and subsequent actions would fail to resonate with us if we did not share some common notions as to Christian concepts of sin, adultery, and the general tenor of seventeenth-century New England spirituality. Hawthorne's tossed off references to the "sainted Ann Hutchinson," "good Governor Winthrop," or the "apostle Eliot" and his "Indian converts" would be devoid of context if these weren't figures already taught in history and literature classes throughout the nation.[9]

What we take for granted when studying western narratives, however, can unravel in interesting ways when we encounter indigenous narratives where even common notions such as "original sin," "adultery," and "patriarchy," historically speaking at least, have no cultural foothold. Native narratives are very likely to invoke historical and spiritual touchstones that not only are unfamiliar to contemporary audiences, but that pose compelling challenges to the core values asserted by western culture. When Joy Harjo, for instance, tells of a "woman who fell from the sky" in her poem by the same name, readers may not realize how this "rather ordinary, though beautiful" woman bears resemblance to a figure from countless indigenous creation stories.[10] In Native stories, it is often woman, not man, who stands at the cosmological center of the universe and, rather than claiming dominion over the four-legged beasts, the swimmers, and the feathered beings, she works in cooperation with them to create the world in which we live. By the same token, when the Blackfoot protagonist of James Welch's novel *Fool's Crow* spiritually consummates his relationship with his father's third and youngest wife, there is no further moral recrimination or lingering concern for the state of his eternal soul. Monogamy is not a cultural expectation—the nineteenth-century Blackfeet world that Welch recreates for us operates under a system of values for understanding honor and right action that could not properly register in the world of Hester Prynne.

Therefore, in preparing to teach a semester (or even just a shorter session within a semester) of Native literature it is important that one tread with care and respect. At the very least, it must not be assumed that the same set of cultural materials and strategies that inform dominant interpretive strategies will translate seamlessly into the landscapes of reading "Native space." One may be highly critical of the imperialist aims of manifest destiny (the belief system by which the U.S. morally justifies its expansionist proclivities) and yet still not fully apprehend the deep structures of narrative bias embedded in the contiguous flow of representation, language, and thought by which the *settler colonial* world is constructed. Ubiquitous images of Indianness found in movies, books, advertisements, wall calendars, and sporting nicknames form a kind of cultural wallpaper around our lives, but bear little relation to the actual identities that Native peoples inhabit either in the past or present. In most cases, such representations of Indianness lack not only sensitivity, but any remote vestige of tribal specificity, lumping all "Indians" into a single monolithic group whose actions and tendencies are somehow all perfectly predictable to the modern sensibility. There is an expectation that Indians will be brave, fierce, noble, incapable of telling a lie, at one with nature, insensible to pain, and, of course, willing to fight to the death—which is also, not coincidentally, the Indian's fate in most of the stories told about them. As Thomas Builds the Fire points out in the movie *Smoke Signals*, however, despite the presumed cultural cachet of being perceived as a buffalo hunter, some Native people, such as the Spokane/Coeur d'Alene tribe to which he belongs, made their traditional livelihoods fishing for salmon—an occupation not nearly as romantic or picturesque.

So what does it mean to be Native on the North American continent in the first part of the twenty-first century? Muskogee critic and educator Daniel R. Wildcat has simply but elegantly noted that to be "indigenous means 'to be of a place.'"[11] What is suggested by this, is that indigenous lifeways, traditions, stories, and material culture are typically rooted in an intimate relationship with a particular geographic location—a relationship forged, most often, over thousands of years. That intimacy allows for an intricate understanding of local ecosystems, knowledge of plants and roots, a long-established sense of kinship with the other animated beings of that locale, and a tendency for the stories themselves to be rooted in the region's geographical features and peculiarities. There is nothing essentially supernatural or mysterious about these relationships, despite attempts by the dominant culture to romanticize or essentialize Native identity in such a manner. It is better understood as deep, layered knowledge passed from generation to generation—a knowledge that cannot be readily usurped or assimilated by the colonizing culture that has blustered in and attempted to project its own usages upon the landscape. The results of western culture's comparatively recent imperialist project have, in fact, been disastrous for both the ecology of North America and for the indigenous peoples who have long lived here.

It is, in part, owing to this disastrous intrusion that Native people have become such vigilant keepers of their local histories. Although mainstream educational programs will cautiously skirt around a small handful of "representative" histories—events such as Sand Creek, the Trail of Tears, Wounded Knee—such moments can often serve as a kind of shorthand that ostensibly pleads forgiveness for the isolated wrongdoings of a colonial past before sweeping them under the rug of memory. They are problematic labels that invoke pity while also laboring to hurry Native peoples off the historical stage to make room for a seemingly more upbeat and progressive narrative of American modernity. Students I talk to have, perhaps, heard of the above-mentioned events and even think of them as ready exemplars of the irresponsible use of American power, but, upon further interrogation, they really have no inkling of what actually transpired in these moments or how sustained and systemic was the brutality by which the Americas were torn from indigenous hands. For Native people, these histories are much more difficult to forget, and this often makes them bearers of what Anishinaabe scholar Gerald Vizenor calls "tragic wisdom." In other words, Native people are often forced to bear witness to a history that the rest of America has willfully displaced.

This is why it is so important for those who teach Native literature to take time to try to see and understand this literature from a very local, indigenous perspective. Recent Native scholars such as Robert Warrior, Lisa Brooks, Craig Womack, and Daniel Heath Justice have urged instructors to find ways of centering their work in the epistemological underpinnings of the tribal worlds they are studying—to understand that not all indigenous experiences are the same, and to think about the cultural, historical, spiritual, and even legal concerns so deeply influential on the construction of Native literatures within disparate tribal settings. For instance, when I teach the writings of nineteenth-century Pequot author William Apess, I begin by informing my students of how the Pequot and Mohegan were initially one nation driven apart by the pressures of colonization. We discuss how this division occurred in a conflict that has come to be known as the 1636–37 Pequot War, and how that war, although purportedly waged to stem Pequot aggression, had much more to do with the historic position the Pequot held in the Northeast wampum trade. To understand the significance of all this, however, students will also have to know something of the spiritual significance of wampum to the Native Northeast as well as the commercial implications of the wampum trade in the colonized world. Apess mentions none of these things in his writings, and yet (as will be discussed in more detail in Chapter 2) they are essential to comprehending the economic and cultural fragmentation of the Pequot people when Apess emerges on the scene in 1829, becoming the first Native of North America to write and publish a book-length narrative of his life.

My sense is that a lot of us who teach Native literature classes want to jump quickly to the 1970s and 80s—a time known as the Native American Literary Renaissance, where a great deal of important and beautifully crafted literature was introduced to American audiences by authors such as N. Scott Momaday, Leslie Marmon Silko, Simon Ortiz, and others. Instructors may choose to begin with a few indigenous origin stories, and certainly Zitkala-Sa's nineteenth-century boarding school narrative, "School Days of an Indian Girl," has firmly lodged itself in the canon, but then it's on to the late twentieth century. I would like to make an appeal here, however, in the opening passages of this book, for educators to consider the importance of recognizing earlier contributions by Native writers, going all the way back to the nineteenth and even the eighteenth and seventeenth centuries. This earlier literature often appears more challenging to teach as it typically comes wrapped in what today may seem like dreary antiquated conventions of early American rhetorical style. But it remains useful to demonstrate how Native people, such as Katherine Garret, have been fashioning their messages to meet the demands of western audiences for a long time.

Once students get past the unfamiliar rhetorical terrain of the writing styles adopted by individuals such as Mohegan minister Samson Occom or the Pequot activist William Apess, they will be able to discover what is particularly indigenous about these texts and how Native writers fought to insert themselves into the national dialogue in creative and compelling manner. It is instructive for students to see how Native peoples of earlier centuries were not simply "children of the forest" or hunter-gatherers living off the fruits of the land. They were not exclusively the tomahawk-wielding savages enshrined in the *Last of the Mohicans* frontier genre of nineteenth-century narratives. They were, rather, family members, inhabitants of villages, communities, political systems, and nations, intellectually engaged in the events unfolding around them, and resisting colonialism through every means available to them, using diplomacy, wit, and on occasion forceful retaliation, as they struggled for cultural survival in an age of great and violent upheaval. In some cases, as one student recently commented after reading William Apess, they were even "*super woke.*" And, like the rest of us, they saw the value of converting their experiences into literature. When we are introduced to this earlier literature, we not only gain a deeper appreciation for how Native people have articulated their struggles over time, but we are provided a stronger foundation for engaging with the rich body of literature that follows.

Although it would be impractical, if not impossible, to detail the literary contributions of all of America's 570 plus recognized and unrecognized Indian nations, *Introduction to Native American Literature* will attempt to provide a helpful overview allowing for a deeper engagement with the narrative traditions many Native writers draw upon as they come forward to tell their stories. Rather than simply offering an author-by-author analysis, however, or focusing on a handful of specific books as case studies, this *Introduction* intends to engage with a larger network of cultural, historical, and critical concerns that will assist readers in beginning to comprehend and unpack the complex legacies of narrative tradition and colonial encounter that inform so much of contemporary Native literature. In the process, it will not only detail a pattern of colonial abuses and attempted genocide against Native peoples, but it will offer a kind of rhetorical road map of the literary and critical landscapes many Native writers and intellectuals traverse in their efforts at forging a *decolonized* literature and identity. Such a road map should prove useful in helping teachers navigate whichever Native texts they wish to incorporate into their semester's lesson plan or syllabi.

Of course, such a rhetorical roadmap would be devoid of orientation if it failed to identify a number of prominent critical landmarks to help define the current topography of Native Studies today. Native literature is not exclusively situated around these points, but nevertheless they will help give form to the overall landscape one passes through when encountering this body of work. At times, it may even be necessary to expand our view of what constitutes "literature" in order for us to apprehend these landmarks as more than simply inert earth, tree, and rock formations on the horizon, but rather as vital and animated elements of the overall story of tribal identity. Some of the issues considered most relevant to today's scholars and that this book intends to survey in its mapping of Native literature are as follows:

Sovereignty
Treaty rights
Tribal recognition
Repatriation of indigenous remains and artifacts
Education
Language preservation
Enrollment (who gets to call themselves "Indian"?)
Gender identity
Conditions on reservations (poverty, drug abuse, alcoholism, suicide rates, sexual abuse)
Continuance
Survivance
Kinship

Most of the themes enumerated here begin and end with recognition of America's indigenous peoples as *sovereign* entities whose relationship with the land is not so much spiritual as it is bound to their very sense of traditional, political, and legal identity. It is of utmost importance to understand that the designation of sovereignty is not simply a product of wish-fulfillment wrapped in a politically correct reimagining of settler colonial–indigenous relations. Rather, it is settled law founded in the constitutional framework of the U.S. government and in the structure of how indigenous groups define themselves. This is why, today, Native people living on reservations have their own tribal governments and law enforcement, even as they remain within the oversight of federal bureaucracies. Native peoples understand that they are the original caretakers of a particular space and that they hold what western systems of jurisprudence have come to recognize as "aboriginal title" to the lands they occupied prior to colonization. Continuously emphasizing the sovereignty of Native nations is a powerful way for Native people to keep their claims to the land and self-governance front and center while reminding the federal government of its obligations to America's first peoples.

As violent as the legacy of colonial appropriations has been, it has always relied upon the veneer of lawful action to legitimize its conquests. As such, some of the earliest engagements that indigenous peoples of North America had with western literacy can be located in land deeds and treaties, stretching back to the early seventeenth century. As David J. Carlson points out in his essay on "U.S.–Indian Treaty Relations," one of the first things William Bradford recorded when he stepped off the *Mayflower* in 1620 was the treaty the Pilgrims established with the Wampanoag leader Ousamequin (more popularly known as Massasoit). Treaty literature is an important component of Native literary history that includes both the written treaties preserved by colonizing forces and the indigenous record preserved in wampum belts and other mnemonic devices by Native peoples themselves. Wampum (which will be discussed in more detail in Chapter 1) was misunderstood by European colonizers as a kind of currency, or "Indian money" as it is often called, but it actually holds deep spiritual and diplomatic significance for eastern nations and was essential to the maintenance of peace in Native space. Whenever treaties were negotiated in this space, either an exchange of wampum was involved or it was simply not understood as binding by Native negotiators. It is instructive, in any study of this history of shared space, to note how western powers conformed to these diplomatic protocols in their relations with Native people and found themselves active, if unwitting, practitioners in the rhetorics of wampum exchange.

Western powers did not make treaties with Native people out of the goodness of their hearts or out of pity for a declining race. Treaties, properly understood, are agreements between sovereign nations, and they were orchestrated whenever matters could not be resolved through other means. Many of the earliest treaties that the U.S. made with indigenous peoples were necessitated by the fact that the new colonial government was depleted after 7 years of bloody conflict in its war for independence and needed to know that the Indian nations siding with the British would cease hostilities. It was from this position of indigenous strength that treaty law was instituted in U.S.—indigenous relations and Native people throughout the country have insisted, whenever possible, on compliance with these terms ever since. Of course, as Carlson points out, "reciprocal relations were not a nineteenth-century American goal," and many treaties were not negotiated out of a position of indigenous strength.[12] But even in such later cases, as Scott Lyons points out, Native people were often seeking the best terms they could extract from a difficult, often impossible, situation. With an eye toward future preservation, Native individuals left their "x-marks" on the pieces of paper pushed before them, often giving up great chunks of land and resources, but all the while maintaining their integrity as a coherent political entity or nation.[13]

It is largely through these treaties that Native landholdings, governing structures, and enrollments are defined and understood today. Often, one's right to claim a tribal identity is founded upon blood quantum and whether or not a family name can be traced back to a particular treaty roll. Treaties also form the basis for what the federal government apportions to indigenous nations in terms of goods and services. Far from taking advantage of what many have erroneously termed "Indian welfare," the bulk of benefits provided to Indian nations are given as lawful reparations for contractually promised goods and services that trace back to earlier treaties.

Even for tribes that have not been able to legally establish federal recognition (a prerequisite for receiving such federal reparations), the maintenance of treaty obligations remains an important legal and symbolic gesture. As I write today, the Mattaponi and five other Virginia Indian tribes have just received federal recognition after decades of lobbying for this status. The Mattaponi were once part of what the colonies came to refer to as the Powhatan confederacy and, as mentioned earlier, they count Pocahontas among their ancestors. But, as a result of records lost to history and a deliberate effort in the 1920s and 30s to eradicate Indian identity in Virginia by legally classifying all people of Native origin as "colored," the road to recognition was strewn with difficulties for this indigenous group, despite more than 400 years of uninterrupted tribal continuity that can easily be tracked back through the literature of the Jamestown colony. Even before federal recognition, however, the Mattaponi continued to observe the terms of a 1677 treaty made with the Virginia colony that, in return for land and protection, calls upon them to each year deliver a deer to the governor's mansion. By upholding their end of the treaty all these years, the Mattaponi maintained their historic and political relationship with the nation-state, perhaps to the chagrin of the state itself.[14]

The fact of the matter is that the U.S. has done a poor job of honoring its treaties with Native people and often makes no bones about the fact that it would like to be able to terminate those treaties altogether, even if, from a point of jurisprudence, that has proven extremely difficult to do. As will be recounted in further detail, the U.S. has a history of trying to eradicate Native culture through any means available, including war, murder, massacre, the deliberate disruption of families and communities, the outlawing of religions, disruption of languages—the list goes on. As a result of this complex stew of neglect, abuse, prejudice, and outright violence, Indian nations suffer high rates of poverty, drug abuse, alcoholism, suicide, and other indicators of second- or third-class citizenship that speak to the legacies of generational trauma that persist under a colonial regime. Restoring communities to their rightful places within fractured structures of traditional life is a major endeavor today and a concern reflected in a great deal of the literature that will be reviewed here. Cherokee scholar Jace Weaver refers to these efforts at strengthening the bonds of Native community as "communitism," an underlying ethos behind so many Native literary engagements. It is an endeavor also helpfully summed up in the word "survivance," which, as Vizenor notes, suggests both survival and resistance rolled into one. It remains a difficult path and one that is still daily obstructed by the power of the nation-state.

This *Introduction to Native American Literature* cannot hope to be comprehensive in its scope, but it will attempt to provide a thorough summation of what are generally thought to be the important periods and contributions relative to Native literary thought, being sure to provide relevant cultural contexts along the way and to point to the most authoritative additional resources wherever necessary. Moving chronologically, and ranging geographically over the entire North American continent, the book will begin with a discussion on oral and literary traditions preceding colonization and will, in effect, trace how Native people have carried many of those traditions forward, through various literary expressions and encounters, into our own times. Each chapter will focus on a specific era, to the extent that such eras can be defined and bracketed. The intention, however, is to provide enough of an overview so that readers will feel sufficiently confident to begin tracking their own course through the rich literary traditions of America's indigenous peoples.

This *Introduction* intends to make available for both student and instructor a refined set of tools for decolonizing our approaches prior to entering an unfamiliar literary landscape. Throughout, this book will privilege indigenous perspectives and traditions as articulated by indigenous authors who have been projecting their voices into the national dialogue for a period of roughly 400 years. Paramount to this consideration of Native-centered reading is the understanding that literature was not something bestowed upon Native peoples by the dominant white culture, either through benevolent interventions or violent programs of forced assimilation. Native literature precedes colonization. Native stories and traditions have their roots in both the pre-colonized and the decolonizing worlds. And, almost without fail, when Native writers elected to enter into the dominant discourse of written western literacy, they did so with the intention of maintaining some vestige of indigenous culture and community. Writing was and is a strategy for cultural survival.

Notes

1 Louise Erdrich, *The Round House* (New York: Harper Perennial, 2012), 319.
2 Eliphalet Adams. "The Confession and Dying Warning of Katherine Garret," *Early Native Literacies in New England: A Documentary History and Critical Anthology*, Eds. Kristina Bross and Hilary Wyss (Amherst: University of Massachusetts Press, 2008), 142–148.
3 Ibid.
4 *Maze of Injustice: The Failure to Protect Indigenous Women from Sexual Violence in the USA* (New York: Amnesty International, 2007), 14.
5 Lisa King, "Sovereignty, Rhetorical Sovereignty, and Representation: Key Words for Teaching Indigenous Texts," *Survivance, Sovereignty, and Story: Teaching American Indian Rhetorics*, Eds. Lisa King, Rose Gubele, and Joyce Rain Anderson (Logan: Utah State University Press, 2015), 214–215.
6 For a good source for Pocahontas-related cultural artifacts, see Robert S. Tilton, *Pocahontas: The Evolution of a Narrative* (New York: Cambridge University Press, 1994).
7 See Philip Barbour, *Pocahontas and Her World* (Boston: Houghton Mifflin, 1970), 24–25.
8 For more on Pocahontas and the Jamestown Settlement, see Dr. Linwood "Little Bear" Custalow and Angela L. Daniel "Silver Star," *The True Story of Pocahontas: The Other Side of History* (Golden: Fulcrum Publishing, 2007); Robert S. Tilton, *Pocahontas: The Evolution of an American Narrative* (New York: Cambridge University Press, 1994); Helen C. Rountree, *Pocahontas, Powhatan, Opechancanough: Three Indian Lives Changed by Jamestown* (Charlottesville: University of Virginia Press, 2005); Kathleen Donegan, *Seasons of Misery: Catastrophe and Colonial Settlement in Early America* (Philadelphia: University of Pennsylvania Press, 2014); John Smith, *Captain John Smith: Writings with Other Narratives of Roanoke, Jamestown, and the First English Settlement of America* (New York: Library of America, 2007).
9 Nathaniel Hawthorne, *The Scarlet Letter*, Ed. Ross C. Murfin (Boston: Bedford/St. Martin's, 1991), 54, 129, & 146.

10 Joy Harjo, "The Woman Who Fell from the Sky," *The Woman who Fell from the Sky* (New York: W.W. Norton, 1994), 5.
11 Daniel R. Wildcat, "Understanding the Crisis in American Education," *Power and Place: Indian Education in America*, Eds. Vine Deloria Jr. and Daniel R. Wildcat (Golden Co.: Fulcrum Resources, 2001), 31.
12 David J. Carlson "U.S.–Indian Treaty Relations and Native American Treaty Literature," *The Routledge Companion to Native American Literature*, Ed. Deborah L. Madsen (New York: Routledge, 2016), 111–122.
13 Scott Richard Lyons, *X-Marks: Native Signatures of Assent* (Minneapolis: University of Minnesota Press, 2010).
14 Michael E. Miller, "400 Years Is Long Enough: Virginia Indian Tribes Demand Federal Recognition," *The Virginian Pilot*, May 30, 2017, p. 1.

1

ORAL ENCOUNTERS

Moving the Forest and Rocks by Song

Finding Your Origin Story

In his book *The Truth About Stories*, Cherokee writer Thomas King opens each chapter by saying, "there is a story I know." What he proceeds to tell is not always what we might traditionally think of as a "story," but then again, his intent seems to be to encourage a more expansive view of what actually constitutes a "story" and to wonder whether, as he prompts, "the truth about stories is that that's all we are."[1] The suggestion is that life itself—culture, history, religion, civilization, race—these are all stories, and how we tell these stories actually has great implications in regards to the lives we lead.

So, here is a story I know.

It is sometime in the fall of 1663, and a young scholar sits at his roughhewn wooden desk in his room at Harvard College, quill in hand, staring at a sheet of paper which takes on a ghostly glow in the candlelight before him. He is pensive for a moment as he scans the two words he has previously penned, *Honoratissimi Benefactores*, "Most Honored Benefactors." He is writing to a man (to a group of men really) he has never met and will never meet in his lifetime. But it has been impressed upon him that he owes them something—a measure of gratitude if nothing else—and, although tried and true forms exist for expressing such gratitude, there is always, apart from everything else, some degree of artistry involved in the gesture, a flourish demonstrating both humility and expertise. He knows these protocols well and has often seen them in action, as exhibited by his father and grandfather before him—polished diplomats both who understood the significance of fashioning the proper word to the proper moment, how a sentence spoken one way might result in war, whereas the same words offered in a slightly altered arrangement might ensure yet another generation of peace. It is because of his place in this lineage of wise men and diplomats that he has been sent here to Harvard to study the classics, ancient philosophy, the mysteries of the cosmos, to master Latin, Hebrew, and Greek, and become intimate with the word of God as professed in the Congregationalist meeting houses of the Massachusetts Bay Colony—to become a proselytizer of that faith, in fact, should he ever manage to complete his studies and return home to his village.

Outdoors, a rush of wind shakes the tall oaks, rattles the windows, and calls up a low moan from the channel of the hearth where the fire flares to life for a brief moment, before settling once more to its guttering flame. As though attuned to something the wind has foretold, he turns his head slightly to one side, absorbing some sensory transmission from the sudden shift in the ether. He dips his pen in the well and begins scratching away at the paper, exercising his most precise penmanship and taking care not to rest his hand and smudge the ink. From time to time he pauses, sends his breath over the page to harden the tracks he has left upon its surface, and references the primer sitting open on the table beside him. During these pauses, he unconsciously uses his free hand to stroke the leather hide of the medicine bundle he wears fastened around his neck, running his thumb and forefinger along its worn, pliable surface and feeling the resistance of the objects within. He writes:

> Historians tell of Orpheus, the musician and outstanding poet, that he received a lyre from Apollo, and that he was so excellent with it that he moved the forests and rocks by his song. He made huge trees follow behind him, and indeed rendered tamer the most ferocious beasts. After he took up the lyre he descended into the nether world, lulled Pluto and Proserpina with his song, and led Eurydice, his wife, out of the underworld and into the upper. The ancient philosophers say this serves as a symbol to show how powerful are the force and virtue of education and refined literature in the transformation of the nature of barbarians.[2]

The young man who writes has been tasked with his assignment by none other than John Winthrop Jr., governor of the Connecticut Colony and son of the late, revered, Massachusetts Bay Colony governor of the same name. And, like most advanced students, he has a pretty good idea of what he is being asked to perform. After all, he has been living among these intruders upon his land for nearly a decade, learning their language, their customs, their beliefs, and biases. He knows they have a dim view of the people of the morning light, the Wampanoags—his people—holding in utter contempt the traditions and beliefs he has cherished since childhood. But he has been sent here to learn the ways of these foreigners and he is growing in the art of diplomacy. And so, he places a great deal of carefully crafted pious talk in his letter, thanking his "benefactors" for their "wisdom and infinite compassion" in the work of "bringing blessings to us *pagans*" and for leading himself and his people toward Christian light and salvation. He wonders for a moment if they will even notice how, in congratulating them for their refined arts and letters, he draws upon an example from western culture's *oral* tradition—the Greek bard—a figure he readily equates with the storytellers and medicine men (he knows them as "powwows") of his own people, who, like Orpheus, are capable of making water burn, rocks move, trees dance with their arts.[3]

He concludes his letter by informing his far-off English patrons that they are, in their mercy, like "aqueducts in bestowing all these benefits on us." In his own culture, too, water is sacred, the sustainer of life itself, and he is grateful for the gifts it brings. He has never seen an aqueduct, but he has read enough about them and feels his readers will appreciate the allusion. And finally he signs off, "Most devoted to your dignity: Caleb Cheeshateaumauk." The letter will be handed over to Governor Winthrop and soon travel overseas to London, where it will be received by Robert Boyle, president of the Society for the Propagation of the Gospel in New England, where it will serve as an impressive proof of the progress being made in educating the "poor Indians" in Christian knowledge. The letter will be preserved in Boyle's papers, where it will be rediscovered a few centuries later and held up as the earliest known extant example of writing by a Native American in the English colonies. The letter is written entirely in Latin.

I will often begin a semester by throwing Cheeshateaumauk's letter, untranslated, up on the big screen and asking students to guess at what it is. The point, of course, is not necessarily to stump them, but to begin to break down preconceived notions of what it meant to be Native American during the early era of colonial contacts. Typically, one or two students will recognize (or make a lucky guess) that the text is in Latin. But it will take a while, even in a class specifically devoted to Native American literature, for anyone to hit upon the notion that this is, in fact, a letter written by a Native American, and they will be surprised to learn it is the first such piece of writing on record. It is, put quite simply, a story they have never heard before.

In the discussion that follows, and with translation in hand, I will ask them to unpack the allusions to Orpheus. We will think through some of the Christian language and consider the explicit denigrations of Cheeshateaumauk's own people as grateful "pagans" and "barbarians," asking how much of this is sincere and how much is performance? Students will want to know what Cheeshateaumauk was doing at Harvard in the first place. Was he forced against his will to learn English ways and letters, or would he have his own reasons for being there? Is Cheeshateaumauk truly grateful for the education he has undertaken, or is he withholding his true feelings for the sake of expediency? If one reads between the lines, is it also possible to locate an implied critique of colonialism in his letter? Why, for instance, does Cheeshateaumauk use a figure from oral tradition to represent his gratitude for learning English "letters?" And why, if the allure of western tradition as represented by Orpheus is so powerful and persuasive, does Cheeshateaumauk go on to suggest that the "barbarians" need be "secured like tigers and must be induced to follow"?[4] Does this not imply coercive force rather than a charm offensive? I do not have definite answers to all these questions myself, despite my ability to draw informed inferences based on my knowledge of this era, but I am always interested to see where the conversation will lead and if students can come up with persuasive interpretations on their own that help to decolonize the text of this letter.

Cheeshateaumauk certainly does not fit the model most people hold in their heads for seventeenth-century Indians. But by no means was he a complete exception either. Harvard College was founded with the express intent written into its charter to educate the "poor heathen" and bring them out of their presumed state of eternal darkness.[5] The Wampanoags, who, for better or worse, were neighbors to the new colonists and had to devise ways of getting along with them, found it in their interest to send emissaries, such as Cheeshateaumauk, from established leading families, to learn the ways of western culture and form a first line of political and diplomatic defense against settler ambitions. As we've already witnessed in the case of Pocahontas, this was a practice put in motion by many Native people, independent of one another, across the Northeast. Caleb was, in fact, joined at Harvard by a number of other Native students. They were housed in what became known as the Indian College, the first structure of brick and mortar to be erected on the newly founded campus. This same building would also come to house the Cambridge Press, the very first press in North America, which was manned by a young member of the Nipmuc tribe named Wowaus, but known in the colonies by the Christian name given him, James Printer.

Interestingly enough, given how Native people are rarely equated with literature and printing, the Indian College became the center of literary production in the colonies. Not only were sermons, broadsides, and Harvard commencement speeches printed there, with James Printer himself setting the type, but in 1663 the first Bible to be printed in the colonies was birthed from the press at the Indian College. The Puritan preacher John Eliot, so-called Apostle to the Indians, is listed as the editor and translator of this ambitious production, but, in reality, the greater part of that work was done by a group of writing Indians such as Cheeshateaumauk, Joel Hiacooms, Job Nesuton, John Wampus, James Printer, and others. The Bible was printed in a local dialect of the Algonquian language with the goal of using it to convert Natives to Christianity.

It didn't work.

Not really. It would take war, disease, fragmentation of families and communities, and ultimately decades of marginalization and economic isolation to finally accomplish this goal. But the Algonquian Bible nevertheless stands at the forefront of Native North Americans picking up the pen in the seventeenth century and beginning their long engagement with western notions of literacy.

Orality and Literacy

I say "western notions of literacy" because it is a mistake or misnomer to regard Native peoples prior to European contact as "illiterate." Although it is true that the Native culture was primarily an oral culture, it is perhaps misleading to define

FIGURE 1.1 Interpretation of Caleb Cheeshateaumauk commissioned by the Harvard Foundation Portraiture Project and on display at Harvard University's Annenberg Hall. Image used with permission of the artist, Stephen Coit. All rights reserved

orality and literacy as polar opposites. Oral traditions are much more layered and complex than those of us steeped in western notions of literacy are typically willing to acknowledge. In the western tradition, everything that occurs before the emergence of writing is considered "prehistorical" (a trope that, intentionally or not, reduces Natives to a people without history). And yet, the foundational texts of western literacy are themselves oral narratives—or at least they started that way: the Homeric epics, Gilgamesh, the Christian Bible, Beowulf, stories about Orpheus, and so on. These narratives were in circulation for centuries before being committed to writing, and even then, they remained fluid, subject to translation, interpretation, and alteration. Wars have been fought over these differences. The idea that written texts are somehow more stable than oral narrative is one of the great myths of settler colonial discourse. The reason it seems that way, however, is that a dominant colonial culture has edged out any familiarity with the oral traditions of America's indigenous peoples, alongside the types of inscription routinely practiced in support of those traditions. By the same token, Natives, over time, have become extremely wary of sharing their traditions because of the way western ethnographers and historians have subsequently warped and denigrated them in their published retellings.

A visit to any university library will reveal no shortage of volumes recounting the "manners, customs, and traditions" of the so-called red man, explicating the cultures of hundreds of indigenous peoples throughout the Americas. Many of these works were compiled in the early twentieth century when the fields of ethnography and anthropology were just taking off, fueled by the notion that Native peoples were "vanishing," and their lifeways needed to be recorded for posterity before it was "too late." These works might come across as scholarly, comprehensive, and replete with all the authoritative approbation that accredited colonial institutions of higher learning can bestow, but often the researchers in question, despite spending months and even years with the communities they studied, were incapable of shedding their biases or fully gaining the trust of their "subject material." Even the best of them wrote as outsiders and were often incapable of unpacking the layers of cultural meaning that resonated throughout a given narrative. As Muskogee Creek author Craig Womack suggests in his book *Red on Red*, the effect of a great deal of turn-of-the-century ethnography was to reduce indigenous stories and traditions to mere artifacts, trapped in amber, effectively erasing the essential connections "to a living human community" that ensured such traditions would retain their vitality over time. Often in these scholarly works there is no mention of the narrator of the story being reported or of the ceremonial structure within which the story is to be performed—both essential components to participating in oral tradition. Because western ethnographers either could not comprehend or were simply unconcerned with how such stories retained significance in the contemporary lives and practice of Native peoples, the traditions published became sealed in a decontextualized vacuum and, as Womack asserts, proved self-fulfilling evidence of the "popular 'Vanishing American' theory."[6]

The problem with constantly conjugating Native tradition in the past tense is that it forecloses on the fact that Native peoples are still with us today and that they still draw meaning, sustenance, and spiritual strength from the customs that white scholars treated as mere museum pieces. Today we have at least partial access to a great many oral traditions as related, written, and brought to publication by Native peoples themselves. Whenever possible, in teaching such narratives, it is best to begin with those that are Native-authored or to seek out multiple sources concerning a story or tradition, in order to get a sense of the many variations in circulation. Oral narratives can be rich in cultural detail, even though, like many stories from the Christian Bible, they may, if stripped of context, appear quite opaque or random in their organizational structure. Although it may be tempting to read oral narratives as self-contained pieces of literature, most Native scholars would maintain it is essential to supply as much context as possible when teaching these narratives and to pay attention to when the narrative was recorded and who is doing the telling. Often, storytellers have two audiences to keep in mind at the moment of performance—their own people (the traditional caretakers of the story to whom the storyteller is accountable) and the white audience that is "collecting" the story for whatever purposes. How the Native storyteller decides to negotiate these dual audiences, to a large degree, determines the structure and quality of the tale.

One story that I return to quite often in my teaching and my scholarship is a Seneca creation story, as told by Arthur Parker, first published in 1923 and entitled "How the World Was Made." When I teach this story (let us not denigrate it with the title of "myth," which would imply its spiritual and cultural fabrication), I make sure to tell my students a little something about Parker himself, because his role as a carrier of both Seneca and Haudenosaunee (Iroquois) tradition is as significant, in some ways, as the tale he relates. Parker was born in 1881 to an influential Cattaraugus Seneca family, his father a Native of that tribe and his mother a white missionary and teacher from New England. His great-uncle, Eli Parker, had been an important figure in Seneca affairs and went on to become an aide and secretary to General Ulysses S. Grant during the Civil War, rising to the rank of general himself and present at Appomattox when Robert E. Lee signed the papers of surrender to the Union Army. Arthur Parker (who also went by his given Seneca name, Gawasowaneh or Big Snowsnake) spent much of his life seeking out ways to preserve Seneca practices and culture through the means of both indigenous and colonial institutions. He carefully consulted with other members of the Six Nations of the Iroquois to compile written versions of Haudenosaunee customs and beliefs. But he also used his position as trained ethnographer to write authoritative texts on Haudenosaunee culture and history. He eventually attained the position of staff archaeologist at the State Museum of New York in Albany and installed himself as curator of indigenous objects in colonial keeping. He became a founding member of the Society of American Indians, a progressive political group that advocated for indigenous rights in the early 1900s and that included other important Native authors such as Gertrude Simmons Bonnin and Charles Eastman who will be discussed later in this book. Much of this information can be uncovered in a simple Google search.

In Parker's version of the creation narrative, the world is formed when a young woman, Iagĕn″tci′, falls from her home in the clouds, having been pushed by her husband through a great cavity made by his uprooting of the celestial tree. Rather than plummeting to her death, however, the woman is preserved through the efforts of animal beings from the world below. Her fall is suspended by the interknit wings of waterfowl who fly to her rescue, and, as she is gently lowered to the watery surface of this world, a great turtle rises from the deep to make accommodations for her on its broad shell. At this point, a number of creatures in the water gamely endeavor to plumb the depths to scour a little piece of earth from the ocean floor in order to create a more fitting world for the sky woman.

Taking turns, a duck, a pickerel, and many other "earth divers" make the attempt but fail, until finally the lowliest of creatures, the muskrat, proves successful. The dollop of earth, once procured, is placed on the back of the turtle, which then expands in size to become the world we live in today, or Turtle Island. There is much more to the story. It turns out the woman was with child when she fell through the hole in the sky, and that the child, in turn, is mysteriously impregnated, giving birth to twins but perishing from her labor. From her remains (and the bits of seed and root that Grandmother Sky Woman pulled down with her from the upper world) spring the agricultural gifts of corn, squash, beans, and tobacco, as well as the materials to plant a new celestial tree here on Earth. The twin sons take over the story at this point, one being of "good mind" and the other "flinty" in his ways, and their activities and conflicts give shape and form to the more defined geographical features of the world as we know it.

As Cherokee author Thomas King observes, "it's a neat story," but one we are probably inclined to treat as a quaint novelty or passing amusement. Western audiences aren't likely to invest it with the gravity that seems to cohere around the creation story recounted in the Christian Bible, although there are distinct similarities as well as important differences. King notes how "the elements in Genesis create a particular universe governed by a series of hierarchies—God, man, animals, plants—that celebrate law, order, and good government, while in our Native story, the universe is governed by a series of co-operations" involving Sky Woman, her daughter, and the animals in a manner that celebrates "equality and balance." In one world, creation is a "solitary individual act" that "begins in harmony and slides toward chaos" and, in the other, "creation is a shared activity" that, according to King "begins in chaos and moves toward harmony." As King implies, these differing creation stories reflect different epistemological worldviews and, to some degree, account for divergent cultural values between western and indigenous cultures.[7]

Whenever I assign Parker's creation story, students are quick to notice how the work is packed with narrative elements that might easily be equated with Christian cosmogony. As in Genesis, a fallen woman, a tree, and talking animals occupy the center of the story, as well as two brothers in dire conflict with one another, and a virgin birth thrown in for good measure. A worthwhile exercise is to explore these and other similarities and question why they might be present. Quite possibly, elements of Christian narrative have woven their way into the story over many centuries, as the Haudenosaunee have been living under a system of Christian domination for nearly 400 years. This shouldn't be so remarkable to consider, given that Christian tradition has also incorporated older traditions into its ceremonial life, including the decorating of evergreens at winter solstice and the celebration of fertility and regeneration in spring with fetishized egg-laying bunny rabbits. On the other hand, the similarities may simply be part and parcel of the elemental materials of which human stories consist, or it may be that Parker exaggerated certain corresponding details to make the story more relatable to white Christian audiences, even mimicking in some places the cadences of biblical text. Just as these similarities should be investigated, however, it is equally important to explore the differences (such as the notable absence of "man" in the Earth's initial creation) and to pursue King's line of thinking, pointing to an indigenous world that relies more on balance and cooperation between all beings rather than a hierarchical order of creation that places dire cosmic penalties on those who challenge or doubt its prescribed system.

It is interesting to note that the French Jesuits, in their attempts to convert Native peoples to Christianity in the early seventeenth century, dwelt with the Montagnais, Huron, and Iroquois of New France (Canada) and recorded versions of creation stories that prove to be quite similar to Parker's story. Such tales were regularly related to the Jesuits by their indigenous hosts. Needless to say, the Jesuit fathers viewed these stories as abominable fantasies and often perceived themselves to be in heated opposition with the spiritual leaders of the indigenous communities with whom they lodged—referred to unceremoniously in their writings as "jugglers," "sorcerers," and "charlatans." These Jesuits offered up the written Bible as powerful proof that their system of creation was true, boasting that the technology of writing allowed for God's word to be preserved intact over many centuries whereas the oral versions disseminated by Native peoples were presumably prone to memory lapses and corruptions. The Native communities to whom the Jesuits proselytized listened politely to such arguments, but were hardly persuaded and, in many cases, can be seen teasing the Jesuits and gently poking holes in their logic. These small personal conflicts took on cosmic proportions in the minds of the Jesuit fathers, however, as they found themselves cut off from the affirmation of their own discourse communities and embroiled in epistemological quandaries that ultimately could not be resolved within their trained system of thought. For them there could only be one Truth, handed down directly by God—not a "story" among stories, but the absolute Word and the Law. But, for the Natives, their more flexible belief systems founded in stories of cooperation with all the world's beings enabled them to accommodate and even stitch together worldviews seemingly in opposition to one another.

Coyotes, Ravens, and Corn Mothers

Indigenous oral narratives may appear to the casual reader at first glance as safe havens of literary encounter, set apart from the more complex issues of contact, colonialism, land theft, disenfranchisement, and genocide—a location where classrooms can engage with mystical and fantastic stories without having to become embroiled in the tricky identity politics of our current times. But keep in mind that storytellers such as Arthur Parker were well aware of the violent consequences of colonialism and threaded this knowledge into their stories. Parker himself uses the term "holocaust" to describe the impact of the settler world on Haudenosaunee civilization, and this some 25 years prior to events that would irrevocably equate this term with Nazi death camps.[8] Because storytellers kept white audiences in mind when crafting their tales, it wasn't unusual for them to insert narrative innovations into their performances, such as when the so-called "evil" twin of Parker's creation tale confronts his "good-minded" sibling and cries,

> My elder brother, I perceive that you are about to call forth men-beings who shall live on the island that we here have inhabited. I propose to afflict them with disease and to make their life difficult, for this is not their world but mine, and I shall do as I please to spoil it.[9]

The not so subtle implication is that the "evil" twin assumes the role of the white settler who will claim the land for his own spoil, bringing diseases with him that will devastate indigenous communities. By fixing this element to the tale, Parker incorporates western colonialism into the system of Haudenosaunee cosmology, demonstrating how it is always already, in fact, a component of an ongoing narrative concerned with placing a world beset with destructive forces and personalities back into proper balance.

Oral narrative has the power to collapse time and space, bringing the past in synch with the present, connecting the animal world to the human through the invocation of dance, movement, and song, and realigning the world of the spirit with that of the physical. Susan Berry Brill de Ramirez observes of the oral narrative form that it "has far greater capabilities in regards to symbolic and metaphoric richness due to the added possibilities inherent in performative, auditory, visual, and intersubjective language."[10] Some stories, of course, are meant to be playful, or serve as reminders of cultural mores and imperatives, but, when the storyteller relates the creation of the world in a ceremonial setting, it is perceived not as mere invocation of ancient occurrences, but rather as an indispensable component of the world's continuance. It is the ceremony that keeps the world in motion, informing all its beings of right action and a proper ordering of events. The story itself is generative and it may change with each telling, just as the world itself is changing and reshaping the narrative order of our existence, but it is framed within a certain form and tradition that must be properly understood and enacted for the ceremony itself to be successful.

Although I often assign Parker's version of the Haudenosaunee creation story, there are many others that will reward careful presentation and interpretation. It is up to instructors to familiarize themselves as much as possible with the tradition that informs the tale, but there are also helpfully explicated stories such as Marilou Awiakta's poignant reflections on the origin of corn in her book *Selu, Seeking the Corn-Mother's Wisdom*. Awiakta excavates surprising layers of meaning in what, on the surface at least, appears to be a pretty straightforward tale recounting the original gift of agriculture to the Cherokee. Within the narrative, concerning twin brothers who defy their mother's prohibition concerning how corn is made, Awiakta draws meaningful analogies for our own times concerning responsibility, respect, and process, with deep implications for the atomic age. Like Parker, her narrative sensibility engages both the traditional past and the conditional present. If the twins, in her story of the world's milky origins, go off into the woods carrying hunting rifles, she cautions we should not concern ourselves with such anachronisms—the tale is not meant to convey historical accuracy so much as mold itself to the exigencies of our current moment. It is a recognition that, to some degree, origin stories are always about the present.[11]

Another such resource is N. Scott Momaday's story of "The Arrowmaker," from his collection of essays *The Man Made of Words*. The accompanying exegesis offers Momaday's sense of how a timeless story involving a Kiowa arrowmaker and his wife helps define his own relationship with literature and language, illustrating "more clearly than anything else in my own experience something of the essential character of the imagination."[12] In the story, a couple's existential vulnerability as human beings in this world is brought into sharp relief when they are made aware of a presence just beyond the protective skin of their lodge. In determining the nature of that presence, whether it be friend or foe, the arrowmaker must ultimately announce and expose himself. But perhaps more powerful than the offered story is the way that both the arrowmaker of the story and Momaday, the storyteller, become conjoined in the telling, both existing within the framework of language, both enunciating themselves to an unfolding universe, both of them, at once, the man made of words.

Thomas King, on the other hand, relishes Coyote stories and tends to cast them in a playful mode that often takes the edge off their underlying seriousness of purpose. In one King story, it is Coyote, rather than Abner Doubleday, who invents baseball and teaches it to Columbus when the Admiral of the Seas comes blundering into the western hemisphere—this is, in fact, in keeping with Native traditions where games of stickball, similar to baseball in some cases, preceded colonization.[13] In another story, Coyote devises a protection racket scheme in which he persuades the ducks to hand over to him their radiant feathers to safeguard from the strange, recently encountered human creatures. Coyote, an elemental figure appearing in the stories of many Native cultures, is, like all trickster figures, capable of snaring himself in his own traps, but, in King's telling, his antics also bring into relief certain human tendencies that, when left unchecked, create trouble for everyone involved, such as when strangers come to your homeland and begin claiming everything for themselves by right of "discovery."[14]

Another traditional trickster is Raven, who much like Coyote, has a tendency to fall in and out of trouble even while playing a central role in important world events. In her book *The Tao of Raven*, Tlingit author Ernestine Hayes recounts how Raven craftily infiltrates the fortress of the old man on the Nass River who kept sunlight horded away in a box in his home. Raven ultimately escapes through the smoke hole of the old man's dwelling place, sunlight lodged precariously in his beak, thereby bringing light to the world. With every victory, however, comes sacrifice, and Hayes locates poignant parallels in Raven's story to her own lifetime balance of gains and losses, navigating us along the misty shorelines where creation and present-day existence seamlessly merge.

In his book *The People Named the Chippewa*, Gerald Vizenor relates the story of the Annishinabe culture hero and "trickster" Naanabozho, outlining a tale that contains familiar elements from the earth diver portion of Parker's story, but also entertains the possibility of human folly and accident. Vizenor is a different kind of storyteller than Parker and has his eye focused on elements of irony and instability that make each telling a new encounter, a new beginning, and a new present that challenges the stolid granite bulwark embedded in the word "tradition." For Vizenor, the teller of oral narratives is an "artist, a person of wit and imagination, who relumes the diverse memories of the visual past into the experiences and metaphors of the present."[15] The manner in which stories are told, the narrative materials assembled, is of utmost importance to Vizenor who recognizes how Native peoples have too often been the tragic subjects of colonial stories rather than the agents of their own narrative destinies in modern times. He calls specifically for Native storytellers to embrace the flexibility of oral narrative and imbue their stories with what he calls a "trickster hermeneutics" or the imperative of "survivance." What he means by this is that Native people should take charge of their own stories and fashion those stories as "repudiations of dominance, tragedy, and victimry."[16] In Vizenor's works, the "trickster" remains an unstable being, standing outside the accepted mantras and creeds of both colonial and indigenous institutions, ready to shape the world anew based on his or her perception of the shadows rising up from a tribal past that can never be fully encountered or articulated, but only reimagined along the trail of reconstituted stories in the present.

Vizenor, although theoretically challenging, can be very useful in the classroom as his scholarship helps to tease out and provoke the highly predetermined view of Native identity that prevails within the dominant culture. In Vizenor's post-structuralist view, history itself, as told and written by colonial power, is a kind of story or performance, and in that performance Indians have been typecast in a persuasive but self-defeating role that, despite its artificial origins (beginning with the misnomer of "Indian" itself), has proven difficult for "Indians" to escape. But he asserts it is up to Native people to play the role of "post-Indian warriors," recasting for themselves an identity that pulls from their own rich traditions and positionality rather than the manufactured "manifest manners" produced by colonial doctrine. In teaching the stories, we too must be mindful of their provenance, of the appropriate tribal contexts, meanings, and responsibilities that the tales incorporate and, as Cherokee scholar Qwo-Li Driskell states, comprehend their radical potential to generatively "transform the memories for both indigenous and non-indigenous people."[17]

Of Birchbark, Wampum, and Winter Counts

Oral narrative, therefore, might be regarded as a force and practice that endeavors to keep the world in balance. If the ligaments of storytelling are inherently flexible, they remain bound to principles, the roots of which trace back through tribal history. It is also important to keep in mind, however, that oral tradition is not solely dependent upon human memory and word of mouth. Native Studies scholars such as Lisa Brooks, Hilary Wyss, Birgit Brander Rasmussen, and others have recently brought a revived analytics to indigenous customs of preserving history and culture through various media such as hieroglyphs, petroglyphs, wampum belts, quipu, birchbark scrolls, and winter counts. Although such forms of history-keeping may not register to the modern western mind as "writing," they nevertheless represent practices that perform a role similar to that of writing in western culture, such as preserving religious narratives, diplomatic exchanges, migration routes, events of historical significance, and, of course, stories. The Mayans and Aztecs, in fact, had great libraries in their urban centers containing thousands of codices (a fancy word for "book"), of which only a handful survived the devastation of Spanish conquest. Although the uninitiated may be hard-pressed to decipher these texts for themselves (just as indigenous individuals during initial colonial contacts were confounded by alphabetic script), we can at least appreciate that these media constitute an indigenous archive that has historically received very little informed scholarly attention and has rarely been considered "literature."

In his book *Broken Spears*, Miguel Leon-Portilla presents, from a variety of sixteenth-century indigenous sources, accounts of the Spanish conquest of Mexico transcribed from the Nahuatl language. In many cases, these are histories recorded by firsthand witnesses. They include initial encounters between Cortés and Motecuhzoma in Tenochtitlan (Mexico City) in 1520, the brutal massacres that Cortés perpetrated on unsuspecting villagers after being repulsed from the Aztec capital, and the horrific onset of pandemic diseases that decimated Tenochtitlan and allowed Spanish forces to finally take the city and overthrow the Aztec regime. Not only are these gripping historical narratives, but they are also, beyond a doubt, literary compositions, recounting moments of supreme human drama, crafted with an aesthetic sensibility meticulously cultivated by the Aztec scribes who forwarded their accounts.

Although issues of ethnocentric interpretation arise from our modern attempts at translation, these texts nevertheless offer an important and poetic counterbalance to Spanish accounts from the same time. One scribe reproduces the scene where Cortés and his men first encounter Motecuhzoma's storehouse of treasures in Totocalco (the Palace of the Birds). He writes how the Spaniards "searched everywhere and coveted everything; they were slaves to their own greed." The Aztec hosts, in the meantime,

> shied away as if the Spaniards were like wild beasts, as if the hour were midnight on the blackest night of the year. Yet they did not abandon the Spaniards to hunger and thirst. They brought them whatever they needed, but shook with fear as they did so.[18]

The account, freighted as it is with knowledge of the horror that would ensue, paints an indelible picture of the Aztecs attempting to maintain their cultural bearings while confronted with the insatiable greed of the conquistadors.

As explained in the foreword to Leon-Portilla's edition, the Nahuatl language texts were made possible because "inscriptions based on a partly ideographic, partly phonetic mode of writing" were extremely abundant from the fourth and fifth centuries onward, particularly among the Mayans. "They testify to the fact that these cultures possessed a profound sense of time and history."[19] The individuals who recorded and preserved accounts of Cortés's actions were already highly trained priests and scribes prior to colonial contact, with specialized skills in the documentation and relation of cultural events. As such, they were able to quickly learn the Phoenician alphabet under Spanish guidance. In the words of one Spanish instructor, "if one did not see, one would not believe" how within a few short years these indigenous scribes had "become teachers and preachers of their parents and elders."[20] Converting their relations to Christianity was likely a low priority for the scribes, however, as compared with preserving a record of their own culture and history. Many of their writings were supplemented with hieroglyphic versions of events, and these, too, have been preserved in the *Florentine Codex* and elsewhere and offer a helpful companion to the alphabetically rendered accounts.

Most people have no conception that the Mayans and Aztecs were first-hand reporters of the infamous events more famously documented by the conquerors themselves—individuals such as Bernal Diaz, a foot soldier in the armies of Cortés who wrote *The Conquest of New Spain*, or Cortés who reported on his campaigns in reports written to King Charles V of Spain, or even the late nineteenth-century historian William H. Prescott, whose famous 1843 work *The History of the Conquest of Mexico* continues to be influential and lionizes Cortés as an unparalleled military genius. What the Nahuatl versions help us understand is not only the richness and complexity of the cultures undermined by western rapacity (Tenochtitlan was an urban center of one quarter of a million residents when Cortés arrived, replete with pyramids, aqueducts, botanical gardens, zoos, and, as earlier noted, libraries), but that Cortés would have been unable to effect his improbable victory had it not been for the emergence of debilitating pandemic diseases that essentially rendered Aztec military resistance inoperative. As one scribe recounts, the plague began to spread in the thirteenth month and it lasted 70 days.

> Sores erupted on our faces, our breasts, our bellies; we were covered with agonizing sores from head to foot ... The sick were so utterly helpless that they could only lie in their beds like corpses, unable to move their limbs or even their heads ... a great many died from this plague.[21]

In the aftermath of conquest, every imaginable effort was made to reduce all trace of Mexico's indigenous culture to waste and rubble. It is a testament to the strength, will, and tenacity of these peoples that their stories have survived these most brutal attempts at erasure.

The highly centralized civilizations of Central and South America can often appear a strange anomaly or historic exception to what otherwise has been regarded as the "prehistoric," "primitive," and "stone-age" woodlands and plains cultures of North America. Few Americans are ever taught of the urban complexes of "Mississippian culture" that flourished sometime between 900 and 1300 A.D. in the heart of the North American continent, such as Cahokia, a city in the vicinity of modern day St. Louis consisting of massive earthworks, a population larger than that of London or Paris at the time, and the agricultural technology and productivity to support the expansive population. One can catch glimpses of these indigenous hubs in the works of early Spanish adventurers to the continent, including Cabeza de Vaca, Garcilaso De La Vega, and Hernando de Soto, but knowledge of these sites has been largely erased from western history-keeping, even though, in many places, great earthen structures still loom over the landscape, rising seven stories in height in some cases, to remind us of the civilizations that once lived there.

Little consensus exists among historians and anthropologists concerning what became of these cultural epicenters or how they dispersed. A subtle change in climate, often referred to as the little ice age, may have rendered such dense population bases agriculturally unsustainable, or it is possible that pandemic diseases arrived through the exchange of trade goods, well in advance of actual European settlement in the region, causing residents to abandon their more centralized existence. Whatever the case, this rich and unexpected history is strategically forgotten, or *unwitnessed*, in the United States, contributing to the more pervasive, dominant belief that Native peoples were scattered nomads and foragers, pursuing primitive hunter-gatherer livelihoods prior to colonization.

Chadwick Allen has written extensively on North America's little-known indigenous earthworks, observing that these structures, in their various manifestations across the continent, "represent achievements in science and aesthetics on a monumental scale. They integrate the precise observation of natural phenomena with

FIGURE 1.2 Artist's rendition of Cahokia by Lloyd K. Townsend. Courtesy of Cahokia Mounds State Historic Site

geometry and other abstract forms of knowledge, as well as with practical skills in mathematics, architectural design, engineering, and construction." He adds that "particular works were often aligned with specific celestial events, such as an equinox or solstice sunrise or sunset point on the horizon."[22] One has to wonder why it is that we teach our children about the pyramids of Egypt but remain absolutely in the dark concerning the pre-contact wonders in our own backyards.

But even apart from the Mississippian "mound cultures" (as they are sometimes called), Natives throughout the North American continent were participants of thriving village communities, different in many ways from the organizational structure of European society, but still anchored in deep-rooted, familial, traditional, religious, and agricultural customs. They harvested medicines that we still rely upon today to cure the sick. They manufactured durable goods that were remarkably well suited to indigenous lifeways and proved highly marketable throughout Europe as well. They managed their ecosystems with alacrity and mindfulness, developed agricultural innovations allowing them to equal or surpass colonial productivity with considerably less labor, and cultivated systems of good governance that, according to some, inspired the English colonists to attempt a cooperative league of independent states in the 1770s in which citizens chose their own leaders and devised their own laws.[23]

Arthur Parker, for one, dedicated himself to educating Americans about these poorly understood historical facts and, among his other works, published *The Constitution of the Five Nations*, in which he details the laws by which the Five (now Six) Nations of the Iroquois have lived for a period of some 600 years since the founding of their league. Their laws were first introduced to the warring nations of the Northeast by a figure known as the Peacemaker, in partnership with the culture hero Hayonwhatha (variant of Hiawatha). Through the invention of wampum and by advocating for a philosophy of good-mindedness, the two were able to "comb the snakes" from the hair of their opposition. The once warring nations were persuaded to bury their weapons of war and bond together under the tree of peace. A physical record of the league's initial founding (believed by some to have occurred around the year 1390 A.D.) still exists in the form of a wampum belt often referred to today as the Hiawatha belt. The Great Law of Peace itself continues to provide the foundation of present-day Haudenosaunee governance and is recited each year in a longhouse ceremony that takes 5 days to perform.

Wampum belts are made of beads manufactured from the quahog shell and strung together with sinew and other fibers to form intricate designs patterned from the contrast of the white and dark sections of the shell. The production of these beads is painstaking, delicate labor, but no diplomatic agreement or treaty was considered operative in the indigenous Northeast without an exchange of wampum to bind spoken words into law. Colonial representatives and authorities were frequent participants in ceremonies of wampum exchange, "wiping the tears from their eyes, removing the dirt from their ears, and the obstructions from their throats" in accordance with the dictates of the condolence ceremony. Such events form a crucial chapter in North American history, as colonists would mimic the necessary phrases and poignant cadences of the ceremony in order to clear a ritualized space for mutual understanding and to "bury the hatchet." They were impressed by the ritual aspects of wampum exchange, while little suspecting the layered history and tradition of the ceremony standing behind the outward custom. Benjamin Franklin, who reported on many of these diplomatic exchanges for his newspaper, *The Pennsylvania Gazette*, famously noted that,

> Having frequent Occasions to hold public Councils, they [the "Savages"] have acquired great Order and Decency in conducting them … they preserve Traditions of the Stipulations in Treaties 100 Years back; which, when we compare with our Writings, we always find exact.[24]

The indigenous nations of the Northeast understood wampum exchange as central to their spiritual and civic well-being, and any perusal of early colonial history in the region will find wampum playing a central role in all indigenous dealings, even when the settlers themselves were in the dark as to what they were actually describing. Once they did come to appreciate the significance of wampum to indigenous communities, the colonists immediately stamped their own value upon it, realizing they could trade these seemingly worthless shell fragments for valuable furs and other trade goods. In order to secure this trade advantage against the French and Dutch settlements, the New England colonists launched an offensive war against the Pequots in 1636, known today as the Pequot War, because the Pequot were located geographically in the area of the Long Island Sound where the coveted shells were most likely to wash up on the beach.

The great council belt of the Five Nations. Each square represents a nation and the heart in the center represents the Onondaga.

FIGURE 1.3 The Great Council Belt of the Five Nations as depicted in Arthur Parker's *Seneca Myths & Folktales*. Courtesy American Antiquarian Society

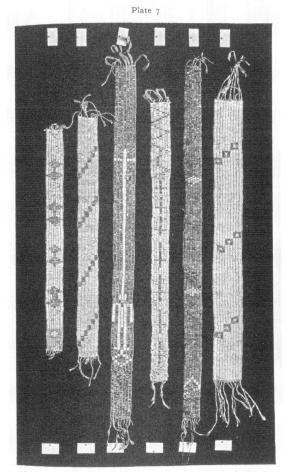

FIGURE 1.4 Commemoration Belts of the Five Nations recording events and alliances, from "The Constitution of the Five Nations," *Parker on the Iroquois*. Courtesy American Antiquarian Society

The unsuspecting Pequot were all but annihilated in the ensuing conflict, as many as 600 of them destroyed when the Puritan army ambushed their village at dawn, burning it to the ground along with everyone in it. Those not present at the massacre were hunted down and either killed or sold into slavery, and a decree was passed that the Pequot name be struck from the history books, never to be spoken again, and that their remains were fit only for "dunging the ground."[25] Some of the surviving women and children were made to live out the balance of their days in Puritan households where they were forced to practice

Christianity and become laborers for their conquerors. The result was that the New England colonies were able to seize control of the wampum trade, and wampum became the de facto currency of the colony for the next two decades, replacing the English pound. As such, wampum became known, and even today is largely understood, as "Indian Money." It is important to understand, however, that Native cultures were not organized upon the capitalist system of economic enrichment, and, for indigenous peoples of the Northeast today, wampum's value remains ceremonial, diplomatic, historical, ornamental, and even literary, but never as currency.

Although practices varied from tribe to tribe and nation to nation in North America, most, if not all, had cultivated forms of communication that relied upon inscription or some other representative means to supplement the oral encounter. The *waniyetu wowapi*, or winter counts, of the Lakota provide yet another such example. Winter counts are a compilation of discrete drawings on animal hide, usually made by a trusted leader of the community in the winter season, each drawing or "count" representing an event that serves to recall and, perhaps, ideographically encapsulate the year past. Winter counts might depict a military victory, the death of an important leader, or some other event regarded by the community in a significant light, but they also served as calendric markers to which individuals could routinely refer in order to identify the year of their birth or some other important happening, regardless of whether or not it corresponded to the image depicted in the count for that particular year.[26]

Early ethnographers greeted the discovery of the Lakota winter counts with a predictable brand of ethnocentrism, noting that, "if they [the Lakota] had exhibited a complete national or tribal history for the years embraced in them, the discovery would have been in some respects more valuable." As it was, winter counts remained "interesting to anthropologists because they show an attempt before unsuspected among the northern tribes of American Indians to form a system of chronology."[27] This summation, rooted as it is in western notions of historical representation, fails to take into account how oral and written narratives work in tandem with one another, rather than existing in exclusive spheres, and how the unrolling of the winter count might lead to a fairly comprehensive historical rendering of the life of the community, in most cases reaching back many generations. Although white observers are sometimes confounded at how little impression their own arrival on the scene seems to have made in the ideographic record-keeping of the Lakotas, with the winter counts we can accurately work our way back to mutually observed occurrences such as the appearance in the heavens of the great Leonid meteor shower of 1833, noted in many of the existing winter count rolls, or the 1869 solar eclipse.

That winter counts were used, in part, to call up long-standing oral tradition is evidenced by the winter count of a Brule-Dakota named Wapocta-xi, or Brown Hat, but known among the English as Batiste Good. Good's winter count, properly understood, traces Lakota history all the way back to the period between 901 and 930 A.D. and tells of the emergence of White Buffalo Woman, a figure from Lakota tradition responsible for bringing the sacred pipe to the people and teaching them important ceremonies and ways of good living. As such, Good's winter count documents an American story that, as Birgit Brander Rasmussen reminds us, is at least as old as *Beowulf*.[28]

The Ojibwe or Anishinaabe, too, preserved a record of their history as well as their spiritual narratives on scrolls of birchbark, preserved over generations by their "medicine men," or members of the Midéwiwin society. In one birchbark scroll, kept by James Red Sky, one can follow the actions of the spirit bear who completes his journey through three worlds before finally emerging into the fourth, the one which is destined to become occupied by humans. In the scroll, each of the four worlds penetrated by the spirit bear is represented as a lodge or wigwam, and each new "breakthrough" into the subsequent world might be seen as a kind of birthing process, the bear leaving the womb, or the sort of rebirth that is also a component of the sweat lodge, which many indigenous cultures use in ceremonies designed to heal both physical and spiritual wounds. Other scrolls serve to recall the migration stories of the Anishinaabe, described by Timothy Powell as a "form of *aadizookaanag*, which translates roughly to empowered stories about legendary ancestors or dream spirits." Such stories begin in primordial times and recount "the actions of the *manidoog* (spirits)."[29]

Native communities of the Northeast, aside from their use of wampum, also left pictographic records of their travels and exploits known as *awikhigans* scraped onto trees and other surfaces. These signs might offer details of a recent hunt or supply vital information for parties traveling along the same trail. In the Andean cultures of what is today South America, indigenous peoples kept intricate records by a system of knotted strings known as quipus, capable of communicating vast quantities of information, both narrative and numerical. When the French Jesuits first encountered the Micmaq tribes of eastern Canada in the early seventeenth century, they were amazed at the ease with which the tribes developed their own system of hieroglyphic writing, little suspecting that, just as with Aztec scribes, they were drawing from a form of communication that long preceded the Jesuits' arrival on these shores.

Scholars today, such as Brander Rasmussen, observe how pictography, although denigrated as "primitive" by anthropologists and historians, is making a triumphant comeback in the twenty-first century, becoming a "global language on smartphones and in other digital media."[30] Damián Baca goes so far as to suggest that contemporary scholars working in the digital humanities have missed an opportunity by not considering what he calls the "obvious connection between ancient non-alphabetic story systems and the twenty-first century graphical user interface." Mesoamerican codices that relied upon "multimodal pictographic and logographic inscription systems" could serve as a model for how to create more complex graphic communication systems for international software systems.[31] Many of us use emoticons as a kind of shorthand to relieve the necessity of composing drawn-out sentences. Simply an expedient in our own times, such practices could prove of particular use in a region where many different language groups were massed together, needing to interact and correspond with one another in an effective and efficient manner. Onondawaga scholar Penelope Myrtle Kelsey also observes of

Lakota winter counts that they "are the equivalent of Dakota writings and for that reason should be understood as an assertion of Dakota equality and civilization."[32] We should not doubt that these customs constituted forms of literature, and that the stories and traditions embedded in these literatures are still known and passed along by indigenous peoples today.

When Caleb Cheeshateaumauk wrote his letter to Robert Boyle in 1663, he was employing a new technology on the North American continent, that of paper, ink, and alphabetic literacy. But the idea that important communication could travel over distances independent of the human voice was nothing new to him or his people, and he could hardly escape drawing from his own traditions and understandings of the world, even as he attempted to translate such meanings into a form that his English correspondents would recognize. In my mind, Cheeshateaumauk's story is one of the most compelling origin stories we can relate in the classroom. It helps to map out the origins of Native peoples' picking up the pen in a colonized world. Cheeshateaumauk had grown up in a traditional Wampanoag community and came of age in a world undergoing rapid and violent transformation. He carried inside of him the stories, the language, and the culture of his people, and when he put pen to paper, even in the cause of acknowledging his colonial patrons, something of his traditional life and knowledge stood behind his words and the impression they made.

One of the projects we can engage in as readers, students, and instructors is an act of imagination—trying to imagine how individuals such as Cheeshateaumauk navigated these spaces between his traditional world of belief and the colonial epistemologies he was positioned to represent. Historically speaking, there has been a tendency to read such documents as tacit acknowledgment of the supremacy of western ways and the complete stranglehold they exercised on indigenous figures. This was always a naïve and self-interested reading—one that could only exist by outright denying the integrity, value, and tenacity of indigenous belief systems. Cheeshateaumauk's letter of thanks to Robert Doyle was a performance—one with poignant implications for the success of his endeavor to master western codes of thought and behavior as part of the diplomatic mission he was sent to conduct by his own people. Although there was undoubtedly coercion involved in Cheeshateaumauk's circumstances, there was also agency. And, just like Ernestine Hayes notes of Raven, as he stole sunlight from the old man on the Nas River, escaping through the smoke hole with the bright prize lodged in his beak: "he resisted, he battled, he prevailed."[33] To successfully negotiate such moments was tantamount to guaranteeing another season of peace.

Notes

1 Thomas King, *The Truth about Stories: A Native Narrative* (Minneapolis: University of Minnesota Press, 2003).
2 This translated extract is taken from Wolfgang Hochbruck and Beatrix Dudensing-Reichel, "'Honoratissimi Benefactores': Native American Students and Two Seventeenth-Century Texts in the University Tradition," *Early Native American Writing: New Critical Essays*, Ed. Helen Jaskoski (New York: Cambridge University Press, 1996), 5.

3 These were feats attributed to the "powwow" or "shaman" Passaconaway in William Wood's account of his time in colonial New England. William Wood, *New England Prospect*, Ed. Alden T. Vaughan (Amherst: University of Massachusetts Press, 1977), 100–101.
4 Hochbruck and Dudensing-Reichel, 5.
5 This sentiment is expressed (among other places) in the 1643 tract entitled "New England's First Fruits," an anonymously authored bit of propaganda meant to detail, for an English audience, the presumed success in converting Natives to Christianity in the New England colony. The tract was written to raise financial support for the newly instituted Harvard College and voices sympathy for the "poore Indians, who have ever sate in hellish darknesse, adoring the Divell himself for their GOD." The evidences for conversion were, in fact, pretty thin, and the only Natives who might be counted as converts had also died at the time of "First Fruit"'s being written and therefore could not contradict the claims being forwarded. "New England's First Fruits," *The Eliot Tracts: With Letters from John Eliot to Thomas Thorowgood and Richard Baxter*, Ed. Michael P. Clark (Westport, CT: Praeger, 2003), 58.
6 Craig Womack, *Red on Red: Native American Literary Separatism* (Minneapolis: University of Minnesota Press, 1999), 98.
7 King, *Truth*, 23–25.
8 Arthur C. Parker, *The History of the Seneca Indians* (Port Washington: Ira J. Friedman, 1926), 126.
9 Arthur C. Parker, "How the World Began," *Seneca Myths and Folk Tales* (Lincoln: University of Nebraska Press, 1989), 69–70.
10 Susan Berry Brill de Ramirez, "The Historical and Literary Role of Folklore, Storytelling, and the Oral Tradition in Native American Literatures," *The Routledge Companion to Native American Literature*, Ed. Deborah L. Madsen (New York: Routledge, 2016), 329.
11 Marilou Awaikta, *Selu: Seeking the Corn-Mother's Wisdom* (Golden, CO: Fulcrum, 1993), 15.
12 N. Scott Momaday "The Arrowmaker," *The Man Made of Words; Essays, Stories, Passages* (New York: St. Martin's Griffen, 1997), 10.
13 Thomas King and William Kent Monkman, *A Coyote Columbus Story* (Toronto: Groundwood Books, 1992).
14 King, *Truth*, 122–127.
15 Gerald Vizenor, *The People Called the Chippewa: Narrative Histories* (Minneapolis: University of Minnesota Press, 1984), 7.
16 Gerald Vizenor, *Fugitive Poses: Native American Indian Scenes of Absence and Presence* (Lincoln: University of Nebraska Press, 1998), 15.
17 Qwo-Li Driskill, "Decolonial Skillshares: Indigenous Rhetorics as Radical Practice," *Survivance, Sovereignty, and Story: Teaching American Indian Rhetorics*, Eds. Lisa King, Rose Gubele, and Joyce Raine Anderson (Logan: Utah State University Press, 2015), 58.
18 Miguel Leon-Portilla, Ed., *Broken Spears, The Aztec Account of the Conquest of Mexico* (Boston: Beacon Press, 1992), 68–69.
19 Miguel Leon-Portilla, "Introduction," *Broken Spears*, xxix.
20 J. Jorge Klor de Alva, "Foreword," *Broken Spears*, xv.
21 *Broken Spears*, 92–93.
22 Chadwick Allen, "Serpentine Figures, Sinuous Relations: Thematic Geometry in Allison Hedge Coke's *Blood Run*," *American Literature* 82:4 (2010), pp. 807–834.
23 The argument that American democracy was modelled after the government of the Haudenosaunee has long been in circulation. For a good summation of these ongoing debates, see Bruce E. Johansen, *Debating Democracy: Native American Legacy of Freedom* (Santa Fe: Clear Light, 1998).

24 Benjamin Franklin, "Remarks Concerning the Savages of North America," *Heath Anthology of American Literature*, Ed. Paul Lauter (Boston: Houghton Mifflin Harcourt, 2009), 855.
25 John Mason, "A Brief History of the Pequot War, Especially of the Memorable Taking of Their Fort at Mistick in Connecticut in 1637," *History of the Pequot War*, Ed. Charles Orr (Cleveland: Helman-Taylor, 1980), 35.
26 Garrick Mallery, *Picture-Writing of the American Indians*, Vol. 1 (New York: Dover, 1972), 269–270.
27 Mallery, 271.
28 Birgit Brander Rasmusssen, 2017 SEA conference paper, Biannual Meeting of the Society for Early Americanists, Tulsa, OK.
29 Timothy Powell, "The Role of Indigenous Communities in Building Digital Archives," *Afterlives of Indigenous Archives: Essays in Honor of the Occom Circle*, Eds. Ivy Schweitzer and Gordon Henry (Dartmouth College Press, 2019), 33.
30 Birgit Brander Rasmussen, "Indigenous Literacy and Language," *The Routledge Companion to Native American Literature*, Ed. Deborah L. Madsen (New York: Routledge, 2016), 304.
31 Damián Baca, "Writing the Digital Codex: Non/Alphabetic, De/Colonial, Network/Ed," *Afterlives*, 212.
32 Penelope Myrtle Kelsey, *Tribal Theory in Native American Literature: Dakota and Haudenosaunee Writing and Indigenous Worldviews* (Lincoln: University of Nebraska Press, 2008).
33 Ernestine Hayes, *The Tao of Raven: An Alaska Native Memoir* (Seattle: University of Washington Press, 2017), 129.

2

"STILL THE SAME UNBELIEVING INDIAN"

Native Voices in the Emerging Republic

If we limit ourselves for a moment to thinking of literature as the publication and circulation of alphabetically constructed manuscripts, then, without a doubt, the major literary event for Native America in the eighteenth century was the 1772 publication of Samson Occom's *A Sermon Preached at the Execution of Moses Paul, An Indian*. Like a great deal of published Native American literature to follow, Occom's sermon presented something of a paradoxical public spectacle for colonial readers who were fascinated by the novelty of an ordained Indian preacher presiding over the execution of an accused Indian murderer. Real life didn't often serve up such oddities for public consumption, but Occom's sermon proved so popular that it underwent some 22 reprintings over the next few decades and, according to Joanna Brooks who compiled the first edition of Occom's collected works in 2006, it made him "the sixth leading author in the American colonies during the 1770's."[1] Many found the sermon such a perfect expression of "Gospel Sincerity" that newspapers advertised how it "induced most Families in Connecticut to purchase" a copy, urging those in the other 12 colonies to do the same.[2]

Although Caleb Cheeshateaumauk's letter to Robert Boyle and Katherine Garret's written confession may suggest earlier examples of Native individuals engaging with western forms of literacy, Occom's collected works present the earliest examples we have of a Native American of this continent entering into print discourse in such an intentional manner. We might, in fact, say of Occom what has often been said of his contemporary Benjamin Franklin—that he was "a man of letters" whose reputation and accomplishments depended a great deal on how he presented himself in writing.[3] As such, he is a figure worthy of our attention, not only in Native American literature classes, but in classes dealing with early American, or simply *American*, literature as well. Aside from his 1772 sermon, Occom also published a book of hymns in 1774 and prepared a short autobiographical narrative for publication in 1768 that has since been widely anthologized. He kept many correspondences throughout his life with both whites and other Natives, and roughly 100 of those letters still exist. He kept journals of his travels throughout his lifetime, as well, most of which have survived and sit in colonial archives at both Dartmouth College and the Connecticut Historical Society. A number of his sermons and other small prose pieces have also been preserved. Occom's collected writings constitute an unprecedented archive of indigenous activity, thought, and community engagement in the eighteenth century.

The event of Occom's most famous publication is easily misunderstood, however, as, to an untrained ear, the text can sound precisely like the kind of execution sermon one might have expected from a white preacher of the times. In fact, a portion of it was lifted verbatim from just such a sermon preached by the Puritan minister Sylvanus Conant, a decade earlier.[4] But there are a number of flourishes in Occom's text that allow us to see how he, like Cheeshateaumauk and Garret before him, is negotiating the expectations of his very public performance against his awareness of multiple audiences. And even more importantly, there are things occurring offstage that, when better understood, bring the performance into a more poignant light.

This is why, when addressing Occom's role in Moses Paul's execution, we should be careful to place it within a context of indigenous community and kinship. It is important that students are able to see beyond the necessary genre conventions presented by the text and tackle the complexities of the cultural event taking place—the performative moment in which Occom engages. We should not take for granted, for instance, that Occom's presence at the pulpit signifies his belief in Moses Paul's guilt or even his tacit complicity in Paul's public condemnation. The execution sermon was part of a sturdy New England tradition and, as with any genre of literature, there were built-in norms and expectations. Part of Occom's success as an "Indian Preacher" in these times was his ability to meet such expectations while, at the same time, subverting them into missives of Native advocacy. Had Occom not met the generic conventions of the sermon we would probably not know of him today, he would not ever have found his way into publication, and we certainly would not be discussing him in our classrooms. So, if Occom does not at first come across as the eighteenth-century Indian orator most people hold in their minds, his significance as a Native American writer becomes readily apparent when we begin to decode and decolonize the demands of the larger discursive fields in which he labored.

Although the execution sermon frames an important and compelling cultural moment, I generally find that Occom's 1768 short "Autobiographical Narrative," which remained unpublished in his lifetime, is the more accessible and effective reading for appreciating the complex dynamics surrounding Occom's life and his contribution to Native literature. Not only is it considerably shorter and therefore easier to fold into a class lecture, but it offers a window into other aspects of

Occom's career and better conveys his range, as his tone vacillates between earnest appeal and sardonic critique of colonial hypocrisy. Works such as Occom's "Autobiographical Narrative" and *A Sermon Preached* are, perhaps, best understood as sites of cultural negotiation, in which Native people, out of necessity, are actively engaging with western literary practices, but in a way that pushes back against colonial appropriations and incursions. In fact, such negotiation is always a facet of cross-cultural engagement and can often be seen operating on either side of the cultural divide.

As our reading of Occom usually comes early in the semester (typically in the second or third week), it can be helpful to close the gap between Cheeshateaumauk and Occom by talking briefly about John Eliot, the "editor" of the Algonquian language bible mentioned in Chapter 1. Tradition has it that Eliot, the Puritan "apostle to the Indians," preached to the Natives in their own language from a pulpit-like rock in the deep, dark, forested wilderness. But, when we go back to the original source material, it becomes clear that no such performance ever took place. Eliot was actually invited into the village longhouse of Waban, a sachem of the Massachuset Indians, to deliver his sermons. Eliot's grasp of the Algonquian tongue was so poor, particularly at this early stage of his career, that he had to employ Native helpers (who, for whatever reasons, had a much easier time mastering English) to translate for him as he proselytized.[5]

The story from tradition is a powerful bit of colonial myth-making and is meant to perform a kind of "cultural work." It suggests that Natives lived like brute animals in the forest rather than in villages, it subsumes their intellectual involvement in the encounter, and it purposefully erases the fact that Eliot entered into a space of Native spirituality and tradition, the longhouse, when he preached to the local Natives, and that, as such, he was invited into a kind of syncretic spiritual arrangement that colonial tales later erased. Nevertheless, allusions to Eliot's preaching in the wilderness abound. We can find them sprinkled into the works of Hawthorne, Thoreau, Whittier, and others. A plaque at the church of Roxbury, Massachusetts, where Eliot was preacher, still celebrates one who, with the zeal of Saint Francis, "traversed the land for forty years in perils of the wilderness, in perils of the heathen, in hunger and thirst, with gentleness and fearlessness to bear the gospel to the children of the woods."[6]

Ironically, given all the hype, Eliot did little actual trekking through the wilderness. The Indians he visited were his neighbors and themselves frequent visitors to the Puritan settlements. Although Eliot is often made to seem a lone agent of religious zeal and conviction, in truth, he travelled with a contingent of colonial authorities and Native translators who assisted him in his outreach. We can see how such historical distortions perpetuate themselves in productions such as the nineteenth-century illustration of Eliot by Felix Octavius Carr Darley. I will often throw this image up on the screen and have students unpack the colonial symbolism—how it depicts Eliot preaching from a rock in the forest, his position in terms of height and centrality indicating his elevated status in relation to the Natives. Whereas Eliot is bathed in light, the Natives are crouched in darkness, close to the ground, their heads bowed either in meek submission or, in some cases, sullen scowls. In the background we can see a few painted tipis scattered amongst the trees, although tipis were used primarily by Natives of the plains and were never a feature of the New England landscape. The actual longhouse where Eliot first preached to the Massachuset Natives was, by his own account, capacious enough to accommodate a few hundred people.[7]

n fact, everything about the illustration is exactly wrong and contributes to a larger sense of cultural dislocation informing most popular impressions of Native civilization. To provide a bit of contrast, it is helpful, after unpacking the image of Eliot on his rock, to compare it with the paintings of John White, an early English explorer of the Roanoke colony who made lush representations of Native villages based on his eye-witness encounters. This may help students form a better idea of what an actual seventeenth-century east coast Native community might have looked like, complete with longhouses, cornfields, and other village features. Because, once you strip away the romantic hyperbole, what you will find is that the Native space into which Eliot was welcomed was largely a peaceful village world, sustained by the agricultural labors of indigenous families and their extended kinship networks, as well as by long-standing customs of governance and spiritual observance. Eliot was forced, throughout his 40-year career, to make strategic accommodations with Native communities that, although confronted with sustained colonial aggression, remained extremely committed to their own spiritual practices and traditions.

FIGURE 2.1 Felix Octavius Carr Darley, "John Eliot Preaching to the Indians," Drawings: 1999.368.2, Metropolitan Museum of Art

FIGURE 2.2 John White, "Village of Secoton," Watercolor, circa 1685, British Museum, London

Throughout his life, Samson Occom was forced to find resourceful means of engaging with western spiritual conventions while, at the same time, combating harmful stereotypes about Natives and attempting to serve the goals of his indigenous community. For Occom, this started at a young age. He became a member of his tribal council when he turned 16 and was required to weigh in on the incessant land battles in which the Mohegans were embroiled. These battles played out in the colonial courtroom and were mostly connected to what became known as the Mason Land Case, a legal dispute in which the tribe contested the Connecticut colony's practice of appropriating their lands. The Mohegans understood they held sole right to lease or sell off their lands, and this right had been codified in a seventeenth-century agreement between their sachem Uncas and the Connecticut colony. What the Mohegans discovered, however, is that the interpretation of written legal documents, unlike the diplomatic agreements sealed through wampum diplomacy, were fluid and typically favored the biases of those in power.

In part to get a better handle on the nature of such written transactions, Occom elected, sometime in the winter of 1743, to receive instruction from a local minister, Eleazar Wheelock. At around the same time, Occom, according to his autobiographical narrative, converted to Christianity. This confluence of events in Occom's life led to his remarkable journey from a self-described heathen "brought up in heathenism" to becoming something of a preaching sensation on both sides of the Atlantic.[8] As much as Wheelock, along with the evangelical missionary societies that supported him, believed himself to be molding an ignorant "child of the forest" to useful colonial ends, Occom proved to be master of his own agenda. If his conversion to Christianity may strike some as a betrayal of his indigenous heritage, in the same breath that he relates of it in his narrative, he also states "I use to think if I Coud once Learn to Read I Would Instruct poor Children in Reading,—and used frequently to talk with our Indians Concerning Religion."[9] To be successful in his presentation of self to eighteenth-century colonial powerbrokers, Occom had to speak the language of Christianity. But it is clear that he was also in deep discussion with his Native brethren about how to better prepare the next generation of Native leaders for life in a colonized world. In almost every instance where Occom might be seen as capitulating to colonial rule, one might look harder and find acts of what Cherokee scholar Jace Weaver refers to as *communitism*, a community-minded activism showcasing Occom's desire to do good for his people.[10]

After spending many years employing his skills as teacher and preacher for the Long Island Montauk and Shinnecock tribes, and a shorter stint as teacher and missionary to the Oneida, Occom journeyed to England in 1765 to raise money for a proposed Indian school. He was well received in England and Scotland, drawing admiring crowds wherever he preached, and his two-and-a-half-year campaign resulted in his acquiring the start-up funds for Wheelock to found Dartmouth College. Dartmouth, however, did not prove to be the kind of institution Occom felt he had enlisted to promote, and he became understandably embittered by his one-time mentor's misallocation of the monies that he had sacrificed so much to procure. In a 1771 letter to Wheelock, Occom wrote "I verily thought that your Institution [Dartmouth] was Intended Purely for the poor Indians" and,

> with this thought I Cheerfully Ventur'd my body & Soul, left my Country, my poor young Family all my friends and Relations … to help forward your School, Hoping, that it may be a lasting Benefit to my poor Tawnee Brethren.

Instead, however, Occom concluded that Wheelock's newly formed "alma Mater" was become "too much alba mater," a play on words suggesting that Dartmouth had abandoned its original mandate and gave nurture to white students only.[11]

This was precisely the same lesson Occom had learned two decades earlier in the Connecticut general courts arguing the Mason Land Case. He realized that he could no longer place his faith in colonial institutions to supply the needs of his people and he used this opportunity to break his ties with the evangelical concerns of the colony. Drawing together members of various southern New England indigenous nations, Occom helped to spearhead the 1785 formation of a new Indian settlement, *Eeyawquittoowauconnuck*, or Brothertown, in upstate New York. Instrumental in the forging of this new Native space were the diplomatic ties Occom had forged years earlier in his mission to the Oneida. Occom's hope was that this new homeland would be removed enough from colonial intrusions to allow his community to thrive on its own industry and merits. But the pressures of colonial westward expansion were already pushing at the edges of this dream, and Occom died in 1791 at 69 years of age realizing that colonial efforts to subsume and erase Mohegan identity would continue on relentlessly.

Because Occom's autobiographical narrative was completed in 1768, upon his return from England, it cannot address the Moses Paul execution or the immigration to Brothertown, both of which occurred afterwards. But an engaged reading of the short narrative allows students to locate moments of tension in Occom's self-presentation—moments where the text seemingly pulls in two different directions at once. In my experience, students are inclined to initially fix upon Occom's conformity to settler norms—the fact that he refers to himself in the text as a "heathen" and a "poor Indian," as well as his conversion to Christianity, which is often seen as a betrayal of his own culture—students, after all, have mostly been taught to value a highly romanticized notion of "pure" and "wild" Native identity. Some will even accuse Occom of being a "whiner" based on his complaints concerning unequal compensation for his years of missionary outreach. But these initial impressions can be redirected, and students can be encouraged to also notice how every action Occom narrates is precisely animated with the intent to serve his Indian brethren. His conversion to Christianity through English literacy is balanced by his desire to educate the "poor" Indian children. His decision to apprentice under Wheelock to learn dead languages such as Latin is offset by his need to understand legal nomenclature, also in Latin, by which his people were being disenfranchised of their lands. It is also useful to bring attention to Occom's 11 years serving as a missionary in Montauk and how those years are defined by an almost impossible accumulation of responsibilities to the tribe that far exceeded his role as minister and educator. Occom describes how he,

> kept school as I did before and Caried on the Religious Meetings as often as ever, and attended the Sick and their Funerals, and did what Writings they wanted, and often Sat as Judge to reconcile and Deside their Matters between them, and had visitors of Indians from all Quarters; and as our Custom is, we freely Entertain all Visiters,—And was fetchd often from my Tribe and from others to See into their Affairs Both Religious [and] Temporal.[12]

One can see that Occom, because of his literacy skills and his ability to leverage those skills to some extent with colonial authorities, performed the offices of preacher, teacher, diplomat, judge, medicine man, and scribe. He tends to the sick, writes letters and petitions for the tribe, and is obliged, owing to Native customs of hospitality, to entertain tribal dignitaries from other nations. His overall significance to the Montauk is marked by his marriage to Mary Fowler, daughter of one of the leading families of the tribe, and Occom must balance his many responsibilities with the necessities of maintaining his own family. On top of his official duties, Occom catalogues the exhaustive domestic chores he must take on, doing his own sowing, hunting, and reaping, and making pails, brooms, and other crafts to sell to white neighbors to supplement his income. He observes that, during this whole time, he received only one-twelfth of what a typical white missionary would be compensated despite his having a great many more responsibilities.

However, in the final analysis, it is not the lack of compensation to which Occom truly objects. He already accepts this as part of the ingrained institutionalized prejudice against Native peoples in colonial America and the price of desiring to serve his community. Occom's autobiographical narrative is an attempt to expose the hypocrisy of the evangelical societies that spoke endlessly of uplifting the "poor Indians" from heathen darkness, but whose actions actually had the exact opposite effect of keeping Native people in "their place." Unlike the world Benjamin Franklin describes in his more famous autobiography, frugality and industry do not naturally lead to prosperity when one is an Indian. As in the parable Occom tells of the indentured Indian child, forced to drive the plow of his white master and continuously whipped for his perceived shortcomings, it matters not how well the job is done or how faithfully the work is executed. "I drive as well as I know how," the child says, but "I believe he Beats for the most of the Time, because I am an Indian."[13] Occom felt his own labors, despite his demonstrable successes, were viewed in the same regard, constantly slamming up against a wall of racial designation prescribing just how far his efforts could take him. His narrative is a declaration of independence of sorts, announcing his intention to no longer abide by the demands and expectations of the white missionary establishment that sought to govern and constrain his actions.

In this light, we might understand Occom's presence at Moses Paul's execution as an act of defiance. Moses Paul's fate was to hang, regardless of who preached at his passing. But, by usurping the role of the white ministerial establishment, Occom was able to stand as an ally at Paul's moment of truth, rather than yet another adversary at the gallows. The court records from the case demonstrate that Paul was more victim than aggressor in the events culminating in his fateful act of violence.[14] But the conditions informing colonial discourse were virtually incapable of maintaining the innocence of an Indian implicated in the death of a white man. The public sentiment, expressed in the press and elsewhere, was "Hang the Indian! Hang him! Hang him!" and, as with Katherine Garret's trial some 40 years earlier, there was little public appetite for delving into the gritty details of the case.[15] Under these circumstances, it was Paul, himself, who requested Occom's presence at the pulpit, undoubtedly seeking a friendly voice of comfort to ease his passage from this world. Rarely could a seventeenth-century Native be afforded such an opportunity. Occom signaled his reluctance to attend this sorry spectacle, calling it an "unwelcome task," but he noted, "in conscience I cannot deny him. I must endeavor to do the great work the dying man requests."[16]

One should keep in mind that Occom, too, was in a precarious situation. He faced constant assaults on his reputation and well-being from unprincipled white educators, ministers, and ne'er-do-wells who seemed to gravitate towards the work of Indian conversion for the easy pickings to be gleaned by those placed in positions of authority over Indian affairs. These predators recognized Occom as a threat to their livelihood as, indeed, Occom's popularity and effectiveness in both Native and white communities negated the work they had signed on to exploit. Far-flung conspiracies were attached to Occom's name. He was accused of both excessive pride and public drunkenness, a charge to which Natives were particularly vulnerable. Such claims could quickly ruin any aspirations someone like Occom might have in the public realm, and so Occom learned to tread carefully in these situations, holding himself at all times with a forthright humility that was not easily provoked. Nevertheless, turning his attention to the audience at Moses Paul's execution, Occom reminded them that it was white men who had introduced alcohol to the Indians, and that written in scripture was "a wo [woe] denounced against men, who put their bottles to their neighbors mouth to make them drunk ... And no doubt there are such devilish men now in our days, as there were in the days of old."[17]

In later years, Occom would grow even more openly critical of the white establishment, speaking out forcefully against "oppressors, over reachers, Defrauders, Extortioners, with holders of corn." There is little question of whom he speaks when he charges,

> *they* Covet everything that their Neighbors have, Yea This Sort of People I think are Monopolizers; don't you think so? For these Men will Buy up every Necessary of Life in the Town or State, even of the Whole World ... especially in Time of great Want and Distress, and When they have Horded up What they can they will set an Extravagant Price upon their Commodities.[18]

Such sentiments did not find their way into print in Occom's lifetime, but they can be found among his unpublished papers and apparently they reflect the kind of subjects that were a staple of Occom's preaching.

Abenaki scholar Lisa Brooks has noted that, in the second half of the eighteenth century, "a group of literate Mohegans banded together, using writing to reconstruct their body politic, re-member their collective history, and reclaim their Native rights."[19] Although Occom's standing as a public advocate for the Mohegan community was second to none, he operated among a wider network of literate Christian Natives with whom he lived, loved, and corresponded. David and Jacob Fowler were two close associates who also were educated by Wheelock at the short-lived Moor's Indian Academy. They accompanied Occom on many of his missions, and David was among the first settlers to break ground and establish his home in the Brothertown community. Occom was related to the Fowler brothers through his marriage to Mary Fowler, who remains an interesting and little-known figure in her own right. Despite her being intimately connected to the most prominent figure in the Native Christian community, she maintained her traditional lifestyle throughout their marriage, refusing to abandon her traditional attire and insisting on speaking her Montauk dialect of the Algonquian language, even when white visitors came calling, which was often. Joseph Johnson was yet another member of the Mohegan community who, after falling afoul of Wheelock's missionary agenda, energetically pursued the cause of the Brothertown settlement, petitioning authorities all along the eastern seaboard to support the "removal" of the southern New England Natives to a new home in upstate New York.

Johnson, too, wrote a short plea to Moses Paul prior to the execution, which was published in the local newspapers and is interesting in its own right—demonstrating a certain level of solidarity in the Mohegan community in their concern and support for Moses Paul. Johnson's tract would often appear tacked on to later published editions of Occom's Sermon and is more openly sympathetic to Paul's plight. Like Occom, Johnson tried to use his talents to benefit other Native communities he encountered in his travels, writing petitions for them, "pricking out" hymnals, and, upon being asked, reading aloud to them Occom's famous execution sermon—a publication in which Native people of the Northeast clearly took pride. Johnson would eventually marry Occom's daughter, Olive, and so sealed kinship ties to the Mohegan preacher, although he would die only a few years later while serving as a diplomatic go-between for General George Washington's continental army and the Haudenosaunee at the dawn of the American Revolution. Some years later, Moses Paul's son would marry one of Occom's daughters in Brothertown, suggesting even further the hidden ties of feeling and kinship that are rarely apparent in the colonized text. Nevertheless, Occom's *Sermon Preached at the Execution of Moses Paul* serves as one more example of how Occom's seeming acts of assimilation are more often than not deeply informed by his dedication to Native community and cohesion.

There are a number of resources one can turn to when teaching about Samson Occom and the dynamics of Native existence in the eighteenth-century Northeast. I will often pair Occom's "Autobiographical Narrative" with readings from *Dawnland Encounters*, an anthology of writings from New England Natives edited by Siobhan Senier. The readings in this volume are organized by tribal identification, and the "Mohegan" section includes a petition written by Occom on behalf of the Shinnecock tribe, extracts from the diaries of Occom's son-in-law, Joseph Johnson, traditional recipes recalled by tribal members, as well as writings from contemporary Mohegan authors such as Melissa Tantaquidgeon Zobel, the medicine woman and tribal historian of the Mohegan at the time of this writing, and a direct descendant of

Samson Occom. These offerings not only fill out our engagement with Mohegan lifeways, but they remind us that the Mohegans and other New England Natives are not just a historical curiosity—they continue to survive and identify themselves as sovereign indigenous nations.

Most of Occom's writings can be accessed online through an excellent website entitled *The Occom Circle Project*, which, ironically perhaps, is run out of Dartmouth College. The website is fully searchable, and so not only can documents such as Occom's "Autobiographical Narrative" and the execution sermon be accessed here, but it can be useful to have students conduct their own searches for materials that might help round out a section plan on Occom. Dartmouth College has made strides in recent years to correct its role in exploiting the labor and wishes of Native peoples who helped fund the institution, but it is also instructive to note that Melissa Tantaquidgeon Zobel, speaking for the Mohegans, has suggested that Occom's letters, journals, and tracts, many of which remain archived at Dartmouth, are themselves living *beings* with spirit of their own, and their rightful place is with the Mohegan people.

William Apess: Removing the Son From the Forest

On January 31, 1798, a child was born to the small, newly sprung, backwoods settlement of Colrain in the hills of Northeastern Massachusetts. His father, we are told, was the son of a white man and a Pequot woman, and his mother, whose ethnic identity is unclear, was most likely born into slavery, despite being affiliated with the Pequot tribe. This, of course, was the same Pequot tribe that, during the 1636–37 Pequot War, colonial forces had done everything in their power to completely annihilate in their bid to control the wampum trade. From this complicated union, vexed by the racial politics of the early republic, and out of this shattered past emerged William Apess, one of the more radical American voices of the nineteenth century. Apess was raised under conditions of brutal poverty, as was the case for so many Native people at this time, uneducated, and the victim of terrible abuse at the hands of his maternal grandparents and, later, from the white families to whom he was indentured. He was forced to join the United States Army in the war of 1812, seeing many bloody sights on the battlefield before he ever reached the legal enlistment age of 18. And then he was cut loose into the world, without compensation for his service or any means, other than his two feet, to complete the journey home. Nevertheless, he would go on to forge a role for himself as author, intellectual, and advocate for Native rights in yet another era of great violence and upheaval for indigenous peoples throughout the continent.

Unfortunately, none of Apess's letters or effects are left to us, or his oeuvre would certainly match Occom's in regards to its breadth and intimacy. We can only assume that Occom's papers were originally swept up by Dartmouth College historians in their overall zeal to memorialize Eleazar Wheelock's founding of the college. Occom's very public role in raising the monies that birthed the

FIGURE 2.3 Engraving from William Apess's 1831 *A Son of the Forest*. Courtesy American Antiquarian Society

institution, fortunately for us, made him a necessary component of that archival initiative. Because Apess never fully served any colonial institution, and was more often than not perceived as an irritant, he was not deemed worthy of such archival preservation. All that remains, at the moment at least, are the five works that he published in his lifetime between the years 1829 and 1836 and a couple of petitions that he penned on behalf of other New England tribes. Even so, these alone were remarkable achievements for any individual of the time and particularly for one who had endured such personal, cultural, and historical trauma.

What we know of Apess, we mostly know through his own writings. His 1829 memoir *A Son of the Forest* details his harrowing childhood and bravely confronts the cultural traumas facing so many Native communities, including self-inflicted wounds of domestic abuse, prostitution, and alcoholism, which Apess would have us understand were the direct outcomes of ongoing economic and cultural depredations imposed by white colonial rule. But the memoir is also a narrative of personal triumph, as Apess uses a platform of Christian uplift to rise above the stations of poverty and decline mapped out for his people. Properly read, *A Son of the Forest* offers a full-throated resistance to the colonial machinery of oppression against people of color in the nineteenth century, forging rhetorical strategies that would echo throughout the abolitionist movement and in subsequent struggles for indigenous rights. As Weaver observes, Apess's works should be viewed in the tradition of "resistance literature, affirming Indian cultural and political identity over and against the dominant culture."[20]

Apess's rhetoric requires a bit of unpacking in the classroom, but a reading informed by the same sort of decolonizing techniques employed with previous works will readily make available how Apess, too, is primarily concerned with advocating for the indigenous community and creating a space for indigenous agency. I believe the challenge in reading Apess, Occom, and so many other Native writers of this period is in making available for students the critical tools that will help them remove *themselves* from the dark forest of dominant discursive practices. Just as it is important to continuously emphasize that Native people were agricultural and lived in village worlds rather than as hunter-gatherers, it requires something of a constant effort to decolonize the reading practices our students have inherited, to coax them out of the primeval wilderness in which they unconsciously place narratives of indigenous identity (that place in the woods where Eliot endlessly preaches from his rock) and into a kind of cognitive cornfield where the green shoots of lived Native experience can push through the soil. Too often, when reading about early indigenous life, we find ourselves entrenched in the rhetorical "howling wilderness" mapped out by colonial captivity narratives or find ourselves engulfed by the soundtrack of tom-toms and pan flute from old Hollywood westerns. As in the Haudenosaunee condolence narrative, we have to, in effect, learn to wipe our eyes of tears, clear our ears of dirt, and remove the obstructions from our throats before we can begin to effectively approach these works (see Chapter 1).

Arguably, Apess does not help this effort by referring to himself in his memoir as a "son of the forest." The irony of course, whether intended or not, was that Apess knew next to nothing of forest existence, was raised in white towns, often laboring as a farmhand for white families in rural communities, and made a name for himself speaking in the churches and meeting halls of Boston and New York City. The closest he gets to the wilderness is when he loses himself in a swamp at a crucial moment in his narrative and almost perishes as a result of his lack of wilderness skills. Barry O'Connell, who first collected and published Apess's works for modern audiences in 1992, reminds us that Indians were not supposed "to get lost in the woods—at least not in American literature and stereotype."[21] But Apess, too, must speak in the jargon of his time, and, in the early nineteenth century, the term "son of the forest" was a standard euphemism for "Indian." Like the rest of us, Apess also had to continuously labor to recover himself from the cognitive forest in which colonial representation had positioned him.

For students, the interpretive dangers of reading Native lives from that dark forested space is that they will fixate on the negatives, having absorbed an unconscious "blame the victim" mentality that is so much an undercurrent of American identity discourse. They will see the struggles that Apess and his family had with alcohol, poverty, and violence and often read this as a cultural failing, cementing the notion that Native existence is inconsistent with modernity. For instance, when Apess tells, at the start of his memoir, of being beaten by his grandmother, she repeatedly demands of him "do you hate me?" It is such a complicated moment, as the grandmother seems to be projecting upon the helpless child the hate she herself has absorbed selling brooms and baskets in the white community. And the child, not properly understanding the question, answers "yes." It is worthwhile, therefore, to fully unpack these moments and work towards the revelation of how difficult it must have been for Apess to publicize his childhood traumas. Most people want to hide or silence domestic abuse of any kind, as the victims of such abuse intuitively understand themselves to be ensnared within the web of a much larger, if always invisible, power dynamic. But Apess leads with it in his narrative, apprehending that the only way to break the cycle of violence is to begin to shine a light upon it and trace it back to its source. Apess understands that the conditions working to destroy his family, as well as the larger Pequot community, were not the result of personal failings so much as impossible pressures, both historical and present, being applied from without. In a passage that invokes Occom's sermon, he writes how he attributes these ills "in a great measure to the whites, inasmuch as they introduced among my countrymen that bane of comfort and happiness, ardent spirits—seduced them into a love of it and, when under its unhappy influence, wronged them out of their lawful possessions."[22] Apess is fully aware that alcohol is not solely to blame for these injustices, but temperance sermons were the coin of the realm in the evangelical movements of this time, and Apess recognized an opportunity to usefully channel this rhetoric into addressing the social ills confronting Native peoples.

A Son of the Forest takes us through Apess's early career as he finds his voice as a preacher and prepares for ordination in the Methodist Episcopal church. We learn how he reunites with his Pequot community after the war and, under the tutelage of his charismatic Aunt Sally George, becomes a devotee of camp revival meetings, which George frequently led in the forested groves, referred to as "God's first temples."[23] Sally George teaches Apess how to tend to the practical and spiritual needs of the community, performing a role much like Occom did among the Montauk. Such a role was implicitly political, the health of the fragile community depending greatly on being able to advocate for rights that were routinely denied those living on Indian "reservations."

Native reservations in the Northeast were maintained under a system of colonial overseers who held the power of feudal lords over their subjects, routinely availing themselves of the fruits of indigenous land and labor. At most, all tribal members could do under this system was appeal for better treatment, either to the higher courts or to the overseers themselves. But such appeals were, in general, quickly swallowed up by a legal system that, after all, was expressly designed to disenfranchise Natives from the last of their holdings. Apess's Aunt Sally George stood at the cultural center of the Pequot community, keeping hope, culture, and tradition alive through syncretic spiritual practices that she passed along to her energetic protégé. Apess harnessed many of these skills over the next decade to rise up through the ranks of the Methodist organization. Although, at the close of his 1829 narrative, he was ultimately denied ordination into the Methodist Episcopal Church, he published his memoir shortly after and continued to pursue his goals of indigenous advocacy through other means, finally achieving ordination within the newly formed Protestant Methodist church in 1831.[24]

A Son of the Forest is a great introductory text for understanding the lives that Natives of the Northeast led in the 1800s, as Apess's experiences are representative in most ways of what other Natives of the time were going through: having their childhoods mortgaged out to white property-holders, fighting in wars of imperialist expansion, warding off extreme poverty and cultural disruption, and finding ways to keep tradition and culture alive under the platform of Christian worship. Although Apess, in his writings, must make accommodations to the discursive demands of his time, his critique of colonial power and, in particular, the corrosive manner in which Christianity was imposed upon Native communities remains pointed and at times even groundbreaking. Apess always assumes the sovereign rights of Native peoples in his writings. His texts, despite being informed by Christian belief, often insinuate the legitimacy of traditional Native customs and spirituality, regarding such practices as a more perfect expression of pure Christian faith than what was being promoted by the white missionary establishment.

In *A Son of the Forest*, Apess discreetly acknowledges the effects of Native spirituality upon his thinking. While wandering through Canada after the war and falling in with other groups of Natives, he encounters a mysterious "unfathomable" lake on the Bay of Quinte, alongside a rock of "a most beautiful and romantic appearance" that seemed to have been "hollowed out by the hand of a skilfull artificer." These natural features inspire him to reflect upon "the wisdom of God in the order, regularity, and beauty of creation" and, in the same breath, he turns around and equally admires "the sons and daughters" of the forest who appeared to achieve the "utmost order and regularity in their encampments."[25] It is an ambiguous and entrancing moment, one referred to by Lisa Brooks as the scene of Apess's "rebirth," as it "connects the Christian God to the spirit of creation, to the forest and its network of relations, which contained all the Native inhabitants of the region, including Apess himself."[26] It would be impossible for Apess to speak openly of such things within the bounds of nineteenth-century print discourse, but his mysterious encounter with nature in this passage is one that is steeped in indigenous ceremony.[27]

Apess continued to grow as both writer and rhetorician, and his works become increasingly more political as he progresses. In his essay "An Indian's Looking-Glass for the White Man," for instance, he once again demonstrates his courage and savvy, as he depicts the bleak conditions suffered on Indian reservations in the Northeast. "It may be that many are ignorant of the situation of many of my brethren," he observes in a statement that is as profoundly true today as it was then.

> Let a gentleman and lady of integrity and respectability visit these places, and they would be surprised; as they wandered from one hut to the other they would view, with the females who are left alone, children half-starved and some almost as naked as they came into the world ... while the females are left without protection, and are seduced by white men, and are finally left to be common prostitutes for them and to be destroyed by that burning, fiery curse. rum.[28]

In this scene, and many others that Apess paints, we begin to catch a glimpse of the painful existence his grandmother must have eked out living in these conditions.

And who else was writing about domestic abuse and the sexual exploitation of women in 1833? The men, as Apess notes, had been forced to go elsewhere for work, many of them employed on whaling boats that would pass 2 or more years at sea. If they returned from such dangerous labor, their wages were often paid out directly to the overseers who determined what percentage might be passed along to the whaler and his family. These were not the romantic Indians of James Fenimore Cooper novels, but the true Natives of the Northeast among whom Apess lived and labored and about which there has not, until very recently, been a great deal of historical investigation. Although state law mandated churches and schools for Indian edification, these initiatives were rarely followed through with any resolve, and, when Apess arrived to preach to the Mashpee Indians of Cape Cod in 1833, he found the Natives weren't even allowed in the church that had been erected for their use.

Osage scholar Robert Warrior looks at Apess's overtly political commentary in "An Indian's Looking-Glass" as "one of the most vital turns in the history of Native writing," striking at "the heart of American racism" and laying "bare the roots of Native degradation."[29] Whereas in his memoir Apess cautiously rebukes the historical trafficking of distilled spirits and the deleterious effect it has had on Indian nations, here he chooses to no longer mince words, calling out the racism that has reduced his people to such conditions of abject poverty. Why, he asks, are Native people not

> protected in our persons and property throughout the Union? Is it not because there reigns in the breast of many who are leaders a most unrighteous, unbecoming, and impure black principle, and as corrupt and unholy as it can be—while these very same unfeeling, self-esteemed characters pretend to take the skin as a pretext to keep us from our unalienable and lawful rights?[30]

In a fascinating passage where he imagines all the "skins" of the world called together to discover which has the greatest crimes written upon it, he concludes, "I know that when I cast my eye upon that white skin ... I should enter my protest against it immediately." Can you charge the Indian, he asks "with robbing a nation almost of their whole continent, and murdering their women and children, and then depriving the remainder of their lawful rights?" And can you charge the Indian of robbing "another nation to till their grounds and welter out their days under the lash with hunger and fatigue under the scorching rays of a burning sun?"[31] Apess is not invested in singling out skin color as a means of defining character. By holding up his Indian's looking-glass, however, he asks his white audience to view themselves through the same lens they have used to condemn Native people and to reconsider who are, in fact, the true "savages." But perhaps even more important is his willingness to single out racial construction as the single most significant factor in how rights are apportioned in a supposedly free and independent United States where all are presumably "created equal."

In 1835, Apess published *Indian Nullification*, which recounts his experiences in Mashpee and the role he played in challenging the system of rule that had, for decades, treated Native resources as the rightful spoil of white neighbors and overseers. *Indian Nullification* is a long and unwieldy work, but, in many ways, also Apess's most brilliant, as it methodically exposes the system of rampant injustices under which Native peoples lived and details the strategies of civil disobedience that Apess activated in his attempt to dismantle that system. It may be a book that better lends itself to an upper-level or graduate seminar, but the reward of teaching *Indian Nullification* is that it situates Apess at the height of his effectiveness, the strategies for Native resistance outlined in this work foreshadowing arguments later put forward by William Lloyd Garrison, Henry David Thoreau, Frederick Douglass, Martin Luther King, and other civil rights leaders. Some of these tactics are still being used effectively today in standoffs such as the one at Standing Rock in 2016, where Native peoples from across the nation peacefully gathered in their attempt to prevent the Dakota Access Pipeline from running beneath the Missouri River and through traditional Lakota treaty lands.

Apess's insistence on non-violent tactics was designed to bring events at Mashpee to a highly publicized crisis and demonstrates specialized skills he had developed over a decade of advocating for Native causes. Although Apess would go to jail for his actions, narrowly avoiding being lynched by the enraged white community, he leveraged this miscarriage of justice to subsequently inform white New England audiences of abuses occurring right in their own backyards of which they knew absolutely nothing. Apess's cause was given a boost by growing public discontent over the way the Cherokee people were being persecuted by the Jackson administration and the state of Georgia in the wake of Indian removal legislation. And given this perfect storm of political awareness, the Mashpee in 1834 were able to win limited civic autonomy for themselves in the Massachusetts legislature, a marked improvement over their previous situation.

Apess would go on to write and perform the compelling *Eulogy on King Philip* in 1836, a kind of travelling one-man show that he presented live on numerous occasions throughout the Northeast. The *Eulogy* was a retelling of colonization that placed the Wampanoag sachem Philip, rather than the English settlers, at the center of the encounter. But even more than this, it was a sophisticated attempt on Apess's part to dismantle the rhetoric of colonization, an expertly orchestrated deconstruction of the discursive norms by which the violence of conquest had been legitimated, offering in its place an indigenous history of colonial encounter. Until very recently, many believed that the *Eulogy* was Apess's final attempt to assert himself and his writings on the nineteenth-century stage, but new research has shown how Apess continued to find new venues and rhetorical platforms to plead for Indian rights, continuing right on until his sudden collapse, apparently from appendicitis, in New York City in 1839. He was 41 years old at the time of his death, his body most likely unceremoniously cast in a pauper's grave in the old black cemetery that now lies sealed under tons of concrete in the Wall Street district of Manhattan.

Teaching the Trail of Tears

Apess and Occom are both remarkable literary figures of this era, their textual legacies little known or appreciated until fairly recently. But they were not the only Native individuals engaging with print discourse at the time. Aside from the network of letter-writing Mohegans detailed earlier, there was John Norton, a Cherokee raised in England and then transported to Canada after having joined the British Army at the age of 16 and later adopted by Joseph Brant into the Mohawk Nation. Norton wrote of his extensive travels throughout the North American continent and his experiences as a leader of Mohawk scouts for the British in the War of 1812, his completed work numbering more than 1,000 pages of hand-written text. But, aside from his translation of the Gospel of John into the Mohawk language, Norton's works were not published in his lifetime, and his massive history *The Journal of Major John Norton* remains little known even among indigenous scholars.

Jane Johnston Schoolcraft is another remarkable figure from this period, an Anishinaabe woman who married the famous white nineteenth-century ethnographer Henry Rowe Schoolcraft. Johnston Schoolcraft was the daughter of an Irish fur trader and a woman from a leading family of the Ojibwe Nation in the area of what is today Sault Ste. Marie, Michigan. Although she did not seek to publish her work in her lifetime, Johnston Schoolcraft became a prolific writer of poetry as well as penning several adaptations of traditional Ojibwe tales and songs. Her Ojibwe name, Bamewawagezhikaquay, translates to Woman of the Sound the Stars Make Rushing through the Sky, which, all by itself, is suggestive of the poetic proclivities of the Ojibwe, or Anishinaabe, people. Fluent in the literacies of both her communities, Johnston Schoolcraft occasionally wrote versions of her poems in Ojibwa and English, providing a compelling study in translation and contrast. Henry Rowe Schoolcraft marshalled his kinship connections with the Johnston family to establish his authority as an Indian ethnographer and often embellished his wife's tales to presumably make them more palatable for western audiences. From these embellishments we inherit the legend of Hiawatha, a misattribution of cultural stories and namesakes that resulted in the famed poem by Longfellow. Robert Dale Parker notes of Jane Johnston Schoolcraft that, although she shied away from political commentary, her poetry often engaged "the personal and the familial with what we might call a nationalist commitment to place and people that can resonate powerfully."[32]

Other Native writers from the period include David Cusick, who published his *Sketches of Ancient History of the Six Nations* in 1828. Peter Jones and George Copway were both Methodist ministers of the Ojibwe Nation who wrote of their experiences as remarkably self-assured indigenous evangelicals traversing the epistemological gaps between cultures. David Brown emerged as a charismatic Cherokee intellectual in the 1820s but died of "bleeding of the lungs" before he could exhibit his full potential.[33] But perhaps the Native figure with the greatest national reputation of the period was Elias Boudinot, who served as editor for many years of the *Cherokee Phoenix*, a newspaper produced by the Cherokee Nation and printed in both English and Cherokee, using the syllabary invented by Sequoyah only a few years prior.

Boudinot was an outspoken advocate for Cherokee nationhood, touring the eastern seaboard in the 1820s and 30s with his cousin, John Ridge, in an effort to build public opposition to President Jackson's vicious Indian removal policies. Having been schooled from the age of 6 in missionary academies in Springplace, Georgia, and later in Cornwall, Connecticut, Boudinot's worldview was heavily slanted towards a narrative of Christian assimilationist uplift. Civilization appeared to have become synonymous in his thinking with Western culture, and he aspired for indigenous peoples everywhere to raise themselves up out of their state of savagery to receive the fruits of white settler rule if they did not wish to perish by the cultural wayside. Nineteenth-century discourse, in particular, forwarded this dire either/or choice of assimilation or extinction for Native peoples, foreclosing on the notion that, perhaps, they could both change and grow while maintaining their traditional cultural identities. Cherokee scholar Daniel Heath Justice cautions against this form of "antiquated progressivism," rejecting the notion that Native people were ever a "doomed race that sacrificed indigenousness for White civilization."[34] In other words, there is nothing to mandate that being indigenous is incompatible with modernity. But such notions remain powerfully in place, even today, and continue to inform paternalistic legislation concerning Native people.

However steeped Boudinot's rhetoric was in antiquated progressivism, he was still a powerful advocate for Cherokee nationhood, and his 1826 "Address to the Whites" was meant to appeal to western audiences by arguing how the Cherokee, as a people, were taking a step forward, inaugurating themselves as a "civilized" tribe as a result of the new laws and constitutional system of government they were presently adopting, closely modeled on those of the United States. The Cherokee constitution was ratified by the nation in 1827, and John Ross was elected their first president under this system of laws in 1828. The *Cherokee Phoenix*, which Boudinot operated with the assistance of the Baptist missionary Samuel Worcester, became the voice of the nation, publicizing their transformation into "civilized" purveyors of democratic institutions to subscribers on both sides of the Atlantic. But the Indian Removal Act was passed by Congress directly on the heels of these measures in 1830, foreshadowing how futile it ultimately was for the Cherokee to try to forestall settler expansion through such conciliatory means.

It is important that students know about Boudinot, but in my experience the event of Cherokee removal, popularly referred to as the "trail of tears," needs to be comprehended through a wider lens of literary productions. There is no way, of course, to appreciate the full complexity and trauma of this moment in a week or two of class time, but *The Cherokee Removal: A Brief History with Documents*, edited by Theda Perdue and Michael D. Green, remains a very good source for providing historical and cultural context. I tend to focus on the third section of the book, which introduces students to official rationalizations made by people such as President Andrew Jackson and War Secretary Lewis Cass, both of whom attempted to make removal sound like a perfectly benevolent policy. Three petitions to the tribe presented by Cherokee women in 1817, 1818, and 1831 demonstrate how women understood their positionality within the debate and their responsibility to influence public discourse. A selection of Boudinot's editorials can be found here, as well as a defiant letter by Cherokee President John Ross, exemplifying the tone Cherokee intellectuals attempted to set as they made their appeals to an increasingly hostile American government. One successful assignment I have developed is to have my students write a letter to the *Cherokee Phoenix*, assuming their best nineteenth-century voices, that responds to the arguments put forward by Jackson and Cass using specifically cited rebuttals drawn from the Cherokee writers in the volume.

Jackson's removal policies affected not only the Cherokee, but many other Eastern indigenous nations, pressuring these groups to quit their ancestral grounds and push west of the Mississippi to lands that had been set aside for their use, blithely ignoring the fact that other indigenous people needed to be displaced to make such lands available. The case of the Cherokee has become synonymous with Indian removal in the public imagination owing to the simple fact that they had a press and a newspaper and were able to publicize their cause. Their effective public relations battle was accompanied, however, by legal battles that carried all the way to the Supreme Court in two cases, *The Cherokee Nation vs. The State of Georgia* (1831) and *Worcester vs. The State of Georgia* (1832). In the former, Justice John Marshall determined that the Cherokee were a "domestic dependent nation," a ruling that seemed to concede limited sovereignty to the Cherokee and has had lasting ramifications for how the law regards Native people in the United States. *Worcester*, too, ruled that treaties must always be understood as agreements between sovereign nations and, as stated in the constitution, remain "the law of the land." As such, neither Jackson, Congress, nor the state of Georgia had proper authority to force Cherokee people off their lands.

As it became increasingly apparent, however, that the Jackson administration was intent on proceeding with its plans, regardless of the Supreme Court decision, a small group of some 50 Cherokee, including Boudinot and Ridge, determined to make the best of a bad situation. They signed an agreement with the federal government, acting against the wishes of the vast majority of the Cherokee Nation and the laws of their constitution, to abandon their lands in exchange for parcels out west. This is a story that has been turned over again and again by Native scholars, but it will be new to most students. The signed agreement, known as the 1835 Treaty of New Echota, was regarded by the United States as a legitimate treaty, actionable upon the entire Cherokee Nation, and Jackson used this spurious document to effect the brutal removal of 16,000 Cherokee people from their traditional lands in what are, today, Georgia, North Carolina, Tennessee, and Kentucky.

The majority of the Cherokee, led by their president, John Ross, who rightfully resisted the legitimacy of the treaty, were torn from their homes at the points of bayonets, forced to give up their lands and their possessions, often with white families standing by waiting to immediately steal in behind them, and were marched without proper clothing, shelter, or provisions to staging areas near Chattanooga, Tennessee, in preparation for the 1,000-mile march. Language matters a great deal when we discuss these events. I say "staging areas," but Daniel Heath Justice reminds us that these should be properly understood as "concentration camps," and, although "removal" is the term most often deployed, the more modern term, "ethnic cleansing," is a very suitable replacement.[35] Understood in this light, one can begin to see just how much violent erasure is contained within the term "Trail of Tears," by which most Americans understand and characterize this historical event. It is a term that reduces full-blown atrocity on the part of the United States government into a somewhat trite and sentimental catchphrase, suggesting that the occurrence of the Cherokee being violently ripped from their lands, resulting in the deaths of a quarter of their population, was, in the final analysis, a little sad, causing tears.

To my knowledge, there are no existing firsthand accounts of the removal by the Cherokee themselves. Like the infamous Middle Passage of the slave trade, it is a forced journey that maintains many silences. Contemporary Cherokee authors have written eloquently about it, however, including Diane Glancy, who penned the novel *Pushing the Bear*, Robert Conley's *Mountain Windsong*, and Blake Hausman's post-modern treatment entitled *Riding the Trail of Tears*. I can typically only assign one of these works in a semester, so, despite the fact that they each offer strikingly different takes on the "Trail of Tears," I tend to assign them on a rotating basis. I will discuss Glancy and Hausman's works in more detail in Chapter 5.

To supplement the historical documents in Perdue and Green's casebook, however, I always include excerpts from the journal of Daniel Butrick, a Baptist missionary who chose to accompany the Cherokee on the trail and kept a detailed journal. I should note here that I always want my Native American Literature classes to consist solely of works by Native writers, but this section is an exception, where I feel it is necessary to help penetrate the historical silences to some degree. A very useful selection from Butrick's journals can be found in Vicky Rozema's edited collection, *Voices from the Trail of Tears*. Here we can begin to apprehend the true enormity of what was taking place, as Butrick describes the daily horror of thousands upon thousands of people being driven at gunpoint to the concentration camps where they were packed in, exposed to the elements, and held for months while military officials made their preparations. He notes of Cherokee prisoners being marched from their homes that,

> they were obliged to live very much like brute animals, and during their travels, were obliged at night to lie down on the naked ground, in the open air, exposed to wind and rain, and herd together, men women and children, like droves of hogs, and in this way, many are hastening to a premature grave.

Death in the camps becomes such a common sight that Butrick bitterly observes, "had half the infants … and all aged over sixty … and one fourth of the remainder" simply been killed outright, it would have saved "a vast amount of expense and suffering," and the result would have been the same.[36]

A student recently wrote in my end-of-the-semester classroom evaluation (required by my institution) that he wished the class had been less political and just focused more on the literature.

I want my students to appreciate the beauty, inventiveness, and poignancy of so much Native Literature—it is, in many ways, what first attracted me to the field as a scholar. But the idea that you can somehow read this literature and separate it from the politics is to demand the "tears," but not the "ethnic cleansing." It is to desire the dark romantic forests of James Fenimore Cooper novels, but not the fields of green corn planted long before Europeans ever arrived. It is to demand horseback Indians in eagle feathers and deerskin with bow and arrow in hand, but not those in ascot and overcoat, headed to a camp meeting with Bible in hand. It is to desire an "Indian princess" in your distant bloodline, but to disregard the long history of sexual violation of indigenous women that continues to destroy lives and wreak unimaginable havoc. It is the cultural insistence on remaining absolved of any sense of social responsibility for ongoing injustices occurring in Indian country today—a tacit refusal to take Native writers at their word when they say these are their lives and this is their history, and to insist, instead, that they write of topics aesthetically pleasing to the sensibilities of white privilege.

I feel bad that I was not able to get that student to move beyond the entrenched myths and stereotypes that he brought with him into the classroom. But I also know that I cannot always undo a lifetime of cultural programming in one short semester, as much as I always enter into the bargain believing that I might. And, even as I write this in 2020, I am confronted almost daily with images of our current president signing executive orders from the Oval Office with a portrait of Andrew Jackson prominently displayed over his desk and glaring down at the proceedings. Still, in the case of the Cherokee removal, as well as in many other heartrending accounts of colonial injustice that will inform any given semester, there is always room for reaffirmation, always the nod to the present, the reminder that, as Melissa Tantiquidgeon Zobel recalls of the Mohegan, "We survive as a nation ... our circular trail returns us to wholeness as a people."[37] Or, as Robert Warrior says of the Pequots, "they refuse to give up on the idea of [themselves] as a people."[38] Or, as Daniel Heath Justice says of the Cherokee, "our fire survives the storm." Or, as William Apess wryly reminds us in his 1834 *Indian Nullification*, despite all the challenges and obstacles thrown in his path, he's "still the same unbelieving Indian that he ever was."[39]

Notes

1 Joanna Brooks, "This Indian World," *The Collected Writings of Samson Occom, Mohegan: Leadership and Literature in Eighteenth-Century Native America* (New York: Oxford University Press, 2006), 23.
2 See "Advertisement," *Boston Evening-Post*, Feb. 2, 1773, p. 3.
3 Many people have certainly referred to Benjamin Franklin as a "man of letters," but I'm thinking more specifically of Michael Warner's essay here in which he plays with the dual meanings inherent in the phrase, recognizing that Franklin's public print persona is a thing literally constructed of letters. See Michael Warner "Franklin and the Letters of the Republic," *Representations* 16 (Autumn 1986), 110–130.
4 See Bernd C. Peyer, *The Tutor'd Mind, Indian Missionary Writers in Antebellum America* (Amherst: University of Massachusetts Press, 1987), 93.
5 This scene is recounted in Thomas Shepherd, "The Day Breaking if not the Sun Rising of the Gospell with the Indians in New England," *The Eliot Tracts*, Ed. Michael Clark (Westport, CT: Praeger Press, 2003), 82–85.
6 See James De Normandie, "John Eliot, The Apostle to the Indians," *Harvard Theological Review*, Vol. V (Cambridge: Harvard University Press, 1912), 349–370.
7 Shepherd, *Eliot Tracts*, 83.
8 Samson Occom, "Autobiographical Narrative, Second Draft," *The Collected Writings of Samson Occom, Mohegan*, Ed. Joanna Brooks (New York: Oxford University Press, 2006), 52.
9 Occom, "Autobiographical Narrative," 53.
10 See Jace Weaver, *That the People Might Live: Native American Literatures and Native American Community* (New York: Oxford University Press, 1997), xiii. Weaver writes that "Literature is communitist to the extent that it has a proactive commitment to Native community, including wat I term the 'wider community' of Creation itself ... to promote communitist values means to participate in the healing of the grief and sense of exile felt by Native communities and the pained individuals in them."
11 Samson Occom, "Letter to Eleazar Wheelock, July 24, 1771," *The Collected Writings of Samson Occom, Mohegan*, Ed. Joanna Brooks (New York: Oxford University Press, 2006), 98–99.
12 Occom, "Autobiographical Narrative," 55.
13 Occom, "Autobiographical Narrative," 58.
14 See Ava Chamberlain, "The Execution of Moses Paul: A Story of Crime and Contact in Eighteenth-Century Connecticut," *The New England Quarterly* 77:3 (Sep. 2004), pp. 414–450.
15 Chamberlain, 436.
16 Occom, "A Sermon Preached at the Execution of Moses Paul, An Indian (1772)," *The Collected Writings of Samson Occom, Mohegan*, Ed. Joanna Brooks (New York: Oxford University Press, 2006), 177.
17 Occom, "Execution," 193.

18 Occom, "Thou Shalt Love thy Neighbor as Thyself," *The Collected Writings of Samson Occom, Mohegan* (New York: Oxford University Press, 2006), 202. Italics mine.
19 Lisa Brooks, *The Common Pot: The Recovery of Native Space in the Northeast* (Minneapolis: University of Minnesota Press, 2008), 67.
20 Weaver, *That the People Might Live*, 55.
21 Barry O'Connell, "Introduction," *On Our Own Ground: The Complete Writings of William Apess, a Pequot* (University of Massachusetts Press, 1992), lii.
22 Apess, "A Son of the Forest," *On Our Own Ground*, 7.
23 Apess, "A Son of the Forest," 40.
24 See Drew Lopenzina, *Through an Indian's Looking-Glass: A Cultural Biography of William Apess, Pequot* (Amherst: University of Massachusetts Press, 2017), 187.
25 Apess, "A Son of the Forest," 33.
26 Brooks, *Common Pot*, 173–174.
27 For more on the possible significance of this passage, see Brooks, *Common Pot*, 173–175, and Lopenzina, 126–131.
28 Apess, "Indians Looking-Glass for the White Man," *On Our Own Ground*, 155.
29 Robert Warrior, *The People and the Word: Reading Native Nonfiction* (Minneapolis: University of Minnesota Press, 2005), 31–32.
30 Apess, "Indian's Looking-Glass," 156.
31 Apess, "Indian's Looking-Glass," 156–157.
32 Robert Dale Parker, *The Sound the Stars Make Rushing through the Sky: The Writings of Jane Johnston Schoolcraft* (Philadelphia: University of Pennsylvania Press, 2007), 50.
33 Hilary E. Wyss, *English Letters and Indian Literacies: Reading, Writing, and New England Missionary Schools, 1750–1830* (Philadelphia: University of Pennsylvania Press, 2012), 182.
34 Daniel Heath Justice, *Our Fires Survive the Storm: A Cherokee Literary History* (Minneapolis: University of Minnesota Press, 2006), 8.
35 Justice, *Our Fires Survive the Storm*, 56.
36 Daniel Butrick, *Cherokee Removal, Monograph One: The Journal of Rev. Daniel S. Buttrick, May 19, 1838–April 1, 1839*, (Park Hill, OK: The Trail of Tears Association, Oklahoma Chapter, 1998), 6.
37 Melissa Jayne Fawcett, *Medicine Trail: The Life and Lessons of Gladys Tantaquidgeon* (Tucson: University of Arizona Press, 2000), 4.
38 Warrior, 11.
39 Apess, "Indian Nullification," *On Our Own Ground*, 169.

3
RED PROGRESSIVES AND INDIAN "PASS-WORDS"

The Bad Password

At eight years of age, Gertrude Simmons (later Simmons Bonnin), who published under the name Zitkala-Sa, was sent far from her home on the Yankton Sioux Reservation in South Dakota to White's Manual Labor Institute, a Quaker-run Indian boarding school in Wabash, Indiana, that was, likely, as dreary a place as its name suggests. One of her earliest memories of boarding school is of herself and two friends playing in the snow outside in the schoolyard, allowing their bodies to fall outspread in the freshly formed drifts, thereby leaving their impressions on the surface—what is commonly referred to today as making "snow angels." This innocent play had for some reason been forbidden, and, when one of the supervising women happened to see the children at their game, she immediately summoned them inside. As they walked toward the school building, Judewin, the friend with the greater grasp of the English language, cautioned her companions that, "if she [the supervisor] looks straight into your eyes and talks loudly, you must wait until she stops. Then after a tiny pause, say, 'No.'"[1] Luckily for the young Zitkala-Sa, she and Judewin were asked to wait outside the office as the third companion was first to be reprimanded. Listening through the keyhole, they needed no skill in the English language to comprehend that Judewin's advice was not having the desired effect. Each meekly offered "no" led to an escalating round of blows and shrieks, prompting Judewin to recall that this was not the proper response after all. As Zitkala-Sa's narrative observes, her friend had been given a "bad password," and the results were disastrous.[2]

I am reminded, when reading this account, of the situation William Apess faced as a young child in *A Son of the Forest*, confronting his grandmother who had just come in from selling her baskets and brooms among the white households in Colchester,

Connecticut, shouldering her daily burden of humiliation, poverty, and abuse and now drunk on rum or some other spiritous liquor. She repeatedly asked the young child, "do you hate me?" and, somehow misunderstanding the question, Apess continually answered "yes," provoking a beating that left him severely injured, his arm broken in two places. Apess, too, had been given a bad password. His inability to verbally negotiate the deep, layered traumas of colonized space left him vulnerable to unpredictable and explosive acts of violence.[3]

Though their accounts are separated by some 80 years, the situations they faced were similar. Both Apess and the young Gertrude Simmons had to learn to rhetorically navigate a world specifically structured to silence their speech, stifle their identity, and severely restrict their spheres of influence. Their pleas were not meant to travel beyond the closed doors where power worked its will either directly or by proxy. Their speech, if heard at all, was merely meant to echo what power allowed or demanded it to speak. The fact that these individuals, as with a number of others such as John Rollins Ridge, Charles Eastman, Luther Standing Bear, Alice Callahan, Arthur Parker, Sarah Winnemucca, Mourning Dove, Simon Pokagon, and Pauline Johnson, all emerged in opposition to such cultural imperatives in the nineteenth century had something to do with their ability to learn the proper "password"—their fashioning of rhetorical strategies that enabled them to "pass" into the domain of print discourse and have their voices heard and preserved. As Zitkala-Sa wrote of her later school years, "by daylight and lamplight, I spun with reeds and thistles, until my hands were tired from their weaving, the magic design which promised me the white man's respect."[4] Like many of Ztikaa-Sa's pronouncements, it is a layered admission, the significance of which might easily become lost within the disarming, sentimental voice she adopts throughout most of her narrative productions. By comparing the "magic" work of the white man's letters with the traditional indigenous art of weaving basketry, she is placing before the reader two forms of cultural expression, in a sense, stitching them together as though preparing a spell. She knows that she must master alphabetic literacy to forge a path of success for herself and yet she works painstakingly to incorporate something of her Lakota sensibilities into the spells she weaves. There are few clear choices in life, and no single path guarantees success or fulfillment, but, even given the soul-searing loneliness that often permeates Zitkala-Sa's prose, this was also a strategy that served her well, allowing her to move about more freely in her adulthood and advocate for Native people and causes.

Over the years, Native writers from the Progressive Era, often referred to as "Red Progressives," have been critiqued for the painful cultural concessions they appeared to forward in their narratives, their voices seemingly subjugated by the cultural and aesthetic conventions of a settler colonial world. More recently, however, their collective works have come to be viewed as savvy critiques that exploited popular discursive practices to lodge resistant indigenous perspectives. As Susan Bernardin was among the first to recognize, Zitkala-Sa "subversively engages" with popular tropes of sentimentality that were foisted upon Native boarding school students in the form of dominant domestic ideologies centered around the woman's role of mother and housekeeper.⁵ Her narratives left the wounds of forced assimilation exposed, prompting readers to confront the failure of domestic endeavors (such as Indian boarding schools) to provide nurture or comfort for unprotected Indian children. There was a jarring message here for audiences if they chose to receive it.

Mainstream discourse, however, also worked feverishly in this era to absolve its white audiences of any responsibility for shouldering the burden of such indigenous memories. Native people were largely believed to be fading from the face of the planet at the time Zitkala-Sa wrote, and even her own stories, forged out of pain, loss, and resistance, could still be called into the service of settler colonial paradigms, proving, perpetually, how difficult it has been for Native authors to assert their claims of sovereignty, rights, and continuance to a settler nation bent on conquest.

Vanishing Points

The power of the nineteenth-century trope of the vanishing Indian should not be underestimated. It is a persuasive cultural myth that found its aesthetic formation in James Fenimore Cooper's *Last of the Mohicans* but was perpetuated beyond fiction to be given voice in history, ethnography, drama, poetry, painting, sculpture, and legal statute, and, by the time photography, motion pictures, and television came along, it readily accommodated these new genres as well. American audiences were literally bombarded with narratives and images that, at once, fed into their fascination with indigenous culture and yet fully persuaded them of its demise. On a policy level, this aesthetic was hammered out through reform-minded movements that posited assimilation or extinction as the dire choice confronting all indigenous peoples. This false dichotomy became baked into the American imaginary to the extent that nearly every depiction of an indigenous person found itself echoing the formula and typically leaning in favor of extinction. As we have seen already, such beliefs gave intellectual cover to the morally reprehensible scheme of Indian Removal in the 1830s and, following America's Civil War, there was a renewed investment in promulgating this belief as the United States finally found itself in position to forcibly actuate its long-standing dream of manifest destiny.

The form "assimilationist" policies took in this period consisted of a three-pronged offensive against Native peoples west of the Mississippi, all of which will be discussed at some length. The first prong simply involved subduing indigenous nations by whatever means available and containing them on reservations. It took roughly 25 additional years following the war to fully carry out this ambition, and only at great economic and psychic cost to the conquerors (it has been argued that each Indian death cost the U.S. government \$100,000 in this timeframe).⁶ This is to say nothing, of course, of the disruption, heartbreak, and lasting intergenerational traumas such actions inflicted on indigenous peoples. The period in question is adequately summed up by the white reformist, author Helen Jackson, who recognized it in her 1881 publication as *A Century of Dishonor*. Jackson, after carefully laying out the legal traditions of western nations in regards to treaties and international law, concluded unequivocally that the violations of the U.S. government against Native people "convicts us, as a nation, not only of having outraged the principles of justice, which are international law; and of having laid ourselves open to the accusation of both cruelty and perfidy; but of having made ourselves liable to all punishments which follow upon such sins."[7] She wasn't wrong.

This *Introduction* does not have time to go into comprehensive historical detail concerning the many invasions and massacres perpetrated by the U.S. government and its citizens—incursions that were endlessly justified with hyperbolic accusations of "Indian depredations." Certainly, Native people did strike out against white colonizers who intruded on their territories, and there were, no doubt, heinous acts committed on both sides, because this is the long story of human warfare. But Native forces, in nearly every instance, were acting in retaliation to outrages the colonizers had perpetrated against them, even if such offenses were rarely reported, and the Native retaliation was sure to receive relentless press.

We will have opportunity to see how this dynamic played out as we read more closely individual literary works by Native authors. Suffice it for now to say that the military chapter of colonial conquest is perceived to have drawn to a close when, in December of 1890, the Seventh Cavalry opened fire with their Hotchkiss guns on a band of Lakota led by the Miniconjou chief, Big Foot, that had already surrendered themselves to the "protection" of the U.S. Army and were attempting to reach shelter at the Pine Ridge reservation. More than 300 Lakota men, women, and children were gunned down alongside Wounded Knee Creek that winter day, many of them found afterwards with bullets ripped through their backsides as they died trying to escape the gunfire. In the wake of this massacre, historian Frederic Jackson Turner, presenting his views at the 1893 Chicago World Fair, declared the frontier officially closed and projected a bold new era made possible by white European settler hegemony—as though Native peoples and the lands they still legally possessed, either through treaty or indigenous title, had simply ceased to exist.

A compelling reason as to why so many Americans are enamored of the idea of the vanishing Native is that, if we can imagine Native peoples simply disappearing from the landscape, victims of their own incompatibility with ambivalent forces such as "modernity," "civilization," and the "changing times," then we are not left to confront the actual unspeakable violence by which conquest was truly effected. This is, once again, why Gerald Vizenor deploys the term "tragic wisdom," as it is often left to Native people to be the bearers of this awful history that average Americans have either sentimentalized or *unwitnessed* from their own cognitive landscapes.

An iconic image entitled *The Vanishing Race*, by turn-of-the-century photographer Edward Curtis, offered mainstream audiences a stunning visual metaphor for this agentless conquest. The photograph, part of Curtis's 1907 multi-volume pictorial publication *The North American Indian*, presented the forms of six or seven Navajo on horseback, moving single file through the brush in dim twilight, casting their shadows along the path while headed for a canyon pass shrouded in darkness. The figures of the riders are themselves barely legible in the quickening dark, and the photograph comes across almost as a poor exposure, an experiment in light gone awry. Except the effect was intentional, and turn-of-the-century audiences were well versed in how to interpret this image with its suggestion that Native people were leading themselves toward the maw of oblivion, neither hounded nor chased, but simply in quiet submission to the fact that their trail had reached its end. Extinction. Lock the door on the way out and leave the key under the mat, so the white folks can let themselves in. It can be helpful to seek out this image and others like it as a visual tool for students to comprehend the dynamic in question, but one must also be prepared to energetically deprogram this trope by providing images and narratives of Native peoples surviving, continuing, and managing modernity (Lakota scholar Vine Deloria Jr. offers a strong critical framework for presenting such images in his book *Indians in Unexpected Places*). The dissemination of such counter-narratives to vanishing is the essence of what is referred to here as "continuance."[8]

The other two prongs of nineteenth-century social policy designed to enact "vanishing" consisted of the Indian boarding school system, a federally funded program that was, in the famous words of Richard Henry Pratt, designed to "kill the Indian and save the man," and the Allotment Act of 1887, otherwise known as the Dawes Act after its legislative sponsor, Massachusetts Congressman Henry Dawes. These programs were pitched to lawmakers as altruistic endeavors meant to ease the transition of a presumably savage people into citizenship, if possible. In the occurrence that Natives proved unadaptable to civilization as prescribed, the reservations were perceived as places where indigenous peoples and cultures might quietly die off, out of sight of the delicate sensibilities of those who were still inclined to feel pity for the "poor Indian."

Allotment

William Apess once described Indian reservations as "the most mean, abject, miserable" patches of real estate on earth, places of "prodigality and prostitution."[9] Although Apess was speaking of the little-known eastern reservation system of the early nineteenth century, Indian reservations west of the Mississippi, as they came into being in the last two decades of the century, were, for the most part, similarly forsaken places—concentration camps where hunger, disease, and death became familiar guests. As we will see, many Indian nations saw their leaders murdered or imprisoned. Innocent civilians were chased down and mercilessly killed for little or no cause, their homes and possessions put to the torch, and the buffalo, the major means of sustenance on the western plains, were deliberately hunted to near extinction, their carcasses left to rot in the dust for the precise purpose of starving Native peoples into submission. Natives had no rights of citizenship on the reservations, could not vote, could not practice their religions or hold tribal gatherings. They were forbidden to leave the bounds of the reservation without a pass from their assigned Indian agent. And the reservation land itself was often "waterless and inadequate" to support agriculture. Luther Standing Bear, a Lakota living on the Rosebud Agency in 1933, described it as "the Garden of Eden after the fall of man."[10] He observed that his people were in "dire straits," the elders "insufficiently clothed" and, therefore, unable to "endure the cold of winter," and the rest "undermined in health by starvation while the public sleeps on the thought that 'the Government takes care of the Indian.'"[11]

This dismal scene, for the most part, conforms with what people already suspect or care to know about reservation life at the turn of the century; the great, romantic, western plains Indians were now a defeated people living in squalor and forced to rely on the government for handouts or "Indian welfare." End of story. And, although there is certainly some truth in this understanding, it is also a good place to begin to complicate our notions about the "closing of the frontier" and how it came about. The government "assistance" so many Native people were forced to rely upon (and to a certain extent still do) did not come in the form of goods distributed out of a sense of pity or altruism—it is not the equivalent of disaster relief following an earthquake or hurricane. When Native people ceded portions of their traditional estates in treaties, these large tracts of land were ostensibly paid for by guaranteed annuities in goods and services. Trying to get the U.S. government to honor these commitments has been an ongoing problem, and that was particularly true in the 1880s and 90s at the lowest ebb, in terms of population and wealth, of Native civilization in North America. The needlessly desperate situation on reservations resulted from an onslaught of prohibitive laws and restrictions meant to further break up and disenfranchise Native culture. They were also the result of generally corrupt white Indian agents who facilitated these harmful practices and, rather than properly distributing allocated goods, hoarded them for themselves or channeled them toward private profit. Many reform-minded whites, who felt they had the best interests of indigenous peoples at heart, saw the reservations for the death camps they were, but misguidedly promoted the termination of these Native spaces, believing the only path to survival was full and speedy assimilation.

One such reformist was Merrill E. Gates, one-time college president of Rutgers and later Amherst College. Gates argued that to bring the "savage" out of his dejected state, we must make him

> more intelligently selfish before we can make him unselfishly intelligent. We need to awaken in him wants. In his dull savagery he must be touched by the wings of the divine angel of discontent ... The desire for property of his own may become an intense educating force.[12]

Such arguments proved incredibly persuasive to people in the U.S. government who also wanted to break up the reservations once and for all—if for slightly different reasons.

The 1887 General Allotment Act was passed by Congress in response to this brand of rhetoric and was meant to force the issue of detribalization, gently prodding Native communities toward the joys of capitalism. The idea was that Indian land, held communally up to this point, would be carved into individual, privately owned lots, with each family head assigned 160 acres, and smaller lots of 80 and 40 acres for every other individual, depending upon age and status. It was hoped that Natives, newly franchised as landowners, would become farmers and quickly learn to appreciate the values of industry and thrift—attributes thought to be lacking in their culture. It all sounded pretty good—many white people would have salivated, or, indeed, killed, over such "gifts" of land, although it must be constantly reinforced that nothing at all was gifted. These were lands that had belonged, by every dispensation of the law, to Native peoples, and it turns out that, once every Native, counted and placed on government census rolls, received their individual or family allotment, a majority of reservation land still remained unaccounted for. That "excess" land was either placed in trust or bought up by the U.S. government—with the assets set aside until Native residents were deemed comfortable enough with the rituals of capitalism to become their own financial stewards.

Predictably, the "excess" lots fell into the possession of white settlers, as did many of the individually allocated lots, despite the fact that they could not technically be sold off. Suffice it to say that white neighbors found all manner of creative ways, not excluding rape, kidnapping, murder, and outright theft, to claim possession of individual lots from Native people after the passing of the Dawes Act. One report detailing abuses leading to the loss of Native lands listed, among other offenses, a party of speculators waiting

> literally at the bedside of a dying women, and hardly had the breath left her body when her thumb was pressed upon an ink pad and an impression from it made on an alleged will, which was later offered for probate.[13]

As Robert Warrior observes,

> in the early 1880's, more than 150 million acres were held by Natives. By 1890, that number had been reduced to roughly 100 million, and at the turn of the century, only about 75 million acres remained in Indian hands.[14]

The Dawes Act, a presumably benevolent bit of legislation cobbled together by men who called themselves "Friends of the Indian," set in motion a 50% depletion of tribal holdings across the U.S.

To be certain, many saw through the ruse, with a House Committee report stating,

> the real aim of this bill is to get at the Indian lands and open them to settlement … if this were done in the name of greed, it would be bad enough; but to do it in the name of humanity and under the cloak of an ardent desire to promote the Indian's welfare by making him like ourselves, whether he will or not, is infinitely worse.[15]

Nevertheless, the bill passed and set in motion the initial survey of the reservations and their inhabitants, creating tribal rolls that, in many cases, determine to this day who can or cannot legally be called "Indian" and how the newly assigned individual lots would be distributed.

Because tribal governments, as a result of the two Supreme Court rulings concerning the Cherokees in the 1830s, were considered "domestic dependent nations" (see Chapter 2), they retained right of refusal in their specific nations over passage of the Allotment Act. But the U.S. government was not to be deterred, and, just as it manufactured the Treaty of New Echota with the Cherokee, conferring upon their forced removal a false sheen of legitimacy, their agents were able, in most cases, to gather a sufficient number of signatures from Natives, adult or underaged, drunk or sober, dead or living, to ram through their agenda. As usual, many did not know what they were signing or were poorly informed as to the nature of the proposed law. The great Hunkpapa Lakota warrior and medicine man Sitting Bull, for one, strongly objected to the allotment process and argued against carving up what was then known, by the 1851 Fort Laramie Treaty, as the Great Sioux Reservation. In 1889, the Dawes commission could collect no more than 22 signatures at the Standing Rock Agency where Sitting Bull lived, nowhere near the three-fourths needed. In 1890, however, Sitting Bull was awakened from his sleep, surrounded by an armed guard, and, despite his peaceful compliance, shot dead outside his own home, a sure sign that opposition to the Act was not to be tolerated.

The monies that went into trust as a result of the Dawes Act, presumably to be restored to the tribes at a later date, were never in fact surrendered by the U.S government, which has obviously benefitted from rents, leases, sales, and billions of dollars-worth of harvested resources in the interim. In more recent times, as various tribes have pressed legal suits attempting to force the U.S. to honor these earlier agreements, an embarrassing problem has been exposed. It turns out that the interest owed on these initial sums has climbed into the billions of dollars, and the government has no way to make good on its treaty obligations. In 2016, the U.S. government agreed to a $492 million settlement with 17 tribes. Although this does not settle all existing claims and comes nowhere near to what is actually owed, the government takes the stance that it no longer holds these properties in trust, and the case is closed.

When the term "Indian welfare" gets bandied about (even if students don't bring it up themselves, they are often familiar with the concept), it is important to understand why the U.S. government has brought these obligations upon itself. If you were to rent out a room in your own house to someone who subsequently moved in but refused to pay you the money owed, you would not call it "welfare" when the courts finally ordered your full compensation. It's a simple enough concept to comprehend, and yet it is surprising how few are willing to make the intellectual leap when it comes to understanding how the situation applies to indigenous peoples in the U.S.

Distance Education: The Indian Boarding School Era

An additional component of the Dawes Act was that, once tribal lands were dissolved into private lots, tribal governments could also be dissolved. Many resisted this, but, after passage of the Act, Indian people ostensibly lived under the jurisdiction of state and federal laws. It was all part of the general process of grooming Native people for western civilization, which, to westerners themselves, was simply understood as "civilization." In keeping with that goal, a portion of the moneys held in trust was allocated to Indian education.

The aim of assimilating Native peoples through education was hardly a late nineteenth-century innovation. As we have seen, it was a central component of colonial rhetoric from the very start. John Eliot's campaign to convert the Massachuset Natives to Christianity led to the founding of Harvard College, which resulted in Harvard's Indian College, the first brick building to be constructed on campus and the production site of the 1663 "Indian Bible" (see Chapter 1). The endeavor to indoctrinate Native peoples into western discourses continued into the next century through privately funded efforts such as Moor's Charity School, established by Eleazar Wheelock in the 1750s. Through the fundraising acumen of the Mohegan preacher Samson Occom, Moor's Charity School ultimately laid the foundation for Dartmouth College (see Chapter 2). Even Pocahontas, setting sail from England in 1617, was headed back with funds that had been collected for her and her husband, John Rolfe, to begin a school for Indian children—a scheme interrupted by her untimely death at Gravesend before her ship could even take to sea (see Introduction). It is interesting to map out the extent to which higher education in the United States today owes a surprising debt to enterprising Native intellectuals who chose to engage with western literacy in attempts to better the conditions of their people under colonization.

But the education programs themselves had been largely unsuccessful in their stated intentions of converting and assimilating Native communities and, in fact, were never much more than a flimsy pretense to exercise coercive control over Native populations. One of Richard Henry Pratt's innovations when he founded the Carlisle School in 1879 was his notion that, to finally make U.S. citizens out of Indians, it was necessary to indoctrinate students while they were still quite young and to remove them as far as possible from their homes and kinship networks, so that they would be severed from what were perceived to be the corrupting influences of their backwards cultures. In his published account of his efforts, Pratt wrote how, "In [the matter of] Indian civilization I am a Baptist, because I believe in immersing the Indians in our civilization and when we get them under holding them there until they are thoroughly soaked."[16] Today, this might sound more like waterboarding. Nevertheless, the process, as enacted by Pratt and others, was to forbid students from speaking their own languages once they arrived at these institutions. All traditional clothing, blankets, and regalia the children brought with them were replaced with military-style outfits. And every child was required to have their hair cut to conform with accepted western gender norms.

This last practice alone proved an emotional hardship and humiliation for many students who attached cultural significance to their braids and unshorn locks. Charles Eastman, Luther Standing Bear, and Zitkala-Sa all placed particular significance on the moment of having their hair cut as they related their boarding school memories. Standing Bear recalls experiencing a loss of identity, observing, "I felt I was no more an Indian, but would be an imitation of a white man."[17] Zitkala-Sa remembers how she "cried aloud, shaking my head all the while until I felt the cold blades of the scissors against my neck, and heard them gnaw off one of my thick braids." She confides that it was at this precise moment "I lost my spirit," believing, as her mother had told her, that "only unskilled warriors who were captured had their hair shingled by the enemy." Whatever the reason for the powerful memories provoked by this act in so many boarding school survivors, Zitkala-Sa's text makes compelling use of it by equating the situation with one of captivity—the cutting of one's hair becomes a cultural marker of their condition as prisoners of war.[18]

The claim may sound hyperbolic to some, but it is actually dead on. Pratt began his career as a cavalry officer assigned, after the Civil War, to lead an experimental division consisting of freed blacks, who came to be known as Buffalo soldiers, and 25 Cherokee scouts, charged to keep the peace in "Indian Territory" or modern-day Oklahoma. A true reformer in many senses, Pratt argued for the acceptance of black soldiers in the regular army some 80 years before the rest of the U.S. caught up with his agenda. In 1875, however, Pratt was ordered to escort a contingency of 72 mostly Kiowa, Comanche, and Cheyenne warriors some 2,000 miles to Fort Marion, an old Spanish fort in Saint Augustine, Florida. These warriors had been captured amid a desperate attempt to maintain their traditional sovereignty over the plains and live in accordance with the original treaties that had been decided between themselves and the U.S government at places such as Medicine Lodge, in 1867. Their resistance was tamped down, however, and they became prisoners of war under Pratt.

Not content to simply let his prisoners languish in homesickness and boredom in the wake of their long journey to confinement, Pratt was determined to keep military order, dressing the prisoners in uniforms, cutting their hair, requiring them to undergo drilling instruction, and ostensibly placing them in charge of the day-to-day operations of their own prison. He began to school the prisoners in reading and writing and, before long, had race reformers such as Harriet Beecher Stowe invested in his program and sending down New England "school marms" to help in the process of "civilizing" a group that General Nelson A. Miles had once specifically referred to as a "body of wild savage murderers."[19]

An unexpected legacy of Pratt's time as Indian jailer is the ledger-book art his captives produced. The ledger books were likely Civil War surplus issue donated to Pratt to use for educational purposes. It is not clear what prompted the emergence of this syncretic artform, but many of the prisoners began using the ledger books to pictographically communicate their experiences, both of their lives back in their homelands and of their subsequent captivity. The artwork is representative of the artwork of the plains, as seen in winter counts, calendar rolls, and other traditional media, but now making use of colored pencils, crayons, and paints, only barred by the ruled margins of the ledger books themselves. The pictographic artwork generated in this unlikely scenario is strikingly distinctive, gorgeously rich in color and detail, and in some ways enigmatic in its use of traditional symbols and indigenous aesthetic conventions.

Brad Lookingbill, who has written an account of the lives of the captives at Fort Marion, notes that the prisoners also began to hold public dances that became a popular tourist draw for the community. However denigrating this performance of identity and culture might potentially have been for the captives, as it reduced their longing for and expressions of traditional ceremony to mere entertainment, it nevertheless demonstrated extraordinary adaptability to a severe situation. As Lookingbill observes,

> more than passive recipients of parochial knowledge, they [the Native prisoners] displayed amazing insight by imagining a world where Indians still made medicine. They found creative ways to positively channel their deepest and most profound sentiments. Their bravery transformed the casemates into classrooms and heartened almost everyone interested in their fate.[20]

Utilizing the artwork and writings produced by his prisoners as promotional materials, Pratt was able to parlay his successes at Fort Marion into the establishment of the first federally funded boarding school at Carlisle, Pennsylvania, which opened its doors in 1879.

One reason the U.S. government was now so invested in the idea of distance education for Indians, as expressed to Pratt by Secretary of the Interior Carl Schurtz, was the government's understanding that the western tribes, now carefully contained on their respective reservations, would be less likely to revolt knowing their children were being held hostage by their conquerors.[21] The mature Zitkala-Sa fully understood this cynical underlying motive to the boarding school platform, but, by presenting her experiences from the viewpoint of a

FIGURE 3.1 "An Omaha Dance given by the prisoners on the solicitation and to please their new friends in St. Augustine as well as to amuse themselves." Courtesy Beinecke Rare Book and Manuscript Library, Yale University

child ignorant of the larger cultural-historical forces at play, she is able to relate to us her feelings of captivity and trauma through a lens rendered acceptable for white audiences.

From the Deep Woods to Civilization and Back Again

Luther Standing Bear was part of that first class of students at Carlisle. As with Zitkala-Sa, his narrative has an almost epic arc as it relates sweeping historical changes occurring throughout Native space in the late nineteenth century. In *My People the Sioux* and elsewhere, he offers his life as a kind of hero's journey, as he ventures far from his home determined to represent his culture and uphold the values of his people. He recalls,

> I could think of no reason why white people wanted Indian boys and girls except to kill them, and not having the remotest idea of what a school was, I thought we were going East to die ... thus, in giving myself up to go East I was proving to my father that he was honored with a brave son.[22]

Standing Bear lived through transformative times, and his writings remain acutely attuned to the role he plays as witness to so many historic events and transitions, such as the defeat of Custer, the destruction of the buffalo herds, the adaptation to reservation life, and the introduction of the Allotment Act. He notes that his father, on Standing Bear's own advice, was first at the Rosebud Agency to sign the papers, leaving his x-mark, in support of the Allotment Act, though much of the tribe had rallied against it. This support was echoed by many of the so-called Red Progressives who became convinced, rightly or wrongly, that the legislation was the only way for their people to break the downward spiral of conquest. But, as much as Standing Bear ultimately embraced his Carlisle education, even returning to the reservation in later years to recruit more students for the school, he is also a poignant critic who, in accordance with his father's wishes, learned the ways of western culture so that he might "stand up for his rights" and the rights of his people. [23]

Standing Bear was living near the Rosebud Agency in 1890, serving as a teacher for Indian children, when the tensions raised by the Ghost Dance broke out among the Lakota bands. Riding 30 miles through the snow to Pine Ridge to check on his family, Standing Bear came upon the site of the massacre, only recently cleared of its corpses, the field still strewn with tipi poles, cookware, broken-down wagons, and the carcasses of horses. He recounts being greeted with an "oppressive and terrible" silence as he rode through pools of water still stained red with blood. "According to the white man's history," he wrote,

> this was known as the "battle" of Wounded Knee, but it was not a battle—it was a slaughter, a massacre. Those soldiers had been sent to protect these men, women, and children ... but they had shot them down without even a chance to defend themselves.[24]

As horrified as he was by these scenes, Standing Bear nevertheless claims it was his father who brokered the peace in the aftermath of Wounded Knee. Standing Bear's father, some 15 years earlier, had ridden out with thousands of Lakota and Cheyenne warriors as part of the successful resistance to General Custer's ill-advised incursion at Greasy Grass—what most of us know as Little Big Horn. In the year that followed, his lodge was visited by the great Lakota warrior Crazy Horse, who sought to discuss matters with the elder Standing Bear, just a day before he was murdered at Fort Robinson.

Both Standing Bear and his father had witnessed the disruption of traditional Lakota lifeways. Violent change was thrust upon them. But now the former warrior and current head chief declared, "he would carry the peace pipe" to those who had holed up in the Badlands to defend themselves after Wounded Knee. As Standing Bear relates, his father rode to the camp of the Lakota refugees with the pipe of peace carefully displayed in his arms before him. Members of the camp had put out word that anyone trying to approach, regardless of color, would be killed on sight. But, despite being met with initial hostility, the elder Standing Bear's counsel was ultimately heeded, and "after a time these wild Indians calmed down" and agreed to settle with General Miles and come back to the reservation.[25]

It is difficult to know how to read such moments. Luther Standing Bear is an effective advocate for Lakota continuance, and yet he often deploys language that appears to not only denigrate his own people but is callously dismissive of their plight as survivors of merciless violence. Far from behaving as "wild" men, the Lakota at Pine Ridge and elsewhere were caught in a desperate bid to protect their families against a much more powerful and relentless invading force. He recognizes the bitter irony when the dominant culture applies language of conventional military engagement to acts of unprovoked brutality against unarmed innocents—but he fails at times to locate the colonized subtext of his own syntax. It is a discursive understanding that has yet to be fully opened to him or the other Red Progressives of his time and it is something we, as readers and instructors, must grapple with as we seek to decolonize our own language and habits of thought.

Charles Eastman, who was also raised in the sphere of traditional Lakota customs before receiving a boarding school education, presents similar interpretive dilemmas in his various accounts. Eastman was a young child during the 1862 event known as the Great Sioux Uprising or Little Crow's War (yet another military misnomer). The retaliation among the eastern Santee Sioux living in the area of what is today Mankato, Minnesota, was provoked by a slew of treaty violations and other deprivations the Lakota were made to endure, including a corrupt agent who would allow provisions to rot in the storehouses rather than properly distribute them among his hungry charges. Pushed beyond endurance, the Santee bands revolted and quickly met with stiff opposition from the local militia. Although Eastman was able to escape with much of his family, his father, Many Lightnings, was apprehended and sentenced to be hanged, along with 303 other "ringleaders" of the revolt. In the end, his sentence was commuted by President Abraham Lincoln, although 38 Lakota men were still executed in what remains the largest mass hanging in U.S. history. To get an accurate measure of the times, one need only note that the hanging was celebrated as a victory for civilization, and commemorative platters were produced some years later by Standard Brewing of Mankato, Minnesota, bearing a representation of the immense gallows and its victims with which purchasers might decorate their homes.

When, roughly a decade later, Eastman's father returned, as though from the dead, to retrieve his son and put him on the path of a white man's education, it dramatically altered the direction of Eastman's life. Describing it in his 1916 memoir, *From the Deep Woods to Civilization*, as setting out on a "warpath," Eastman made his way to the Santee Normal School in Nebraska, where he became proficient in western literary practices.[26] Upon completing his education, he continued on to Dartmouth where, as an Indian student, he finally cashed in on Samson Occom's efforts to make Dartmouth a center for Indian education, and from there he travelled to Boston College where he became a licensed doctor. Invoking his traditional warrior ethos as a model, Eastman determined to put his education to use in the service of his people, returning west to the Pine Ridge reservation as the agency physician in 1890 and arriving, as fate would have it, just as the Ghost Dance was breaking out. Eastman, now in his 30s, was a complete stranger to reservation life, and, though his sympathies were firmly aligned with the Lakotas, his cultural orientation had largely shifted in favor of dominant western values, and he suddenly found his loyalties and convictions challenged in ways he could not have anticipated.

The Ghost Dance was a popular revitalization movement originating with a Paiute man, Wovoka, who received his vision of the dance in a dream. The movement quickly caught fire across the western plains, spreading from one Indian agency to the next as Native people, culturally disoriented and dismayed under the new reservation regime, found hope and sustenance in this innovative mix of traditions promising to restore the buffalo and drive the white man off the continent. Although the practice of Ghost Dancing was inoffensive in and of itself, calling for peaceful observances, it rattled the nerves of government agents, particularly at Pine Ridge, who felt the dance was preparation for another uprising. As reservation doctor, Eastman felt he had earned the trust of the people, gaining access to all the various camps and factions amid the rising tensions. Although dismissive of the ceremony itself, referring to it as "groping blindly for spiritual relief," he quickly came to understand that behind the dance were many legitimate grievances reflecting the miserable conditions on the reservation. Not least among these is what he described as an "alarming" death rate, particularly among the children of the agency.[27]

I have personally always imagined events such as Wounded Knee unfolding in a vacuum of sorts, so far from the public eye that the shrieks of death were simply swallowed up on the darkling plain, making of such atrocities opaque and, perhaps, unknowable eruptions of confusion, chaos, destruction, rippling through history in perfect traumatic silence. It never occurred to me, prior to reading Eastman, that not only was there a college-educated Lakota witness present to publish his account, but that the lead-up to the massacre was something of a media event, with mission workers, the U.S. military, and the press all converging on the scene, accompanied by profiteers of all sorts hoping to cash in on the circus atmosphere. Eastman recalls how, on the morning of December 29, those stationed at the agency could hear the report of the Hotchkiss guns some 11 miles away. As the casualties began to pour in hours later, the wounded Natives refused to be treated by army doctors, and so Eastman had to clear the pews out of the Pine Ridge chapel, turning it into an impromptu surgery. Outside, a blizzard began to blow, and it would take 3 days before Eastman could accompany a search party to visit the same scene Luther Standing Bear would cross over only a day or two later.

It must have been difficult to know how to write about such moments, even though more than two decades passed before Eastman finally determined to commit his memories to paper. I am reminded of the difficulties Kurt Vonnegut describes in his novel *Slaughterhouse Five* writing about the fire-bombing of Dresden in World War II. Even without the added burden of being a racialized "other" on one's own soil, Vonnegut understood that his Dresden story was not one that many people were eager to receive. This is, in fact, the great throbbing, terrible, chaotic, rupture residing at the heart of the trauma narrative. To bear witness to horrific events is to train one's gaze upon wounds, both physical and psychic, that most would rather keep at a distance. It is to wade against a mighty current while pointing your slender finger at power and saying, "here is the unseemly hidden cost of all your comfort, wealth, and privilege." It is to tear open corpses and tombs and invite the unwelcome horror to come slithering out once more into the light of day. There was a limited vocabulary for this sort of thing in Eastman's day and no public taste for it.

Owing to complicated reservation politics, Eastman was soon drummed out of his job as doctor, first at Pine Ridge and later at the Crow agency. Married to a white woman, Elaine Goodale Eastman (who had served as a teacher among the Lakota prior to Wounded Knee), and starting a family, he tried hanging up a private shingle for a time in Minneapolis, Minnesota. But it was difficult for a Native professional of any sort to sustain a trade in predominantly white communities where walls were adorned with decorative plates depicting "rough justice" toward Indians. Despite Eastman's ideological commitments to notions of progress, his one bankable commodity resided in the public's interest in romanticized tales of vanished Native culture. His value lay in being a remnant, a trace, an authority, in fact, on a topic, the significance of which was its perceived passing. By the time he settled upon a new career as author of books and promoter of Indian life and culture, there were both psychic and economic pressures weighing upon him that went a long way toward determining how the tale could be told. Many of his books were directed at an audience of children, and he geared his tales to the needs and tastes of that audience.

Nevertheless, Eastman could not separate himself from the scenes witnessed at Wounded Knee Creek. His long journey *From the Deep Woods to Civilization*, inevitably, and perhaps unceasingly, leads him to the bodies of the dead, "scattered along as they had been relentlessly hunted down and slaughtered while fleeing for their lives." Further along he encounters Big Foot's encampment, where the violence had initially erupted, with its "frozen bodies lying close together or piled up one upon another." He notes, "I counted eighty men who had been in the council who were almost as helpless as the women and babes when the deadly fire began." But remembering, as well, his audience of primarily white middle-class readers, he reminds how "all this was a severe ordeal for one who had so lately put all his faith in the Christian love and lofty ideals of the white man."[28]

Robert Warrior, for one, remains critical of Eastman's oeuvre, describing his memoirs as "highly sentimental accounts ... in which he portrays Natives as needy for, worthy of, and ready for inclusion in mainstream civilization." While he cautions that we cannot simply view Eastman, Standing Bear, and their cohorts as "misguided, brainwashed, self-hating collaborators," it is clear from his phrasing that there might, nevertheless, exist compelling reasons to do so.[29] Warrior fully appreciates the cultural and historical pressures under which this generation of writers labored, but he also holds them accountable for language and stances that do not sit easily with current cultural and critical understandings of the momentous transformations taking place at this time. Eastman opens his book *Indian Boyhood* with the declaration,

> The North American Indian was the highest type of pagan and uncivilized man. He possessed not only a superb physique but a remarkable mind. But the Indian no longer exists as a natural and free man. Those remnants which now dwell upon the reservations present only a sort of tableau—a fictitious copy of the past.[30]

Eastman seems to concede that the vitality had drained from Native culture, and anyone still holding on to that way of life was participating in a misguided delusion.

Nevertheless, as noted earlier, it has become more critically generative today to seek interpretive stances more appreciative of these authors' attempts to subvert the discursive practices they were forced to appropriate. Lucy Maddox observes that the message of social uplift, with all of its harmful racial implications, was deeply embedded in the times, and to partake in such language was to associate oneself with progressive sentiments believed to be forward-thinking and, in the minds of Eastman and Standing Bear, essential to the continued survival of Native people. Although it may seem their views were deeply affected by their boarding school experiences and the wrong-headed social experiments in cultural waterboarding advanced by Pratt, it might be remembered that the fathers of both Eastman and Standing Bear also adopted progressive views, despite never having attended the white man's schools. In other words, there is a case to be made that these types of arguments had currency in the Native worlds inhabited by Standing Bear and Eastman and weren't simply symptoms of having undergone baptism by fire in the dominant settler colonial sphere. In a time when Native people were relentlessly represented as dying out, the language of uplift was also a language of survivance, even where, to our modern ears, it seems to flirt with notions of social Darwinism promoting a racialized survival of the fittest.

By embracing progressivism, sentimentalizing their accounts, and gearing their narratives toward youthful audiences, the Red Progressives were arguably not much different than those who embraced the Ghost Dance as a means of survival. Neither offered a practical solution to the devastating and intractable issues facing Native people at this time, but they represented strategies of sustaining hopefulness, pointing to the possibility of cultural survival in an uncertain present. If the works of the Red Progressive era arguably lack the ready conviction we typically demand of contemporary authors, we must understand that they lived through unspeakable events, and much of their experience, undoubtedly, goes unspoken. And so they directed their narratives at children or cushioned the blow in sentimental strains, locating ways to brush up against the boundaries of their lived experience without quite inviting the trauma narrative to the fore.

They were up against a competing brand of colonial rhetoric, however, also disguising itself as "uplift," though couched in expressions of genocidal violence (given that genocidal violence must always drape itself in reasonable tones). As another popular children's author of the period, Frank L. Baum, wrote in his capacity as editor of the *Aberdeen Saturday Pioneer*,

> the nobility of the Redskin is extinguished, and what few are left are a pack of whining curs who lick the hand that smites them. The Whites, by law of conquest, by justice of civilization, are masters of the American continent, and the best safety of the frontier settlements will be secured by the total annihilation of the few remaining Indians.[31]

Baum, for those who do not know, was author of the beloved *Wizard of Oz* books.

Defiance Through Compliance

Gertrude Bonnin's published recollections of her own experiences remain the most "literary" of the first-generation boarding school narratives. Appearing in installments in *The Atlantic Monthly* over 3 consecutive months in the year 1900, her stories were carefully designed to appeal to the aesthetic tastes of audiences of her time. She imbued her narratives with rich symbolism and layered metaphors, allowing for a groundswell of intimated meaning and sentiment to ripple through her descriptions of events and landscapes. She presents herself as having been lured away from her childhood Eden on the Yankton Sioux Reservation when missionaries appeared offering red apples and promising to take her to a land of plenty where such fruits hung from the trees ripe for picking. Agreeing, against her mother's counsel, to travel east with the missionaries, she is thrown on a train where she is subjected to the stares of white passengers who have never before seen an Indian. The seduction is completed when she confronts her fallen condition at the boarding school and endures the loss of all outward expressions of culture. With her introduction to Christianity, she begins to apprehend that the missionaries were acting in league with Satan, whose picture she comes across while flipping through the pages of a book one day. Responding to the constant state of surveillance she has been placed under since being "othered" by white civilization, she proceeds to rub away the eyes of the menacing figure in the illustration—but the figure continues to stalk her, nevertheless, taking the form of the missionaries in her dreams.

All of these complex allusions are brought together through the perception of the young child, too innocent and culturally disoriented to comprehend her condition, allowing the reader to bring their own sentimental capacities to bear on the narrative and reflect upon the train of indignities the Indian girl must suffer for the sins of civilization. As she tells it, her one small victory comes when, asked to mash turnips in a clay jar, she pounds the turnips so hard that the bottom of the jar breaks loose. This unleashes a private, internal "war whoop" from the child who has apparently learned that compliance, taken beyond the point of necessity, can transform into a kind of resistance.

Sentimental literature, properly understood, is the aesthetic exploitation of predictable emotional responses. It plays upon the domain of feeling for which language is readily accessible and culturally approved. But Bonnin, too, must hit upon the edge of the unspeakable in her narrative, where her ability to relate her experience through culturally shared emotional archetypes such as the mother–daughter relationship or the fish-out-of-water adventures of her early schooldays brush up against deeper, more complex undercurrents of experience.

The boarding schools were hives of psychological violence, sexual molestation, and poorly ventilated incubators of death for Native children who had no built-up immunities to the kinds of diseases that can circulate in sealed-up, overcrowded, institutional environments. At Carlisle, the mortality rate for children was as high as 25% in some years. Although Bonnin spares us a full accounting of child mortalities, she intimates their silent erasure from the daily record through the "painful cough of slow consumption." She describes inept white doctors who dawdled "while Indian patients carried their ailments to untimely graves." Their collective passing is conflated into the death of one "dear classmate" whose pitiful decline is precipitated by institutional neglect. Bonnin projects a pall of bitter irony upon the scene when she locates an open Bible in the folds of the dead girl's bedclothes. Her battle to land upon appropriate language can be gleaned from the twist of contradictions she forwards in her attempt to cast judgment and yet spare the sensibilities of her white audience. She writes,

> I blamed the hard-working, well-meaning, ignorant woman who was inculcating in our hearts her superstitious ideas. Though I was sullen in all my little troubles, as soon as I felt better I was ready again to smile upon the cruel woman. Within a week I was again actively testing the chains which tightly bound my individuality like a mummy for burial.[32]

In this paradoxical passage, the nurse who attends to her dying friend is at once "well-meaning," "ignorant," and "cruel," accorded a smile but binding Bonnin's individuality in chains. Bonnin's syntax is so tortured, in fact, that the passage resolves itself in her own rhetorical interment. And it is precisely this set of paradoxical memories that forces her beyond the boundaries of acceptable speech. While she maintains her sentimental tone, the narrative dissipates along inarticulate pathways—becomes likened to the whine of the haunted telegraph pole (an earlier allusion from her narrative) whose vibrations are senseless to those not equipped with capacities fine-tuned enough to receive its message. She writes,

> The melancholy of those black days has left so long a shadow that it darkens the path of years that have since gone by … Perhaps my Indian nature is the

moaning wind which stirs them now for their present record. But, however tempestuous this is within me, it comes out as the low voice of a curiously colored seashell, which is only for those ears that are bent with compassion to hear it.[33]

Bonnin never intimates that she was sexually violated during her experience, but it should be understood that sexual violation was an all too common component of the Indian boarding school experience for both men and women. More recent accounts, such as writings by Basil Johnston, Robert Alexie, Richard Wagamese, and others have given voice to this, but there existed no print venue in Bonnin's time for one to offer up such accusations. When she finally returns home after her first 3 years of schooling, she recalls how she "seemed to hang in the heart of chaos, beyond the touch or voice of human aid." Nevertheless, she eventually chose to continue her western education, going to college in Indiana and teaching for a short stint at Carlisle. But Bonnin would emerge a vocal critic of Pratt's educational model, exposing its exploitative practices and standing in condemnation of the low sort of practitioner who routinely gravitated to the Indian boarding school—not just the inept, but the drunk, the opium eater, and other social predators who had proven themselves inadequate to tend to white children. Her experience in these schools brought her to the point where she wanted "to curse men of small capacity for being the dwarves their God had made them."[34]

Bonnin was an incredibly accomplished and outspoken woman for her time, becoming a concert violinist who performed for President McKinley, a published author of stories, poems, and Lakota legends, and, in 1911, along with Eastman, Arthur Parker, Henry Standing Bear (Luther's brother), and a host of other Red Progressives, she helped to form the S.A.I., or the Society of American Indians. The S.A.I. hoped to advance the cause of the Indian by fostering a public presence of Native activists/intellectuals and building coalitions among Natives and non-Natives to assert moral pressure on Congress in order to pass needed legislation. They strongly refuted the notion that the Native "race" was dying out, but, in keeping with the philosophical leanings of its constituent parts, the S.A.I. wanted Native peoples to embrace ideas consistent with the values of western progressivism. The rap against the S.A.I. has been the way its members aligned much of their rhetoric with current strains of social Darwinism and their tendency to define indigenous identity as a monolithic group, distancing themselves from the specific cultural and geographical issues particular to different Native groups. Such views could be interpreted as an abandonment of culture.

These were, perhaps, significant lapses on the part of the S.A.I., although their stances were, in most ways, more nuanced than their boilerplate language sometimes suggested. Arthur Parker, in articulating the mission statement of the organization in 1916, argued that Native people had a right to know that their name as a people is not hidden forever from its place among the nations of the earth. They have a right to ask that the false statements and the prejudice that obstructs historic justice be cast aside. They have a right to ask that their children know the history of their fathers.[35]

As noted in Chapter 1, Parker, who identified with the Seneca Nation, would work to preserve that history by collecting the stories and traditions of the Haudenosaunee and presenting them to the public in published form. As Margaret Bruchac points out in her book *Savage Kin*, however, he also profited by selling Haudenosaunee artifacts to museums and other collectors, thereby stripping his countrymen of part of their heritage.[36]

Another important mission of the S.A.I., however, included lobbying for laws defining the legal status of Native people. The existing legal system seemed to purposefully project Native identity into a state of legal ambiguity, making it easy to exploit and abuse Native individuals without legal repercussion. "Who today, we may well inquire, is the Indian?" asked Parker.

What is he in the eyes of the law? The legal status of the Indian has never been defined. He is not an alien, he is not a foreigner, he is not a citizen. There is urgent need for a new code of law defining the status of Indians and regulating Indian matters so that a definite program replaces chaos.[37]

When Parker, who also served as editor of the S.A.I. journal, finally grew disillusioned with the lack of progress the Red Progressives were making, Bonnin took over the role of journal editor and was the driving force behind the S.A.I.'s continued existence moving through the late 1920s and into the 30s. It is always a mistake to keep Bonnin wrapped in the sentimentalized winding tape of her early publications. She remained a tireless activist for Native reform throughout her life, willing to do the dreary administrative work of editing the society's papers, chairing meetings, endlessly drafting and sending out S.A.I. newsletters and dues collections, and stationing herself in Washington, D.C. in later years so she could be close to the channels of power and influence. In 1924, she joined a commission sent to Oklahoma by the Indian Welfare Committee to investigate systemic abuses by which the Oklahoma tribes were being robbed of their resources, including oil revenues that had, on paper at least, made many Native Oklahomans rich.

It is fascinating to read her singular contribution as "research agent" for this committee in a report entitled "Oklahoma's Poor Rich Indians: An Orgy of Graft and Exploitation of the Five Civilized Tribes" and subtitled "Legalized Robbery," just in case anyone missed the point. Here she not only catalogues the insidious legal devices by which Native peoples were disenfranchised from their holdings by corrupt appointed "guardians," but, as a Native woman, she is also able to collect testimony from a handful of young women who suffered sexual assault alongside being robbed of land and wealth. She doesn't necessarily mince words as she details one Muskogee woman's experience,

> whose little body was mutilated by a drunken fiend who assaulted her night after night. Her terrified screams brought no help then,—but now, as surely as this tale of horror reaches the friends of humanity, swift action must be taken to punish those guilty of such heinous crimes.

Still, as in her earlier narratives, there are limits to what can be articulated in polite print discourse, and Bonnin is left to summarize that "the smothered cries of the Indian for rescue from legalized plunder comes in a chorus from all parts of eastern Oklahoma."[38] How far were those smothered cries from Bonnin's own spiritual anguish, the inexpressible whine of the stripped telegraph pole, or the low moan rising from the sea shell.

There was a hard price for such commitments, for excelling at your conquerors' arts, learning the Indian passwords, being the carrier of tragic wisdom. As Zitkala-Sa concluded in her early biographical narrative,

> For the white man's papers I had given up my faith in the Great Spirit. For these same papers I had forgotten the healing in trees and brooks. On account of my mother's simple view of life, and my lack of any, I gave her up, also. I made no friends among the race of people I loathed. Like a slender tree, I had been uprooted from my mother, nature, and God. I was shorn of my branches, which had waved in sympathy and love for home and friends. The natural coat of bark which had protected my oversensitive nature was scraped off to the very quick. Now a cold bare pole I seemed to be, planted in a strange earth. Still, I seemed to hope a day would come when my mute aching head, reared upward to the sky, would flash a zigzag lightning across the heavens. With this dream of vent for a long-pent consciousness, I walked again amid the crowds.[39]

Notes

1 Zitkala-Sa, "The School Days of an Indian Girl," *American Indian Stories, Legends, and Other Writings*, Eds. Cathy Davidson and Ada Norris (New York: Penguin Books, 2003), 92.
2 Zitkala-Sa, "School Days," 92–93.
3 William Apess, "A Son of the Forest," *On Our Own Ground: The Complete Writings of William Apess, a Pequot* (University of Massachusetts Press, 1992),
4 Zitkala-Sa, "School Days," 101.
5 Susan Bernardin, "The Lessons of a Sentimental Education: Zitkala-Sa's Autobiographical Narratives," *Western American Literature* 32:3 (Fall 1997), pp. 212–238, 218.
6 H. B. Whipple, "Preface," *A Century of Dishonor: A Sketch of the United States Government's Dealings with some of the Indian Tribes*, by Helen Jackson (New York: Indian Head Books, 1993), ix.
7 Helen Jackson, *A Century of Dishonor: A Sketch of the United States Government's Dealings with some of the Indian Tribes* (New York: Indian Head Books, 1993), 29.

8 Philip Deloria's *Indians in Unexpected Places* offers many helpful examples of Native people successfully negotiating scenes of modernity.
9 William Apess, "An Indian's Looking-Glass for the White Man," *On our Own Ground*, 6.
10 Luther Standing Bear, *My People the Sioux* (Lincoln: University of Nebraska Press, 1975), 190.
11 Standing Bear, *Land of the Spotted Eagle* (Lincoln: University of Nebraska, 1978), 245–246.
12 Arrell Morgan Gibson, *The American Indian, Prehistory to the Present* (Lexington, MA: D. C. Heath, 1980), 494.
13 Gertrude Bonnin, Charles H. Fabens, Matthew K. Sniffen, *Oklahoma's Poor Rich Indians: An Orgy of Graft and Exploitation of the Five Civilized Tribes—Legalized Robbery* (Philadelphia: Office of the Indian Rights Association, 1924), 6.
14 Robert Warrior, *The People and the Word: Reading Native Nonfiction* (Minneapolis: University of Minnesota Press, 2005), 75–76.
15 Gibson, 497.
16 Richard Henry Pratt, *Battlefield and Classroom: Four Decades with the American Indian, 1867–1904.* Ed. Robert M. Utley (New Haven: Yale University Press, 1964), 335.
17 Standing Bear, *My People*, 141.
18 Zitkala-Sa, "School Days," 90–91.
19 Nelson A. Miles, *Personal Recollections of General Nelson A. Miles* (New York: De Capo Press, 1969), 180.
20 Brad D. Lookingbill, *Wardance at Fort Marion: Plains Indian War Prisoners* (Norman: University of Oklahoma Press, 2006), 129.
21 Pratt, 220.
22 Standing Bear, *Spotted Eagle*, 230–231.
23 Standing Bear, *My People*, 98.
24 Standing Bear, *My People*, 224–226.
25 Standing Bear, *My People*, 228–229.
26 Charles Eastman, *From the Deep Woods to Civilization* (Boston: Little Brown, 1916), 34.
27 Eastman, *Deep Woods*, 99.
28 Eastman, *Deep Woods*, 111–114.
29 Robert Warrior, *Tribal Secrets: Recovering American Indian Intellectual Traditions* (Minneapolis: University of Minnesota Press, 1995), 8.
30 Charles Eastman, *Indian Boyhood* (New York: Dover, 1971), introductory material, no page number.
31 Frank L. Baum wrote this in Dec. of 1890 as part of an editorial for the *Aberdeen Saturday Pioneer*. Quoted in Jennifer Guiliano, *Indian Spectacle: College Mascots and the Anxiety of Modern America* (New Brunswick: Rutgers University Press, 2015), 65.
32 Zitkala-Sa, "School Days," 96–97.
33 Zitkala-Sa, "School Days," 97.
34 Zitkala-Sa, "An Indian Teacher among Indians," *American Indian Stories, Legends, and Other Writings*, Eds. Cathy Davidson and Ada Norris (New York: Penguin Books, 2003), 111.
35 Arthur C. Parker, "Social Elements of the Indian Problem," *American Journal of Sociology* 22:2 (Sept. 1916), pp. 252–267.
36 Margaret M. Bruchac, *Savage Kin: Indigenous Information and American Anthropolgists* (Tucson: University of Arizona Press, 2018), 48–83.
37 Parker, 263.
38 Bonnin, Fabens, Sniffen, *Oklahoma's Poor Rich Indians*, 26.
39 Zitkala-Sa, "Indian Teacher," 112.

4

SUNSET, SUNRISE

The American Indian Novel and the Dawning of the Native American Literary Renaissance

Oklahoma, Not O.K.

For a brief moment at the turn of the twentieth century there existed the possibility of a 46th state entering the Union, consisting of a majority Indian population and named after the Cherokee visionary Sequoyah, the man who single-handedly reduced the Cherokee language into a functioning syllabary that was rapidly adopted and internalized by much of the Cherokee Nation. Instead of statehood, however, what was known at the time as "Indian Territory" became incorporated into the acceptance of the larger, whiter state of Oklahoma into the Union in 1907, and, for better or worse, the dream of Indian statehood was laid to rest in that precise location where the grass is as high as an elephant's eye and the wind goes whipping down the plain.

Perhaps not surprisingly, a great deal of the Native literature being produced in the late nineteenth and early twentieth centuries came out of this region shown on the maps, right up until 1906, as "Indian Territory." Indian Territory (I.T.) contained not only groups already claiming parts of Oklahoma as their ancestral homelands, including the Osage, Caddo, Comanche, Kiowa, Wichita, and others, but the Indian nations that, during the removal era, were forcibly marched to lands granted them by the U.S. government within these borders. Today, no less than 39 federally recognized tribes are located within the boundaries of the state, all with their own histories, languages, cultures, and traditions.[1] Although they remain within the state jurisdiction of Oklahoma, they nevertheless maintain their own elected governments and tribal constitutions, mostly formed in the early days of forced relocation.

A good number of those living in I.T. during the allotment era had received western-style educations (in books and letters as well as in power and dominance), and it didn't take long for them to establish newspapers, schools, and even colleges

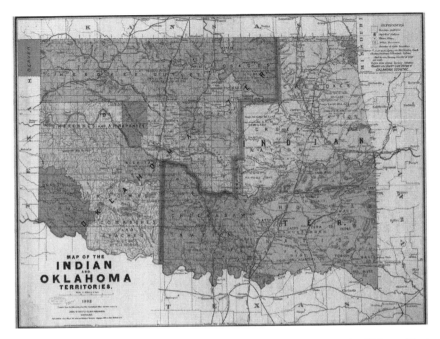

FIGURE 4.1 Rand McNally and Company 1892 *Map of the Indian and Oklahoma Territories*. [Smithsonian Institute, 1892] Map. www.loc.gov/item/98687110/. Courtesy Library of Congress, Geography and Map Division

within their boundaries. Cherokee author Robert Conley claims that, by the time Oklahoma declared statehood, the Cherokee Nation "had produced more college graduates than did its neighboring states of Arkansas and Texas combined," as well as having created "the world's first free, compulsory school system."[2] And the *Cherokee Phoenix* did, in fact, rise again, and continued to publish in both English and Cherokee. Although there have been a few stops and starts, the paper remains in circulation to this day.

It was as a result of this troubled dynamic of displacement, forced assimilation, and western book-learning that what is considered to be the first Native American novel emerged in 1854 — a bandit story patterned on the dime store novels coming into popularity at the time, entitled *The Life and Adventures of Joaquín Murieta, the Celebrated Bandit* and written by John Rollin Ridge. Although the novel is ostensibly about the life of a Mexican bandit whose descent into lawlessness is spurred on by white settler violence, including the rape of his wife and the lynching of his brother, one can also sense the traumas of removal rippling through its pages. Rollin Ridge was, himself, the son of John Ridge, the Cherokee activist and intellectual who was ultimately executed for his participation in the drawing up of the 1835 Treaty of New Echota. Rollin Ridge had come of age just as his people were being forced from their traditional homelands by Jackson's removal policies and he was witness to his father's violent death in I.T. Rollin Ridge was never able to forgive those of the Ross faction who passed the death sentence on his father, and *Joaquin* has been read by Cherokee scholar Jace Weaver and others as a "thinly veiled revenge fantasy" whose confused identities, borders, and nationalities are entangled in the overall dynamics of displacement.[3]

S. Alice Callahan was yet another Native novelist of I.T. whose 1891 novel *Wynema, A Child of the Forest* deals with the dilemmas of removal, assimilation, and allotment. A sentimental tale that tracks multiple love interests around and between Creek–Muskogee students and white missionaries on Muskogee lands, the novel walks a precarious line between celebrating certain aspects of Muskogean culture and offering a progressivist view that regards assimilation to dominant white values as both necessary and inevitable. Seen through the shifting perspectives of the white Methodist schoolteacher Genevieve and her precocious Muskogee student Wynema, the novel is also a polemic on issues of the day such as the passing of the Dawes Act and ongoing events on the Pine Ridge Indian Reservation in South Dakota.

Wynema, A Child of the Forest is identified by Lavonne Ruoff, editor of the modern edition, as "probably the first novel written by a woman of American Indian descent."[4] As with William Apess's *A Son of the Forest*, the title is entirely misleading, as there are no forests to speak of within the work itself, and the evocation is simply a nod to the still powerful and persistent trope of Native peoples eking out a puerile existence in the dense American wilderness of white imagination. Callahan's father was of Irish–Muskogee heritage, a slave owner and an officer in the First Creek Mounted Volunteers during the Civil War, who would later become a rancher and a newspaper editor. Callahan herself went to white schools, attending a year of college at the Wesleyan Female Institute in Staunton, Virginia. Nevertheless, their family strongly identified as Creek–Muskogean, and her father served in tribal government in various capacities over the years.[5]

Despite all this, *Wynema* often voices a stilted view of indigenous identity. It describes the traditional green corn dance with great fondness, but, when talk turns to the implementation of allotments, we hear from Wynema herself that there are too many "idle, shiftless, Indians who do nothing but hunt and fish … so long as our land remains as a whole, in common, these lazy Indians will never make a move toward cultivating it."[6] In what probably seemed like a disarming rhetorical move, Callahan has the white missionary–schoolteacher, Genevieve, voice the anti-allotment sentiment by observing that the legislation will "be the ruin of the poor ignorant savage."[7] Neither of the views expressed seem to locate strength or resiliency in traditional Muskogean culture, although certainly such traditionalist views existed and were strenuously voiced in I.T. at the time. But it is equally true that many of the Red Progressives were in favor of allotment, even if Callahan herself comes across as ambivalent—supportive of the act in theory, but wary of what it might mean for Native peoples unprepared for the intensely acquisitive and unprincipled rigors of "civilization."[8] The novel makes no attempt to resolve these misgivings, but takes an unexpected turn at the end when reports of tensions at Pine Ridge and Wounded Knee suddenly find their way to I.T., offering an opportunity for many of the characters to recertify their commitment to Native rights.

For all its shortcomings, *Wynema* is an intriguing and important work that communicates the concerns emanating from I.T. at the turn of the century. It depicts strong, opinionated female characters of both Anglo and Native extraction, who, despite their ultimate subordination to the expectations of sentimental domestic literature, nevertheless demand that the men they marry be sensitive, informed, and attentive to their views and needs. Even as it denigrates the status of traditional Native identity as static or frozen in the past, it voices strong concern for the rights and autonomy of Indian peoples. We might also keep in mind that Callahan was barely 22 when she wrote *Wynema* and perhaps would have had much more to contribute had she not died of pleurisy in 1894 at 26 years of age.

Also weighing in on the issues of the day from I.T. was Alexander Posey, a Creek newspaper editor, like Callahan's father, and author of what came to be known as the *Fus Fixico Letters*. The Fixico letters, written in the English-language dialect of the Creek people, are satirical sketches that appeared in Posey's newspaper, the *Eufaula Indian Journal*, digesting current events and attitudes in the I.T. and inevitably training their focus on allotment and Indian statehood as these issues came to the fore. Posey's newspaper columns are unique for their unselfconscious representation of Creek voices and attitudes that, in part, drew upon the literary conventions of regionalism and dialect pioneered by late nineteenth-century authors such as Mark Twain and Kate Chopin. Posey, however, employed this aesthetic platform to offer a rare depiction of parochial indigenous life. His staple of homegrown Creek characters, including Fus Fixico, the assumed author of the letters, and his friends Hotgun and Jim Chibbo, gave voice to the various factions in the Creek community, allowing space for humor, conflict, disagreement, sarcasm, gullibility, and a kind of salt-of-the-earth wisdom that, nevertheless, all came together as a vital expression of Creek sovereignty.

The multi-vocality of Posey's literary performance often makes it difficult to determine his actual political stances as an author, and surely this obfuscation was part of his intended process. His Fus Fixico columns were picked up by other papers across the country and widely appreciated for their unique wit and the genuine perspective they promised of the "view from Indian Country." Part of what rendered them successful to broader audiences, however, was that Posey's own opinions were opaque to white readers, who could choose to simply focus on the humor. In some ways, Posey was the Native Stephen Colbert of his day, offering a satirical take on current events through a veiled persona. The Creek critic Craig Womack, who frames each chapter of his book *Red on Red* with vignettes meant to emulate Posey's dialogues, lauds "the power of transgression" in Posey's work, including his ability to "take the stereotypes surrounding full-blood Indians—laziness, illiteracy, simplicity, and so on" and invert them "for his own purposes." As such, Womack sees Posey as a subversive voice, employing what

Gerald Vizenor refers to as a "trickster hermeneutics" that effectively collapses the reductive binary categories of traditionalist/progressivist attitudes. Posey's education and upbringing (including a father who would punish him for speaking his own language) seem to squarely position him in the Red Progressive camp. But, as Womack asserts, Posey engages "in guerrilla warfare, camouflage, and sneak attacks, the battle strategies of disadvantaged opponents facing more powerful adversaries."[9] Although critics disagree about Posey's ultimate intent in the *Fus Fixico Letters*, for Womack at least, his was a voice in concert with the "radical traditionalist movements and the more centrist attempts to achieve statehood for Indian Territory rather than simply annexing it to Oklahoma." It held true potential to sway events and "strike a deathblow to the crooks in Washington trying to take over his nation."[10]

In 1898, the passing of the Curtis Act (an extension of the Dawes Act necessitated by the fact that the major tribes of I.T. had managed to forestall the implementation of allotment for over a decade) signaled that the U.S. government was bent upon forcing the allotment issue. In view of the fact that allotment was to become a reality whether Native people wished for it or not, the so-called "five civilized tribes" made up of the Cherokee, Choctaw, Chickasaw, Creek, and Seminole, came together in the Creek town of Muskogee in 1905 to argue for Indian statehood. Part of the Allotment Act's raison d'être had always been the termination of the tribes as legal and cultural entities. This was designed to occur after a certain grace period in which Native people, once assimilated into the cult of private land ownership and naturalized by newly activated impulses of selfishness and greed, could be counted as full citizens of the United States without need of separate tribal status or identity. The date set for this magical transformation to free-market capitalism was March 4, 1906. The convening of the five tribes was intended to preempt this occurrence and they went so far as to draft a constitution and submit it to Congress in their push for the admission of the State of Sequoyah into the Union.[11]

Achieving statehood would not have proved a direct corollary to maintaining tribal sovereignty—in fact, it would have been a relinquishment of sovereignty by absorption into the U.S. government—but, under the circumstances, it appeared to many as the most effective way to retain some level of indigenous agency over the lives of Native peoples who had already been pushed off their lands and forced to suffer immeasurable losses at the hands of the settler state. And it was clear that, if they didn't take matters into their own hands, the I.T. would be swept up in Oklahoma's concurrent bid for statehood, bringing about the same outcome with even less control. Or, as Posey put it,

> they ain't no rhyme nor reason in giving Injun Territory in marriage to Oklahoma. It was like marrying a duke or prince of a random royal family to the daughter of a rich trust magnate, so he could repair his ancestral home and roll in luxury. The two countries didn't had nothing in common, unless, maybe so, it was a weakness for firewater. So if you put the two together you was had a drunken brawl.[12]

Residents of the I.T. voted overwhelmingly for the ratification of their constitution, and the bill for Sequoyah statehood went through Congress in 1906, but the majority in Congress voted for the single state option, following the wishes of then President Teddy Roosevelt.[13] Oklahoma, with its motto "labor conquers all things," was made the 46th state in 1907, ensuring that the "drunken brawl" Posey predicted would indeed take place.

Sundown

Other important Native writers contributed their literary vision during this era from other parts of Turtle Island, including the Paiute activist Sarah Winnemucca, Cherokee author John Milton Oskison, Mohawk poet E. Pauline Johnson, and the Okanogan novelist Christine Quintasket, better known by her pen name, Mourning Dove. Each of these artists grappled with the violent transition of Native peoples entering into the twentieth century and often found themselves performing their indigenous identities in seemingly reductive ways, donning headdresses, wampum beads, and moccasins in public appearances to signal their Nativeness to white audiences, even while their literature spoke in poignant manner to the complexity, diversity, and modernity of Native lives.

It was an age of racialized pageantry in America, with memorials to the Confederate war dead sprouting up like weeds in every public square south of the Mason–Dixon line, world fairs featuring tourist-friendly reconstructed Indian villages populated by real live unreconstructed Indians, and Buffalo Bill Cody's Wild West Show reenacting the spectacle of Custer's Last Stand at Little Big Horn on a nightly basis, making a white martyr of the officer responsible for the 1868 massacre of the Cheyenne at Washita.[14]

Charles Eastman appeared on stages throughout the Northeast in a full eagle-feather bonnet, capitalizing on his classic Lakota features to educate audiences on "THE TRUTH about the much misunderstood red man." His promotional literature suggested that, in 1909 alone, he gave more than 100 lectures across New England.[15] Sarah Winnemucca pioneered the role of "Indian Princess" throughout the 1870s and 80s, as she lobbied tirelessly in her public appearances against the disastrous forced relocation of the Paiutes. She was even known to pose, from time to time, as Pocahontas, the mother of all "Indian Princesses," in what were referred to as "tableaux vivants" put on by her family members to entertain and enlighten white audiences.[16] Pauline Johnson, billed as *the* "Mohawk Princess" in her speaking tours, typically appeared in Indian costume, wearing ermine, Indian beadwork, and wampum belts. One newspaper described her outfit as "an exact reproduction of that worn by Minnehaha"—an interesting claim given that Minnehaha was a fictional figure from Longfellow's 1855 poem *The Song of Hiawatha*, which itself was a work of the imagination misattributing the Haudenosaunee culture hero Hiawatha as the central figure in the Anishinaabe epic. Gerald Vizenor would refer to such displays as *manifest manners*—the "notions and misnomers that are read as authentic and sustained as representations of Native American Indians."[17] It was performances such as these, and the layers of simulation that congealed around them, that prompted Luther Standing Bear to observe in dismay, "I felt that I was no more Indian, but would be an imitation of the white man. And we are still imitations of white men, and the white men are imitations of Americans."[18]

If Pauline Johnson played up the role of Indian princess for one portion of her act, she became the progenitor of the quick-change artist, appearing in an evening gown for the second part of her performance and sometimes reversing the order if only to confound or defy expectations. Her verse may have evoked a serviceable noble defiance for white audiences of the period, breathing with "the wild fire of departed braves and ... the pathos of later days," as noted by one reviewer, but, as with Winnemucca, Eastman, and others, Johnson also used these performative openings to offer pointed critique of contemporary settler colonial practices.[19] Perhaps Mohawk poet Beth Brant said it best when she observed of Johnson that, "she walked the writing path clearing the brush for us to follow. And the road gets wider and clearer everytime a Native woman picks up her pen and puts her mark on paper."[20]

Following World War I, however, public taste for such displays and performances receded, and the presentation of Native identity in literature entered an ambivalent phase marked most prominently, perhaps, by John Joseph Mathews and his 1934 novel *Sundown*. If it has never quite received the level of scholarly attention it deserves, *Sundown* stands as the gateway to the modern American Indian novel (although, admittedly, it might also be seen as the opening to a dark cavity that one does not fully escape until, perhaps, the final pages of N. Scott Momaday's 1968 novel *House Made of Dawn*). The events of the novel mirror, at least partly, the events of Mathews's own life and, as such, they seem to reflect his conflicted and suppressed notions concerning not only the Osage side of his heritage, but his negotiations with gender normativity—at least as they manifested themselves at the time of writing.

Far from performing Indian identity, Mathews was, outwardly at least, in the words of Choctaw–Cherokee scholar Louis Owens, "the most acculturated of all Indian novelists."[21] Mathews was the beneficiary of the oil boom that gushed through Oklahoma at the turn of the twentieth century and, in most ways, owing to the headrights granted his family, he managed to lead a gentleman's life of leisure that reveled in travel, hunting, drinking, and being a man of letters—a role he cultivated through prolonged institutionalized training in the halls of higher learning at the University of Oklahoma, then Oxford, and during a short stint at the University of Geneva in Switzerland.[22] A geology major, Mathews originally hoped to use his expertise in the employ of the very oil barons who were at once enriching and destroying the Osage people, but he fell into a writing life instead, assisted and encouraged by a network of well-placed friends in the publishing industry acquired throughout his college years.[23]

And yet, Mathews's novel *Sundown* remains highly intriguing for the striking glimpses of historical and cultural context it offers, almost like scenes witnessed from the window of a passing train, forming indelible visual and mental imprints, often with little or no expository assistance. With its modernist pull toward minimalism and the expression of spiritual enervation on both a personal and cultural scale, *Sundown* often reads as though Fitzgerald's *This Side of Paradise* unfurled in and around I.T. But, if it offers its Osage backdrop as just one more casualty of a lost generation, its author is also wary enough to name his protagonist "Chal," short for "Challenge," for "he shall be a challenge to the disinheritors of his people."[24]

The nature of that challenge is ambiguous, even to John Windzer, Chal's "mixedblood" father who, drunk on "*Rock and Rye*" at the moment of his son's birth, perceives how his own "thoughts are not clear; he didn't know what he challenged. As a matter of fact it had never been definite."[25] Mathews, however, is savvy in the ways he introduces the concerns and struggles of the Osage community, rarely drawing undue attention to this world that would be so unfamiliar to his readers, yet understanding its magnetic pull and presenting it from time to time in the most offhand manner. As such, we learn abruptly of how the Curtis Act (never referred to by name in the novel) hovers over the reservation, with Chal's father proud of the role he has played in bringing it about. Windzer boasts to his family, "if it hadn't been for the progressives on the council, they never would have been any allotment, if it was left up to the fullblood party."[26]

Chal, too, although still a child in the novel's early passages, has felt the running tensions between the traditionalists of the community and those of mixed heritage like himself. When he is old enough to be sent to the reservation school, he finds he has to prove himself in battle to avoid being bullied by the "fullblood" Indians. His liminal status is signaled in the loaded words of advice he gets from his father, who instructs him, "yu see, you got to fight an Indian—just enough to show him you ain't afraid."[27] The language of blood quantum remains a disturbing aspect of how Native identity is understood and legitimated even today—a legacy of settler colonial practice that sought to split Native communities along degrees of racialized identity. As Joseph Bauerkemper observes, the status of "mixedblood (pseudo-scientifically defined and designated) came to serve as a proxy for competency" in the eyes of the law. It largely determined the economic autonomy of Native peoples in the wake of the Dawes Act, with "mixed bloods" being extended legal rights that were routinely denied full-blooded Natives owing to their perceived inferiority.[28] Chal is, therefore, caught in a classic conflict of colonization. Given that his father is of mixed heritage and his mother is full Osage, when Chal is told "you got to fight an Indian," he is essentially being advised to wage internal war against himself. This hidden battle over identity is like an underground current that flows throughout the entire work, as it does throughout so much of the subsequent literature to emerge from Native space.

The father's own unsettled identity is a steady pulse running through the early sections of *Sundown*, as his convictions concerning allotment and the presumed short-sightedness of the full-blood Osage community are eventually seen to be highly compromised positions harkening back to his earlier confession in the novel—his inability to fully comprehend the very thing he challenged. In most ways, Chal is the product of this uncertainty and, even as he first hears his father's "dream-talk about the future," he silently wonders "why the fullbloods didn't want this thing, allotment. It seemed to be the very best of things and he couldn't see why they were against it."[29] Such reflective moments draw little attention to themselves in the novel, but we are nonetheless made witness as the father's dream of Indian statehood crumbles, the Osage council is disbanded, and transformation envelopes the reservation. Chal observes how, "slowly from the east the black oil derricks" crept in, "rising above the blackjacks, like some unnatural growth, from the diseased tissues of the earth."[30] Despite these ominous encroachments, the father, along with many others in the community, celebrates Oklahoma statehood and the perceived march of progress. They are briefly enriched by these events, and, as Chal, himself, comes of age, he enters college at the University of Oklahoma and learns to fly planes, finding a new purpose and identity for himself even with the advent of World War 1.

The modernist impulses driving *Sundown* seem to steer it away from gazing too closely upon the degradations increasingly occurring on Osage lands or from taking too definite a stance on them. Later in the novel, Chal barely responds to the fact of his father's murder at the hands of a white man, although it is evidently prompted by the reservation politics occurring off-page as oil-extraction companies sink their roots ever more deeply into the heart of Osage territory. Chal is again mostly ambivalent when his childhood best friend, Running Elk, a traditional "hill Indian" whose life has spiraled into alcoholic despondency, also falls prey to the greed-driven violence sweeping the reservation.

These acts of violence and the period book-ending them are remembered today as the "Osage Reign of Terror," most recently chronicled by journalist David Grann in his 2018 work *Killers of the Flower Moon*. At the time of this writing, there are plans to make a major motion picture based on this book. Native authors, however, have been chronicling these horrific events for much longer and with much less public notice. Osage–Cherokee legal scholar Rennard Strickland, in his condemnation of the extra-legal acts surrounding the "reign of terror," asserts that, "as many as two hundred tribesmen may have been killed in the 1920s in order to transfer their headrights to intermarried whites."[31] Arguably, the concerted acts of unprincipled white opportunists during Oklahoma's oil boom were as murderous as the massacres perpetrated by Custer at Washita or the Seventh Cavalry at Pine Ridge. These ruptures of racialized violence are part of the same hostile dynamic that Gertrude Bonnin, otherwise known as Zitkala-Sa, began to outline in her 1924 investigation of "Oklahoma's Poor Rich Indians," as discussed in Chapter 3.

But, whereas Bonnin, often critiqued for her ineffectual sentimental discourse, was taking an explicit proactive stance against the coercive state-sanctioned violence directed at Oklahoma's Indian nations, Mathews offers a much more aesthetically muted witness. His conflicted protagonist responds to these crises by becoming more and more spiritually adrift, speeding furiously across the backroads of Oklahoma in his red roadster, drinking copious amounts of moonshine whiskey, attending parties with dead-end acquaintances, and feverishly pronouncing to the heavens, "I wish I didn't have a drop of God damn' Indian blood in my veins."[32] At his lowest ebb in the narrative, Chal is taunted by the sudden descent of a flock of jays upon a blackjack tree. He feels vaguely accused by their presence, his sublimated grief, inaction, and complicity rising up like bile from his alcohol-fueled torpor, at which point, "he got up, picked up the empty bottle and threw it into the branches of the tree, and there were many streaks of blue-and-white floating away, each screaming 'murder!'"[33] It is the only intimation offered that Chal emotionally registers the death of his father and Running Elk.

Sundown remains a taut expression of what is often configured as the post-colonial condition, wherein one is driven to a state of internal warfare by the conflicting forces contained within one's own body and blood—the strains of colonization occurring on a biological level. Abenaki poet Cheryl Savageau expresses this state poignantly in her poem "Like the Trails of Ndakinna," where she observes, "We're French and Indian like the war / my father said … French and Indian / still fighting in my blood."[34] Except, as many Native scholars have noted, there is no "post" where indigenous peoples in America are concerned. The settler colonial state continues to stand and wields its influence in a manner that ingeniously exploits historic, economic, environmental, and racialized animosities in order to reduce the claims to sovereignty that all Native people struggle to maintain.

Chal's conflicts are exacerbated even more by his struggle over his sexual identity, never explicitly articulated in the novel, but signaled throughout by his airless courtships and his persistent attempts to express some private aspect of his physical nature—a "devilish urge" that he cannot quite embrace or purge from his being.[35] Mathews clearly did not apprehend an outlet to speak openly about these urges in his writings, but *Sundown* opens itself up to a queer reading within both Native and settler frameworks. Michael Snyder, in his essay on the novel, notes how, in the Osage tribe, "men referred to as *mixu'ga* took on women's gender roles," and this was not something that was stigmatized in traditional Osage life. Mathews was aware of this practice and writes about it in his large volume of Osage life and customs entitled *The Osage*.[36] Still, he retains his ambivalence despite certain moments in his fiction, as in the "devilish urge" cited above, where his apparent struggle over his own sexual identity cannot divorce itself from the narrative.

In interesting ways, Chal's sexual identity in the novel is often conflated with his ethnic identity. He reflects at one point how he had "often wished that he weren't so bronze. It set him off from other people and he felt that he was queer anyway, without calling attention to the fact."[37] His inability to express his nature manifests itself as an internalized self-loathing. We are told,

> he almost despised himself for the feeling deep within him which feebly remonstrated. He kept this feeling subdued; kept it from bubbling up into the placid waters of his consciousness ... to keep them from reflecting the impressions that ought to be mirrored, if one were to remain in step.[38]

In a number of passages, however, he strips himself of his clothes, like shedding a skin, and dances alone in the elements, seeking some expression of his inner self that is not available to him when around others. Towards the end of the novel, this finally becomes an act of tentative self-affirmation when,

> Suddenly he began to dance. He bent low over the grass and danced, and as he danced he sang, and as he sang one of the tribal songs of his people, he was fascinated by his own voice, which seemed clear and sonorous on the still air. He danced wildly and his blood became hotter, and yet that terrific emotion which was dammed up in his body would not come out; that emotion which was dammed up and could not be expressed ... He was in pain and he danced frantically for some kind of climax; that sense of completeness that consummates the creative urge; an orgasm of the spirit. But he couldn't dance fast enough ... He wanted to challenge something; to strut before an enemy. He wanted by some action or some expression, to express the whole meaning of life; to declare to the silent world about him that he was a glorious male; to express to the silent forms of the blackjacks that he was a brother to the wind.[39]

The significance of intertwining his sexual and ethnic identity may seem an act of confusion or, perhaps, even subconscious subterfuge, but it might also be explained to some degree by Mark Rifkin's suggestion that so-called "normative" expressions of sexuality are yet another imposition of settler colonialism, and that, "U.S. imperialism against native peoples over the past two centuries can be understood as an effort to make them 'straight'—to insert indigenous peoples into Anglo-American conceptions of family, home, desire, and personal identity."[40]

These struggles mapped out on the body are also mapped out on the land in *Sundown*, as both earth and flesh grapple with the influx of hostile foreign elements. Mathews's novel, despite its stylistic reticence, offers a blueprint of the environmental despoliation of Osage lands—the slow creeping emergence of western "progress" from the east like a plague, promising vitality and wealth, but ultimately draining the land of its very life's blood, until "the derricks stood black against the prairie horizon in rows, and became husks of a life force that had retreated back along its own trail."[41] By the novel's end, Chal sees his favorite childhood retreat, a particular creek to which he would often return to explore and interrogate his identity, turned stagnant, the water lifeless and colored with green scum, the roots of the old sycamore on the bank seeming to tremble with fear.[42] This spot represents not just a retreat, but a secret source of power bubbling up from the earth, rooting Chal in this specific geographic location. It is what makes him Osage, *Ni-U-Ko'n-ska*, one of the "children of the middle waters" as the Osage call themselves, apart from all of his questions of allegiance and identity, connecting him to the indigenous side of his heritage in a visceral manner.[43] And its degradation speaks to Mathews's own sense that the Osage themselves have been strangled by the engines of modernity into near cultural extinction—sundown.

This strategy of mapping out the traumatic false promises of western "progress" and "civilization" on the land and body will become essential elements of later Native American novels, poems, and short stories, and Mathews inaugurates this tradition with understated skill, allowing layers of meaning to surface through the recurring motifs of the creek in its despoliation, the image of the oil derricks continuously creeping westward, and the disastrous blight it all unleashes. In one dramatic scene early on in the novel, an oil derrick catches fire in the wake of a storm, and the people of the small town, including Chal and his father, gather round, with one astonished onlooker exclaiming that the disaster is a sign, and "everybody ought to make peace with their God." It becomes clear, however, that the derrick, as well as the elements it unleashes from the glowing maw of the earth, has, in fact, become the new God of choice, usurping the sacred fire of tradition, and the townsmen stand reverently before it as the flames light

> up the whole country-side ... The terrific, ground-shivering roar and the light that spread over the whole valley; the light that made the blackjacks on the hills look like ghost trees, appeared to the mixedbloods standing there as a symbol of the indefinite glory that was coming. That light that you could see as far away as the old Cherokee country, and that roar that drowned all other sounds, gave them a feeling of vague greatness and importance in the universe. Here was a manifestation of a power that made the white man stand and wonder; a power that came out of their own hills, and that light, in which you could "pick up a pin a mile away," was certainly the light of glory.[44]

Chal's father and the other "mixedblood" Osage stand in awe of the force they see unleashed from their own land and are seduced by the false idol of the burning derrick that scours them clean of their former traditional beliefs.

For all the tragic wisdom of this scene and the doom that Mathews forecasts, there is *survivance* in *Sundown*, if one seeks it out. Chal makes a visit to the tribe's roundhouse in the novel, to watch the traditional Osage dancers, admiring the beauty of their offering even though he feels hopelessly estranged from the performance. Seeking some grain of meaning and purification in his aimless existence, Chal attends a sweat lodge with a childhood friend, Sun-on-his-Wings, and partakes in the peyote ceremony. But he is already drunk when he enters the lodge, and the full power of the ceremony fails to resonate with Chal or launch him upon a new path. The true sense of *survivance* in the novel, however, is signaled by the blackjacks—the ubiquitous scrub oaks of Osage country that define for Mathews a resiliency and adaptability to harsh extremes of climate. Throughout the novel, and in other of Mathews's writings as well, the blackjacks appear as counterpoint to the life-sucking machinery of the oil derricks and represent a correlative to the traditional "Hill Indians" who have weathered so much violence and change and yet remain steadfast in their sense of cultural identity.

Early in *Sundown*, as the first signs of rampant transformation are being felt, Chal observes of the "fullbloods" that they

> didn't come into the Agency as often as they had before allotment, and that they seemed to be resigned and to keep to themselves. They had made him think of the blackjacks on the hills that surrounded the valley. Blackjacks that had stood there so patiently, as they had always done, and seemed to pay no attention to all the activity of Progress in the valley at their feet.[45]

The blackjacks, throughout the novel, stand in silent, steady defiance to the transformations taking place all around, as though assured their timeless persistence will outlast the crashing wave of so-called "Progress." Just prior to the lightning storm that sparks the dramatic derrick fire, Chal is out riding his pony alongside his favorite creek and can "hear the wind moaning in the blackjacks" on the higher ridge "like a protest."[46] Riding up to gauge the strength of the storm, he stumbles upon three Osage warriors, partaking of the "ancient ritual" of greeting Wah'Kon-tah, the Great Mystery, in the face of the storm. As the gusts gain in force, they all flatten themselves on the clay, each holding tight to the "thin flexible stem" of a blackjack so that, anchored in this manner, they withstand the storm.[47] Robert Warrior, who is Osage himself, notes of Mathews that he was not "a direct participant in Osage ceremonies. He did, however, have great respect for those traditions."[48] Mathews served for many years on the Osage tribal council, was instrumental in the establishment of the Osage cultural museum, and wrote a number of definitive books on Osage history and culture. If he questioned the resiliency of traditional Osage life in *Sundown*, he nevertheless gestures towards an enduring presence, in the image of the blackjacks that still stand with "dignity" as the "all-powerful" force of western progress signaled by "the creeping black derricks began to recede to the east."[49]

Critics up to this point have failed to fully appreciate the layered complexity of *Sundown*. There is a tendency to want to read it in a modernist tradition in the mode of Fitzgerald and Hemingway, but, when one begins to unpack the social and cultural contexts around which Mathews builds his novel in Native space, his symbolism and the spiritual trajectories of his characters take on a whole new host of meanings and interpretations that have yet to be adequately explored. As Warrior observes,

Mathews did not intend *Sundown* to be merely a story of how an individual deals with personal identity. Rather, Mathews evokes a historical period of intense importance for Osage people and communities and attempts to sort out how the political strategies of various groups of Osages played out and what possible future might exist.[50]

These concerns of culture, continuance, gender identity, and environmental sustainability are all incredibly relevant topics for discussion in today's Native American literature classrooms, and *Sundown* deserves another look, especially in the wake of the current oil-extraction and pipeline debates marked most notably by the 2016 movement at Standing Rock, to be discussed in the conclusion of this book.

Sunrise

The publication of *Sundown* in 1934 just happened to coincide with the Indian Reorganization Act (IRA), often referred to as the Collier Act, drafted and championed by Franklin Roosevelt's young commissioner of Indian affairs, John Collier. The Collier Act was inspired by a rare acknowledgment on the part of the federal government that its Indian policies had been an abject failure, empowering individuals and institutions motivated solely by greed to inflict undue suffering upon Native communities. Such public remorse was unlikely to hold the public's interest for long, but Collier proved himself up to the task of seizing the moment and instituting radical reform. He rolled back as many provisions of the 1887 Allotment Act as possible, given the entanglements and interests involved for both indigenous and settler parties, and he encouraged the tribes to adopt or reconstitute their own governing bodies. The results of the IRA, though not universally celebrated by Native scholars, were an actual increase in Native land base and a turn towards greater sovereignty for the tribes that signed on to the suggested reforms. Perhaps the most significant impact of the IRA, however, was its simple acknowledgment that Native peoples were not dying out or vanishing. It was a tacit recognition from the federal government that, despite everything, Indian peoples, along with their tribal identities, had survived the storm.

The literature of the period, however, had yet to fully acclimatize to this notion. Certainly, *Sundown* cannot be viewed as a narrative of cultural uplift, nor were other important works of this period, such as *The Surrounded* by D'Arcy McNickle or *Cherokee Night* by playwrite Lynn Rollie Riggs, which, like *Sundown*, seemed to signal cultural demise in its very title. These works all grappled with the lived experiences of Native peoples in complex ways, but they also served as acknowledgment that there remained cause for caution. White paternalism had not vanished either, and, sure enough, the post-World War II era saw the drafting of "Indian Termination" policies by legislators who, according to McNickle "regarded the Indian programs of the Roosevelt administration as misdirected social experiments that perpetuated the illusion of a future for Indians as Indians."⁵¹ For many white Americans, such an "illusion" still seemed ludicrous.

Termination measures, first adopted in 1953, were quickly followed by Indian relocation programs, seeking to break up tribal communities by encouraging Native individuals, through promises of financial assistance and job training, to relocate to urban areas. Just to offer some sense of the casual cultural insensitivity with which these programs were carried out, it is worth noting that they were spearheaded by the Bureau of Indian Affairs commissioner, Dillon S. Myer, who, prior to taking over this position, had been the head of the War Relocation Authority that rounded up Japanese citizens into internment camps during World War II. Myers was described by one-time Secretary of State Howard Ickes as "a Hitler and Mussolini rolled into one."⁵² Many Natives' lives were left stranded by these programs, alienated from their communities, torn from ties of kinship and culture. In the words of Cheyenne novelist Tommy Orange, "getting us to cities was supposed to be the final, necessary step in our assimilation, absorption, erasure, the completion of a five-hundred-year-old genocidal campaign." But, as Orange also claims, against all odds, "the city made us new, and we made it ours." Spinning this moment as a story of survivance, he maintains,

> we found one another, started up Indian centers, brought out our families and powwows, our dances, our songs, our beadwork … we made art and we made babies and we made way for our people to go back and forth between reservations and city. We did not move to cities to die.⁵³

Even so, just as with the Indian boarding school programs of the previous generation, the termination and relocation measures of the 1950s were devastating for the indigenous communities they impacted, bringing about the loss of hundreds of thousands of acres of tribal lands and causing 61 Native groups to be severed from federal acknowledgement between 1954 and 1961.⁵⁴ As McNickle notes, the measures "prepared the way for almost a decade of turmoil that paralyzed community action" and left tribes such as the Klammath and the Menominee, which had been economically self-sufficient prior to termination, in complete financial disarray.⁵⁵ But, for a variety of complex reasons, including organized pushback from the National Congress of American Indians, which McNickle helped to form in 1944, termination policies ultimately proved unsuccessful and were abandoned by the more forward-thinking Kennedy administration.

McNickle, an enrolled Flathead, was an eloquent voice for indigenous concerns throughout this long, often bleak, period, working for Collier with the Indian bureau, helping to found the D'Arcy McNickle Center at the Newbury Museum in Chicago (which now holds the largest collection of indigenous manuscripts in the U.S.), and continuing to advocate and lecture on Native issues until his death in 1977. But he is probably best known today for his novel *The Surrounded*, which stands alongside *Sundown* as a progenitor of the Native novel as art form and, perhaps, more than *Sundown*, helped lend shape to the narrative landscape of many works to follow. Although there is not space here to go into depth about *The Surrounded*, it tells what will soon become an iconic story of the alienated Native protagonist returning home to the reservation after having been away for many years at Indian boarding schools, fighting imperial wars, or otherwise immersed in white culture, only to find home on the res a difficult place with which to reconnect. This narrative framework, often referred to as the "homing plot" (suggestive of the Greek *nostos*, or the journey home that animates so much of Homer's *The Odyssey*), has been noted and commented upon by a number of critics and, in some ways, is a continuation of the story Zitkala-Sa tells in her biographical sketches—expanding upon the spiritual dislocation and fractured kinship ties she experienced upon returning to the Yankton Sioux reservation after years at boarding school and college. In *The Surrounded*, it is the character Archilde who has experienced some measure of success in the outside world, but finds returning to the place of his origins to be a difficult journey of transformation and self-discovery that lays unexpected claims upon his soul. In the course of the novel, he must slowly reconnect with the rhythms and traditions of his family and extended kinship networks, but he also finds himself trapped in a growing web of white settler hegemony that hems him in and tragically forestalls any opportunity for spiritual reawakening within his own community.[56]

The homing narrative should not be viewed as formulaic so much as a visceral narrative response to more than a century of forced dislocation, relocation, and assimilation. It is a protean narrative that, particularly as a new era of Red Power and indigenous self-determination begins to surface in the 1960s, speaks collectively to a mass of Native people who are looking for a way to reconnect with their roots, their cultures, their stories as mapped out on their ancestral landscapes, however difficult that encounter might prove. Returning to the reservation, both physically and metaphorically, could seem, in some ways, like returning to the source of trauma—the historic sites of massacre, removal, poverty, starvation, and disease. But, if one could push through all this, confront the trauma and plug into the deeper lines of power embedded in these places, then reservations could also prove sites of cultural fortitude and regeneration. Archilde, the protagonist of *The Surrounded*, proves to be presciently named, as he will become the archetype for this narrative structure so indelibly imprinted in the Native psyche of the era. The challenge, however, in both life and literature, was not simply to return to the site of tradition and culture, but to survive the encounter.

Of course, Native peoples weren't the only ones struggling with the return home in this period marked by two world wars and the smaller-scale but still devastatingly brutal Korean and Vietnam Wars. Successive generations were wracked by trauma, and many of the wounded bore invisible scars, though driven to quietly shoulder their anguish in solitude, finding no outlet in domestic life to voice such tortured realities. Many veterans of these wars turned to alcohol and other drugs to assuage their inner turmoil. Many couldn't maintain, losing their jobs and families and taking to the streets. Still others found ways to put an end to their misery through self-inflicted violence. All of these psychic scars were exponentially exacerbated in Native space, where Native men in particular served in the armed forces at highly disproportionate rates as compared with the rest of the population, and existing intergenerational traumas severely compounded the incandescent ruptures of combat trial. These factors taken as a whole rendered N. Scott Momaday's *House Made of Dawn* a momentous literary occurrence when it appeared in 1968, becoming, in 1969, the first, and only, work of literature by an American Indian to win the Pulitzer Prize.

Although one can certainly locate modernist literary aesthetics at play in *House Made of Dawn*, nevertheless, to enter Momaday's book is to enter into Native space, or at the very least a consciousness of Native space, in a way that previous Native literary efforts had not managed to effect (one might argue that Ella Deloria's *Waterlily*, written in the early 1940s, accomplished this as well, although the novel was not published until after Deloria's death in 1988). Even the first word of the novel, "Dypaloh," offers a disorienting greeting for the uninitiated—bringing the reader into the world of Pueblo storytelling and invoking materials, the pollen, the rain, the house made of dawn itself, all of which signal the place, the ceremonial rhythms, the speech act of the story in the moment of its telling. As Louis Owens (himself an important novelist of the period), notes, the reader is offered a "profound awareness of conflicting epistemologies" that show "its ability to appropriate the discourse of the privileged center and make it 'bear the burden' of an 'other' world-view."[57]

The ancient Jemez Pueblo, where much of the story is set, stands alongside even more ancient abodes, where people continue to work the fields in timeless routines, employing handmade plows and hoes, their labor orchestrated by the tracking of sun and moon over enduring features of the landscape. At the start of the novel, the old man, Francisco, strides into the river rushes, devising a simple snare made of hair and reed to acquire bird feathers for a prayer plume which will assist in the annual race—a traditional ceremony to ensure good hunting and harvests. The old man's patient actions speak to the care and hopefulness with which he carries on these practices, and, although his mind wanders back to his youth and his own days as a runner for the tribe, his efforts are fixed upon the future.

It can be easy for readers to miss how every major section of *House Made of Dawn* is framed by ceremony, whether the preserved ceremonies of the Pueblo people, the imposed ceremonies of settler colonial culture that have infiltrated the land, or the hybrid ceremonies sprung up amidst the tensions of colonial and indigenous practice in a place where the cathedral and the kiva stand side by side. However, if the opening passage appears centered in what seem like ageless rhythms of Pueblo life, the protagonist of the story, Abel, is decidedly uncentered, tearing into the narrative like a knife shearing through the fabric of time. When Abel first returns home from the war, the old man, Francisco, is waiting for him at the bus stop, nervously smoothing his shirt with the palms of his hands and glancing about "to be sure that everything was in order."[58] Able, however, stumbling from the bus blind drunk, does not even recognize his grandfather. The old man, despite a crippled leg, must bear the returning veteran's collapsed weight in full view of the other bus passengers, laughing scornfully at them so they will not perceive his tears.

Abel's alienation is keenly felt throughout the novel. Although he tries to speak to his grandfather in days to come, the words will not form. We are told "he had tried to pray, to sing, to enter into the old rhythm of the tongue, but he was no longer attuned to it." If he could have pieced those shattered words and feelings together, however, he would have made "a song out of the colored canyon … it would have been a creation song; he would have sung lowly of the first world, of fire and flood, and of the emergence of dawn from the hills."[59] These traces of Peublo–Navajo tradition remain with him, but he has been jarred loose from these moorings by his war experience and remains a remote presence in the novel, his motivations and feelings opaque, his actions at times seemingly inscrutable.

The narrative itself contributes to that sense of dislocation, moving back and forth in time, taking sudden leaps forward, or spiraling 70 years into the past, grounded more in ceremonial rhythms and the traumatic rupture of those rhythms than in the linear order of the western world. We are left to guess as to why, as a young boy, Abel strangles the eagle he has captured as part of his initiation ceremony into the Eagle Hunting Society. Even as a child, Abel already stands apart from the people of his village, his father unknown to him, though rumored to be Navajo, and his mother and younger brother both dying while he was still a boy. Abel seeks power, a power he evidently found lacking in the eagle, that will protect him against a mysterious malevolent force—a force that still stalks him when he returns to the pueblo all these years later. We catch a glimpse of this mysterious force when Abel is publicly beaten and humiliated by an albino of the tribe during the Feast of Santiago. Later, Abel will confront the albino in a knife fight, resulting in a jail sentence and his further alienation from the place of his birth. Readers will comprehend how these acts are all somehow related, but the reasons cohere nebulously behind a difficult-to-penetrate veil of Pueblo understanding and tradition.

Reading the book as a series of ceremonies—harvests, feast days, sermons, festivals, court trials, last rites, and other rituals, each ordered by the position of the sun on the horizon at dawn and strung together like a makeshift rosary of disparate traditions—will help bring order to some of what is opaque in the novel. Many of the ceremonies are ruptured or corrupted in some way, beginning with the grandfather's attempt to present a prayer plume to Abel upon his initial return from war, with the intent to invite him back into the circle of the long race runners, the race of the dead. Although this initially fails, the book chronicles Abel's journey to reintegrate himself into the Pueblo world. To do so requires not only that he reintegrate his war-shattered psyche, but that he confront forces, mistakes, and violations that precede his own birth. Ultimately, the restoration of order will require a reinvention of self—something Abel begins to catch glimpses of when he is sent to L.A. as part of the Indian relocation program. It is in the city of lost angels that Abel hears the hybrid exhortations of the Kiowa trickster, Tosamah, Pastor and Priest of the Sun, who teaches him that "words were medicine," and the world itself, its order and being, were things called up by words and stories.[60] Abel stitches together other swatches of patchwork tradition from his drunken discussions with the other displaced and disoriented urban Indians who become his companions. One Navajo friend, Benally, talks to Abel about the old ways, the "House made of dawn" and "the stories and the sings, Beautyway and Night Chant. I sang some of those things, and I told them what they meant, what I thought they were about."[61]

Abel is ultimately beaten and brutalized in the city, confronted once more by the ancient malevolent force from his childhood, but, even as he lies a broken heap upon the beach on the outskirts of L.A., ear pressed to the sand, he briefly hears the footsteps of the racers, the runners after evil, and suddenly understands that these remote and seemingly insignificant adherents to an obscure Pueblo ritual were, in fact,

> whole and indispensable in what they did; everything in creation referred to them. Because of them perspective, proportion, design in the universe. Meaning because of them. They ran with great dignity and calm, not in the hope of anything, but hopelessly; neither in fear nor hatred, nor despair of evil, but simply in recognition and with respect.[62]

At his lowest ebb, Abel recovers the words to the song, and he begins to sing himself whole again.

It is this turn toward the land, tradition, and rebirth that marks *House Made of Dawn* as revolutionary in its time, placing it at the forefront of the Native American Literary Renaissance. Other indigenous works would soon seek out similar patterns of cultural regeneration, a revitalization movement taking place in written literary form. In my mind, no novel accomplishes this as well as Leslie Marmon Silko's 1974 masterpiece, *Ceremony*. Silko must have been witnessing many of the same things that Momaday observed when she conceived her work. She would have grown up in the presence of World War II and Korean War veterans rediscovering their place on the Laguna Pueblo reservation and she came of age as even more young Native men streamed home from Vietnam, wounded, disoriented, and disgorged by a federal government that no longer had use of their services. Tayo, the main protagonist of *Ceremony*, like Abel, enters the novel too sick to stand upright, haunted by memories of his experiences overseas and a curse, uttered in a moment of absolute despair, that he believes he has unleashed upon his people. As with Abel, he must spend the duration of the novel trying to reintegrate himself back into Pueblo life in a way that ultimately respects the fluid nature of ancient ceremonies and tradition. What Silko offers, however, is a book more deeply layered and resonant even than

House Made of Dawn, stirring the homing plot with themes of environmental degradation as seen in *Sundown*, the struggle between maintaining cultural identity and the pressure to assimilate, the importance of stories, sophisticated insights into the ways that trauma and narrative become linked, and all of it brought together in a seamless narrative arc tracing Tayo's journey of self-discovery. Silko creates a brilliant, luminous masterpiece that takes us into the unfamiliar indices of Native space, yet persuasively demonstrates how, from that space, there emanate ripples of global consequence that must be restored to balance. The story itself becomes the ceremony in the telling, and it is large enough to embrace us all.

Some have criticized Silko's book, alongside other contemporary indigenous novels, for its reliance on western notions of identity and the importance of self-determined individuals acting to bring about transformation, as opposed to the communally shared knowledge and actions that inform indigenous epistemologies. The genre of the novel itself, as an aesthetic choice, seems to privilege such narrative structures, typically emphasizing individual over tribal agency. These arguments stand and ought to be considered as integral to any discussion of the works discussed here. But *Ceremony* also calls for the very flexibility that western tradition, in its insistence on one God and one truth, often marginalizes. Tayo must operate within a web of competing traditions and hybrid possibilities to bring the world back into balance, making instinctive choices to avoid getting caught in the trap of old patterns, chasing down elusive game with the assistance of spiritual allies, all of whom have a place in the constellation of stories Silko weaves together in her novel. Tayo does not operate alone so much as he yields to the impulses of these forces and becomes their agent, reenacting the many stages of the ceremony that will restore life back to the land. As we find near the conclusion of the novel, he

> had arrived at a convergence of patterns; he could see them clearly now. The stars had always been with them, existing beyond memory, and they were all held together there. Under these stars the people had come down from White House in the north. They had seen mountains shift and rivers change course and even disappear back into earth; but always there were these stars. Accordingly, the story goes on with these stars of the old war shield; they go on, lasting until the fifth world ends, then maybe beyond. The only thing is: it has never been easy.[63]

Tayo is deeply involved in a ceremonial cycle, the value of which is not its evocation of the past, but, in the words of Vizenor, how it "relumes the diverse memoires of the visual past into the experiences and metaphors of the present."[64] As Tayo's blind old grandmother observes, "these goings-on around Laguna don't get me excited any more … it seems like I already heard these stories before … only thing is, the names sound different."[65] The novel, even as it clashes with contemporary issues of global warfare, trauma, uranium mining, and the dawning of the nuclear age, is informed by the awareness that the ceremony is always already ongoing.

Rebirth

The Native American Literary Renaissance would see the emergence of a number of important Native writers, including Simon Ortiz, Louise Erdrich, James Welch, Joy Harjo, Gerald Vizenor, Sherman Alexie, Linda Hogan, the list goes on. In her modern classic, the 1984 novel *Love Medicine*, Erdrich signals both her awareness of and her separation from the homing plot by having her heroine June Kashpaw rise on Easter Sunday from a drunken encounter, awaken suddenly to the desperation of her spiritual condition, and set out for home across a frozen North Dakota landscape. "It was a shock, like being born," for June to step out from the warm car where she had lain with a white oil worker, into the frigid night, intuitively sure of her direction. But June is ultimately unable to endure the "crackling cold" and finds herself caught in a blizzard, the snow falling "deeper that Easter than it had in forty years." The syncretic images of birth and regeneration fail to prepare the reader for the fact that June will not reach her intended destination, even though, as Erdrich tells us, "June walked over the [snow] like water and came home."[66]

Through this bold, enigmatic gesture, Erdrich apprehends the ruptures and complications of the homing narrative and works to resituate her novels in a larger, less prescribed realm of Native identity, culture, and agency. *Love Medicine* is a sprawling multigenerational account that presents the layered dimensions of contemporary Native lives, both on and off the reservation, as compatible with modernity, while also brilliantly allegorizing ongoing tensions created by a settler colonial world. Although her works expertly situate her readers within Native space in ways that will be further explored here, they also tease out the hybrid complexity of Native lives and identities in ways that had yet to be fully examined in the novel form. One of the lessons of *Love Medicine* is, perhaps, that tradition—medicine, the adherence to old cultural practices—is not something easily manipulated for personal gain and does not always work out as planned. As with traditional trickster stories widely circulated among the Anishinaabe and others, things go awry, skid out of control, and bring forth unintended consequences. Erdrich proved willing to explore those consequences with wisdom, lyricism, and humor that proved a successful recipe for reaching mainstream audiences, but also remained respectful to Anishinaabe culture, history, and narrative tradition.

One of Erdrich's greatest creations, and in my mind one of the great literary inventions of the twentieth century, is the character of Nanapush, first introduced in her novel *Tracks*, but appearing in a number of her densely interconnected novels. Nanapush, modeled in some ways after the Anishinaabe culture hero Nanabhozo, is a wholly original character study embedded in the locations and traditions of Anishinaabe narrative and identity while also embodying the radical nature of trickster tales. He is at once the carrier of tradition in Erdrich's novels and yet a consistent reminder of the foibles of human nature—a character who is often, though not always, snared in his own web. Far from being a comic character, however, Nanapush reminds us of the complexity of human nature. He is a character of great understanding, wit, sexual vitality, and deep reserves of compassion and yet one who has been forced to witness the collapse of his people. As he tells it in *Tracks*,

> I guided the last buffalo hunt. I saw the last bear shot. I trapped the last beaver with a pelt of more than two years' growth. I spoke aloud the words of the government treaty, and refused to sign the settlement papers that would take away our woods and lake.[67]

Nanapush is himself a contemporary culture hero who, having survived the catastrophic epidemics that swept through the northern woodland populations like the stroke of one deadly scythe after another, nevertheless continues to represent the values and the culture of his people.

And yet, to conclude, it is important to note how in *Tracks*, a novel where superstition and rumor abound, Nanapush remains the character least susceptible to gossip and unsubstantiated rumor. He is cannily observant of both human nature and nature itself, forming his judgments and practice through patient study of the world and people around him. Nanapush may be a traditional "blanket" Indian who preserves the old ways, but he also allows himself to be converted to Christianity (admittedly—to win the favor of a woman), becomes a member of the tribal council, and keeps stacks of bound newspapers and letters under his bed. He is literate from his time spent at the Catholic boarding school he was forced to attend as a child, and he is the self-appointed keeper of the indigenous archive for his tribe.

In fact, in many of the novels discussed here, it is the character who most represents "tradition" in the work who is also most attuned to western practices. In *Ceremony*, it is the Pueblo medicine man Bettoni, a traditionalist who has accommodated himself to modernity, who sets Tayo on the path toward spiritual healing. His home in the sandrock hills outside Gallup, New Mexico, is cluttered with boxes and shopping bags filled with "bouquets of dried sage and the brown leaves of mountain tobacco wrapped in swaths of silvery unspun wool," standing beside "bundles of newspapers" and "barricading piles of telephone books."[68] In Linda Hogan's 1990 novel *Mean Spirit*, about Osage families coping with the "Osage Reign of Terror" during the Oklahoma oil boom, it is Michael Horse, "the last person in Indian Territory to live in a tepee," who not only tends the sacred fire of his ancestors but keeps a cedar box full of his diaries and letters that keep written record of events taking place within his sphere. In other words, to be a traditionalist does not suggest that one is hermetically sealed off from an ever-changing world. These novels show how orality and literacy, tradition and modernity, Native spirituality and settler religion often occupy the same space at the same time and can be harnessed toward similar ends.

The novel as an aesthetic art form is, itself, a product of hybridity—or what the Russian scholar Mikael Bakhtin referred to as "dialogism" born of social engagements and anxieties that make it necessary to assimilate the discourse of the "other." And perhaps, as some critics have posed, this renders the American Indian novel a subjugated art form, a product of the post-colonial—or perhaps more accurately, settler colonial—condition, mimicking western values of individualism and commodification. Louis Owens opened his study of Native American novels, *Other Destinies*, by noting that, "to begin to write about something called 'the American Indian novel' is to enter a slippery and uncertain terrain" where questions of authority and authenticity quickly arise, often concerning mixed-blood protagonists inhabiting a hybrid art form.[69] But those questions, which seem to assume the possibility of some base-level cultural purity, appear less pressing today. Owens himself ultimately determines that the overall achievement of the Native novel is worth any risk of cultural appropriation it might take on, concluding that, "the shared consciousness in all of these works is that of the individual attempting to reimagine identity, to articulate a self within a Native American context."[70] Creek author Craig Womack takes this conclusion a step further by observing that the idea "of books as a valid means of passing on vital cultural information is an ancient one" and one that, as seen in Chapter 1, is not necessarily inconsistent with traditional Native practice.[71] Womack argues that, "I am more interested in what can be innovated and initiated by Native people in analyzing their own cultures rather than deconstructing native viewpoints and arguing for their European underpinnings."[72] Womack goes on to define "traditionalism" as "anything that is useful to Indian people in retaining their values and worldviews, no matter how much it deviates from what people did one or two hundred years ago."[73]

Womack's objective is not to muddy the waters of culture to the point that all markers of identity or traditional practice become indistinguishable. Far from it. But he is combating the entrenched notion that Native peoples have to always be viewed through a nostalgic lens that considers only what that culture once was or was imagined to be. He argues for the right of Native people to draw upon their own vital traditions, practices, and transformations to define themselves in the present moment and he recognizes the novel as one of the places where this has been performed in generative ways. We shouldn't be surprised or critically alarmed when Native people express themselves in what might be perceived as nontraditional ways or, in the words of Philip Deloria, show up in unexpected places. Even the famous Rogers and Hammerstein musical *Oklahoma*, that quintessential statement of mid-century American whiteness, culture, aesthetics, and manifest manners, was based on a play, *Green Grow the Lilacs*, written by a Cherokee author, Lynn Rollie Riggs.

Notes

1 Stacy L. Leeds "Defeat or Mixed Blessing: Tribal Sovereignty and the State of Sequoyah," *Tulsa Law Review* 43:5 (2013), pp. 5–16.
2 Quoted in Daniel Heath Justice, *Our Fire Survives the Storm: A Cherokee Literary History* (Minneapolis: University of Minnesota, 2006), 90.
3 Jace Weaver, *That the People Might Live: Native American Literatures and Native American Community* (New York: Oxford Press, 1997), 78.

4 Lavonne Ruoff, "Editor's Introduction," *Wynema, a Child of the Forest* (Lincoln: University of Nebraska Press, 1997), xiii.
5 See Ruoff, xiii–xiv.
6 S. Alice Callahan, *Wynema, a Child of the Forest* (Lincoln: University of Nebraska Press, 1997), 51.
7 Callahan, 52.
8 Callahan, 52.
9 Craig Womack, *Red on Red: Native American Literary Separatism* (Minneapolis: University of Minnesota Press, 1999), 152.
10 Womack, 148.
11 Leeds, pp. 1–12.
12 Alexander Posey, "Letter No. 57," *The Fus Fixico Letters*, Eds. Daniel F. Littlefield and Carol A. Petty Hunter (Lincoln: University of Nebraska Press, 1993), 219.
13 Leeds, 6.
14 Washita River was the site of an infamous massacre of Black Kettle's band of Cheyenne on November 27, 1868. Despite having announced their presence to the commander at Fort Cobb, and receiving rations and the promise of protection, Black Kettle's band was attacked at dawn by Custer's regiment. It is estimated that 103 were killed in the surprise raid, most of them women and children.
15 Lucy Maddox, *Citizen Indians: Native American Intellectuals, Race & Reform* (Ithaca: Cornell University Press, 2005), 30.
16 See Carolyn Sorisio, "Playing the Indian Princess: Sarah Winnemucca's Newspaper Career and Performance of American Indian Identities," *SAIL* 23:1 (Spring 2011), pp. 1–37.
17 Gerald Vizenor, *Manifest Manners: Postindian Warriors of Survivance* (Hanover: Wesleyan University Press, 1994), 5–6.
18 Luther Standing Bear, *My People the Sioux* (Lincoln: University of Nebraska Press, 1975), 141.
19 News, "Paddles Her Own Canoe. Miss Pauline Johnson Canoeist, Reader, and Poet," *Jackson Weekly Citizen* (Michigan), September 19, 1893, p. 11.
20 Beth Brant, *Writing as Witness: Essay and Talk* (Toronto: Women's Press, 1994), 7–8.
21 Louis Owens, *Other Destinies: Understanding the American Indian Novel* (Norman: University of Oklahoma Press, 1992), 50.
22 See Michael Snyder, *John Joseph Mathews: Life of an Osage Writer* (Norman: University of Oklahoma Press, 2017).
23 Snyder, 83–103.
24 John Joseph Mathews, *Sundown* (Norman: University of Oklahoma Press, 1988), 4.
25 Mathews, *Sundown*, 3.
26 Mathews, *Sundown*, 45.
27 Mathews, *Sundown*, 31.
28 Joseph Bauerkemper, "Federalism Reconfigured: Native Narrations and the Indian New Deal," *The Routledge Companion to Native American Literature*, Ed. Deborah L. Madsen (New York: Routledge, 2016), pp. 167–180.
29 Mathews, *Sundown*, 45–46.
30 Mathews, *Sundown*, 62.
31 Rennard Strickland, "Osage Oil: Mineral Law, Murder, Mayhem, and Manipulation," *Natural Resources & Environment*, 10:1 (Summer 1995), pp. 39–43.
32 Mathews, *Sundown*, 160.
33 Mathews, *Sundown*, 302.
34 Cheryl Savageau, *Dirt Road Home* (Willemantic, CT: Curbstone Press, 1995), 90.
35 Mathews, *Sundown*, 69.

36 Michael Snyder, "'He certainly didn't want anyone to know that he was queer': Chal Windzer's Sexuality in John Joseph Mathews' Sundown," *Studies in American Indian Literature* 20:1 (Spring 2008), pp. 27–54.
37 Mathews, *Sundown*, 117.
38 Mathews, *Sundown*, 90.
39 Mathews, *Sundown*, 297.
40 Mark Rifkin, *When Did Indians Become Straight? Kinship, the History of Sexuality, and Native Sovereignty* (New York: Oxford University Press, 2011), 8.
41 Mathews, *Sundown*, 304.
42 Mathews, *Sundown*, 285.
43 See John Joseph Mathews, *The Osages: Children of the Middle Waters* (Norman: University of Oklahoma Press, 1961), 7.
44 Mathews, *Sundown*, 84–86.
45 Mathews, *Sundown*, 66.
46 Mathews, *Sundown*, 80.
47 Mathews, *Sundown*, 80–81.
48 Robert Allen Warrior, *Tribal Secrets: Recovering American Indian Intellectual Traditions* (Minneapolis: University of Minnesota Press, 1995), 98.
49 Mathews, *Sundown*, 303.
50 Warrior, 54.
51 D'Arcy McNickle, *Native American Tribalism: Indian Survivals and Renewals* (New York: Oxford University Press, 1973), 104.
52 Richard Drinnon, *Keeper of Concentration Camps: Dillon S. Myer and American Racism* (Berkeley: University of California Press, 1987), 194.
53 Tommy Orange, *There, There* (New York: Knopf 2018), 8–9.
54 Arrel Morgan Gibson, *The American Indian: Prehistory to Present* (Lexington, MA: D.C. Heath, 1980), 551.
55 McNickle, 105.
56 Worth noting is the fact that the tragic ending to *The Surrounded* was only one of a number of endings McNickle had imagined for the novel, and it may ultimately have signaled his bowing to the aesthetic expectations of white audiences more than his own sense of hopelessness for Native people. See Owens, 74–78.
57 Owens, 92.
58 N. Scott Momaday, *House Made of Dawn* (New York: Harper Perennial, 1966), 8.
59 Momaday, 54.
60 Momaday, 85.
61 Momaday, 128.
62 Momaday, 91.
63 Leslie Marmon Silko, *Ceremony* (New York: Penguin Books, 1977), 235.
64 Gerald Vizenor, *The People Named the Chippewa: Narrative Histories* (Minneapolis: University of Minnesota Press, 1984), 7.
65 Silko, 242.
66 Louise Erdrich, *Love Medicine* (New York: Harper Perennial, 1993), 6–7.
67 Louise Erdrich, *Tracks* (New York: Harper Perennial, 1989), 2.
68 Silko, 110.
69 Owens, 3.
70 Owens, 22.
71 Womack, 16.
72 Womack, 12.
73 Womack, 42.

5

"MANY OF OUR SONGS ARE MAPS"

Poetry in the Native American Literary Renaissance and Beyond

"Greif Memorizes This Grass"

So much of Native American literature orients us in a space where the prominent natural features lending shape and definition to the land are invoked in names and places never registered by geological surveys or plotted on western maps. Native language itself is said in many cases to have sprung from the land, and Okanagan poet Jeanette C. Armstrong writes that, "it is their distinctive interaction with a precise geography which forms the way indigenous language is shaped and subsequently how the world is viewed, approached, and expressed verbally by its speakers."[1]

"Hé Sápa" greets us at the start of *Whereas*, Layli Long Soldier's 2017 collection of poems—a place whose name precedes western mapmaking, summoned in a tongue that called forth the Lakota world long before white settlers even dreamed this continent existed or had ever pronounced the word "America." "Hé is a mountain as hé is a horn that comes from a shift in the river, throat to mouth. Followed/by sápa, a kind of black sleek in the rise of both." Readers of the poem must negotiate language and space in ways that are both inviting and disorienting, welcoming us into this new place, but asking us to pay attention—to sit, to be wary, to listen. Because there are stories, too, that attach themselves to the landscape, Hé Sápa, the Black Hills, sacred to the Lakota, heart of everything that is. Long Soldier only presents us with the finest sliver of that history; she lets us know that, if it is foreign to you, it is nevertheless an intimate marker of her own sense of self, rooted in this land, the world she is speaking into being which begins here—"see it as you come, you approach. To remember it, this is like gravel."[2]

With the last quarter of the twentieth century came an explosion of Native poetry, part of the powerful wave that is now typically referred to as the Native American Literary Renaissance. Poets such as Simon Ortiz, Joy Harjo, James

Welch, Lucy Tapahonso, Wendy Rose, Carter Revard, and others seemed to have unearthed a new voice, elevated by a new self-assuredness, that tapped into something deep and in the moment, traditional and contemporary all at once. A critical mass of activism, community resurgence, and an accumulation of literary accomplishments, from past figures such as Jane Johnston Schoolcraft and E. Pauline Johnson to current luminaries such as N. Scott Momaday and Leslie Marmon Silko, cleared space for a profound new idiom that felt aesthetically, rhetorically, and philosophically grounded in indigenous experience and consciousness.

On a political level, indigenous peoples were reasserting their claims to Native spaces—a "Red Power" movement that burst out in the legal battles for fishing rights in the Pacific Northwest during the 1960s and 70s and culminated in the highly publicized occupation of Alcatraz in 1969 and the tense 1973 stand-off between federal agents and those who had thrown in their lot with the Lakotas on the Pine Ridge Indian reservation, at what is sometimes referred to as "the second" Wounded Knee. Less visible battles were being waged elsewhere as Native peoples across Turtle Island began to more vigorously voice their sovereign rights as guaranteed them in treaties with the U.S. government and as their birthright as original guardians of the land. New critical and historical works by Vine Deloria Jr. and Dee Brown suddenly reversed the lens on settler colonial frameworks of knowledge-production in radical fashion. Reservation newspapers such as *Akwesasne Notes* in Mohawk Country took on an activist voice that moved Native rights and concerns to the center of the conversation, rather than along the rarely noticed fringes. And the American Indian Movement (A.I.M.) became a public presence, presiding over chaotic events such as the second Wounded Knee and the take-over of the Bureau of Indian Affairs Office in Washington, D.C. Whatever one thought of these occurrences, it couldn't be denied that there was a new energy rising in Indian country, and in the midst of all this social unrest emerged an Acoma Pueblo poet, Simon Ortiz, who had spent the previous few years traveling the country, visiting with indigenous peoples wherever he could locate them, and who was quietly preparing to play the role of witness to the familiar age-old/new struggles Native communities were facing.

Ortiz's first collections of poetry touched upon many of the same themes of homecoming seen in the novels of McNickle, Momaday, Silko, and others, but, unlike those works, the tone of Ortiz's verse is somehow never as saturated with the alienation and dislocation that pervaded earlier offerings—this despite the fact that Ortiz's life traced a path similar to some of the protagonists of those novels. Ortiz had served in the military, wrestled with alcohol addiction, and found himself, for long stretches of time, stranded in urban outposts and other hostile centers of the white man's world. And yet, his poetic voice is always one that comprehends its place in the spiritual geography of his Acoma homeland. If Ortiz journeys into the uncertain spaces beyond Acoma, it is always, as Anishinaabe poet Kimberly Blaeser observes, a kind of "sacred journey," offered in the narrative framework of a traditional quest.[3] His poetic persona may dance in distant roadhouses, serve as cheap disposable labor for the uranium mining companies, get tossed in the drunk tank, or wander like a lost soul through the Albuquerque bus depot or the L.A. airport, but there is always some portion of Ortiz's consciousness that maintains its rootedness. This is illustrated in the poem "Fragment" when, on the precarious path from jail to the courthouse, the poet picks up a small stone, places it in his pocket, and realizes, while caressing its smooth outer surface with his fingers, that it "is a fragment / of the earth center / and I know that it is / my redemption."[4] This unfailing ability to locate his centered self even in the most hopeless spaces is, in the end, what releases Ortiz from the bonds of colonial aesthetics and informs much of his poetry. As Ortiz suggests in the introduction to his 1992 anthology, *Woven Stone*, no matter how far afield he wandered in life, "I also knew I would never strive to be anything other than an Aacqumeh hahtrudzai, a Native American of my homeland and people."[5]

Ortiz opens his 1976 collection of poems, *Going for the Rain*, with a direct address in which he chants, "Let us go again, let us go for the shiwana. / Let us make our prayer songs. / We will go now. Now we are going. / We will bring back the shiwana."[6] The address is, in fact, a piece of a traditional song invoking the epic of how, following a period of neglect and dishonor, precious rain was finally restored to the land and its people. Tayo's story, in Silko's *Ceremony*, was located in a similar traditional narrative framework, and in each case the rain also serves as a metaphor for cultural regeneration, an ongoing, never-ending process that is always already at the heart of the ceremony. In his verse, Ortiz seeks the simplicity and repetition of traditional song cycles of Pueblo and Diné tradition, the cadences of the storyteller, and the invocation of landscapes at once mythic and yet as contemporary as the interstate highway system binding the country in its snarl of criss-crossing concrete lines. Along that highway, one was likely to encounter old friends and lovers, bus depot derelicts, displaced Indians of the 1950s relocation program, racist white barflies, or perhaps even Coyote, himself, waiting to pass down a creation story or two. All of which, for Ortiz, expressed a "closeness to a specific Native American way of life and its philosophy ... structured in the form of an actual journey on the heeyaanih, the road of life, and its experience."[7]

In "The Creation According to Coyote," we are reminded how "'it's all true.' ... You were born when you came / from that body, the earth, / your black head burst from granite, / the ashes cooling." It is an opening gesture that collapses the space between creation and the poet's own emergence into the world. In the poem, Coyote will tell of the twins, Uyuyayeh and Musaweh, dwellers at the dawn of time, and how they determined, after many exciting adventures, to lead humans into the fifth world, the world in which we now live. Such stories are, of course, treated as "myth" or "savage" fancy by the colonized world in which Ortiz himself had been educated and immersed. Ortiz wryly acknowledges his own misgivings regarding such tales, casting a sidelong glance at Coyote's well-known tendencies—how "he was b.s.-ing probably." Nevertheless, these same stories had been passed along through generations in Ortiz's own family, among his own people—they are tales that emanate from that centered place, and there is little choice but to listen to the old trickster, even if warily, and to finally concede, "you know / how he is, always talking to the gods, / the mountains, the stone all around. // And you know, I believe him."[8]

Ortiz moves seamlessly from such transcendent encounters to the more quotidian world of highways, airports, backroad dives, and other roadside attractions, always with a quiet undercurrent of purpose that unveils itself in the unfolding of one poem into the next. Everywhere he travels there are signs of hope and resurgence interspersed with a steady undercurrent of endemic violence that bursts out into the open air at unexpected moments, threatening to pull the rug out from under any possibility of redemption. At a hotdog stand in Pensacola, Florida, Ortiz is introduced to Chief Alvin McGee of the Creek Nation. McGee gifts Ortiz with a story of the Creek/Seminole leader, Osceola, who once lived in that very place. Upon Ortiz's departure he is embraced by McGee—a blessing that puts Ortiz in remembrance of "my grandfather / the mountains, the land from where I came." Back out on the freeway to Atlanta, however, even as he dwells upon the warmth of that meaningful embrace, news of the killings of four college students at Kent State streams from the radio. Ortiz must swerve off the road "just past a sign which read / NO STOPPING EXCEPT IN CASE OF EMERGENCY." Stumbling from his car, the poet wraps his arms around the nearest tree. It is both an act of despair and a blessing all at once, mirroring the embrace that Chief McGee had given him upon parting.[9] In the settler colonial world Ortiz navigates, the blessings and the violence come close upon one another and nearly succeed in diverting him from his path on the road of life. If he maintains his balance through it all, it is despite the fact that, as he would describe some years later in his collection *from Sand Creek*, "this America / has been a burden / of steel and mad / death."[10]

Although at times Ortiz seems to be offering random snapshots of his "Travels in the South" (as this section of *Going for the Rain* is titled), the outlines of his sacred journey are made visible in his encounters with other Natives and his quiet, sustained advocacy. After stopping to meet with the Alabama-Coushatta people in his poem "East Texas," he agrees to carry word for them to the nearby state penitentiary in Huntsville, a site where too many have died slow lonely deaths for the crime of being Coushatta, Caddo, Kiowa, or Comanche. At the penitentiary, he passes along to the Indian prisoners "what the people said / and thanked them and felt very humble. / The sun was rising then."[11] Passing through Dallas, he later visits a place called Lake Caddo. Here, he asks the park ranger the meaning of "Caddo" and is told, "it used to be some Indian tribe."[12] The dismissiveness with which the park ranger casually wipes out the presence of Caddoan peoples, as though the body of water for which the park was named were the only remnant on this Earth of their continued existence, is left to twist silently from the architecture of the poem. Ortiz had, of course, just visited with Caddoan people in the Huntsville prison. He knows only too well the social mechanisms deployed to silence their lives, their presence, their stories. It is up to the reader of Ortiz's poetry, however, to make these connections and fill in these gaps.

Lodged between and beneath the squalid places through which Ortiz passes are sacred spaces, too, their stories gleaned through some abandoned house of the sun. Like Coyote, Ortiz is both messenger and message. Part of his quest is simply to witness and to learn, but part of it is also to restore balance and put things right again, which his actions initiate, but his prayers and his poetry advance into the sphere of collective mindfulness. If his initial responses to these and other encounters appear muted and opaque, he ultimately intimates their toll when he reports, "after sundown in East Texas, I prayed, / for strength and the Caddo … and my young son at home, and Dallas and when / it would be the morning, the Sun."[13]

Blaeser notes how Ortiz "works to reintegrate mythic stories and personages with contemporary global communities, to verbally transform the lives and realities of a world still entangled within the destructive machinery of colonialism."[14] There are no easy assurances, of course, but, as the cycle of his journey for *shiwana*, rain, returns him once more to familiar ground in "East of Tucumcari," he revels in the hopefulness of "brown water / falling from the rock. / It felt so good / to touch the green moss. / A woman between / the mountain ridges / of herself— / it is overwhelming // I could even smell / the northern mountains / in the water."[15] There is, perhaps, no guarantee of regeneration, but Ortiz's mindful meditations are focused upon action that will renew the cycles even after long periods of drought. As he reminds us in his 1980 essay "Our Homeland, a Natural Sacrifice Area," the people

> insist on talking about the years when there was rain and when the grass was lush and tall. It is not with mere nostalgia that they speak, because it is not memory they refer to. Rather, it is a view of the struggle that they have known."[16]

Ortiz's 1981 collection, *from Sand Creek*, is regarded by many as his masterpiece. The poems in this collection (many critics refer to it as a single long poem) act as a continuation, in some respects, of Ortiz's earlier spiritual journey, although, as he confesses, sometimes "passing through one gets caught into things."[17] For Ortiz, this time, it was alcohol addiction and the Veterans Hospital in Fort Lyons, Colorado, that "caught" him up. His experience, however, becomes a launching pad for him to investigate America's deep psychic scars, centering his investigation upon the Veteran Hospital's geographic proximity to the site of the 1864 Sand Creek massacre—a place where some 130 Cheyenne and Arapahoe were killed by U.S. cavalry members, though camped under the American flag, which they believed to be an agreed upon signal of their peaceful intentions.

Once again, the poems in this collection combine the soft, spare cadences of traditional storytelling with the sharp, gleaming angles of a colonized world, in a manner that at once asserts indigenous stewardship over the land even while it grapples with the long-lasting wounds of settler occupation. "Grief / memorizes this grass," Ortiz tells us. The raw, courageous hearts of those who died here remain a spoken poem whispering over the blades. "Believe it," he tells us:

> red-eyed and urgent,
> Stalking Denver.
> Like stone,
> like steel,
> the hone and sheer gone,
> Just the brute
> and perceptive angle left.
>
> Like courage,
> believe it.
>
> left still;
> the words from then
> talk like that.
>
> Believe it.[18]

The deep resonances of this collection cannot truly be gleaned from a single poem, but acquire their power in the accretion of language and images that, even though barely conjuring the historical event for which the book is named, speak directly to the successive waves of violence that swell from that horrific space and moment. The bloody repercussions of Sand Creek are conflated, in the muted imagery of the poems, with the national trauma of Vietnam, and we see how emotional ripples course through the ruptured psyches of the various patients in the hospital, both Native and non-Native, as they nurse their wounds, their silences, their addictions. Colonialism reveals itself as the corruption at the root, not just of the psychic wounds, but of the very scars on the land—a sickness that has seeped into the soil, infecting all that grows, distorting the souls of white men and Natives alike. Echoes of historic violence trip across the landscape of these nameless poems, "Words stumble / on October stories / the abrupt wind / throttled / on fences / barn slats / spikes / thudding / bad cast iron." Ortiz intimates how the horrific intent of past atrocities can rarely be acknowledged or spoken aloud, but manifest themselves in the lay of the land, how the cold, lifeless machinery of modern life remains fortified against memories that the soil and grass would yield back up if they could. The climate itself seems to have grown hostile to the voicing of such narratives, and Ortiz draws our attention to a "last magpie" gazing over all, ancient storyteller, "determined to freeze" in this inhospitable place.[19] As he reminds us, repression, particularly on a national scale, "works like shadow, clouding memory and sometimes even to blind."[20] But there is hopefulness, too, in Ortiz's vision. The promise of regeneration—a lesson that spring has taught since the awakening of things on Earth—binds this collection of poems together, with the observation that even here, at ground zero of the trauma, "there are flowers / and new grass / and a spring wind / rising / from Sand Creek."[21]

Story Keepers

The difficulty—at times even the impossibility—of giving voice to such stories, invoking such histories, comes into play in the poetry of many Native poets. Poetry is so often a space where the suppressed utterances of our experience find release, and the Native Literary Renaissance, in particular, opened up a door for many to unburden themselves of the psychic detritus of existing under a settler colonial regime. Maidu poet Janice Gould has written about the urgency she felt "to reconstruct memory, annihilate the slow amnesia of the dominant culture, and reclaim the past as a viable, if painful entity."[22] Colonialism, as we have seen by now, was a system that worked to utterly tamp down indigenous belief systems, languages, and lifeways, denoting them as inferior to western epistemological standards. The burden of generational trauma was not simply from having endured sustained physical and economic violence over long periods of time, but was manifest in the wanton destruction of culture, the decimated legacy of a coherent sustained identity rooted in practices organically passed down from one generation to the next—including, of course, the songs, the stories, the languages themselves. The disruption of that natural order and the attempt to, in some way, reclaim it lie at the heart of so much Native poetry, including Wendy Rose's poem "Story Keeper."

Rose, of mixed Hopi, Miwok, and European descent, was trained as an anthropologist at U.C. Berkeley and wrote, among other things, about the cultural appropriation of what she called "white shamanism."[23] She achieved greater recognition as a poet, however, emerging on the scene in the late 1970s and nominated for a Pulitzer Prize in 1980 for her book *Lost Copper*. Like many of Ortiz's poems, "Story Keeper," from her collection *The Halfbreed Chronicles*, seems to collapse the space between the early times of which traditional stories often tell and the quotidian world we now occupy. The processes of silencing are alluded to in the poem's opening lines, where Rose notes how "The stories / would be braided in my hair / between the plastic comb / and blue wing tips / but as the rattles would spit, / the drums begin / along would come someone / to stifle and stop / the sound." The lovely image of stories being "braided" in the hair not only invokes the way that stories we are told as children become enfolded in our physical being, but it transports us to the place and time where the stories are transmitted, tradition passed down in intimate domestic spaces, as a mother braids a daughter's hair, or in a room where elders speak casually while a child only half listens, caught up in concerns and preoccupations of her own. The image of manufactured synthetic hair clips and combs is juxtaposed with the onset of organic rattles and drums—the materials that comprise the pulse of the storytelling performance. But the performance in the poem is arrested even as it begins, and, as a result of this disruption, Rose apprehends how "the story keeper / I would have been / must melt / into the cave / of things discarded."[24]

Rose is not simply speaking of her own personal experience in "Story Keeper," but of the experiences of Native peoples across the continent who have felt their cultural heritage pulled out from under them in so many ways. She recognizes that this stoppage—the unnamed forces in the poem standing between her youthful self and the story keeper she might have been, are a "wound" that can only be healed "in the spin of winter / or the spiral / of beginning." There must be a way back to the source, and she sets herself this task, "to find the stories now / and to heave at the rocks, / dig at the moss / with my fingernails," until her effort draws blood.

As part of this process of excavation, however, Rose also acknowledges the irrecoverable aspect of things that have been so long underground "that they have turned albino," with tongues that have "shrivelled / into blackberries" or become crystallized, fossilized, "frozen hard like beetle shells."

In many ways, the poem evokes Rose's training as an ethnologist, well versed in the discussions of cultural assimilation, post-colonialism, settler colonialism, and the manner in which the interference of settler society has infiltrated, interrupted, and transformed the performative space of traditional tales, the same way invasive weeds overtake a meadow. These conditions, discussed at some length in previous chapters, are recognized by Rose, but she is determined to proceed as what Gerald Vizenor might call a "post-Indian warrior of *survivance*," understanding that tradition is not frozen in the past or bound by scripture, but rather is something each generation must redefine for its own purpose and pleasure—carrying forward that which can be salvaged and shaping it to the circumstances around which people must endure. "To find the stories *now*" (italics mine) is the task she sets for herself, as they live and breathe in the present. Like Ortiz, she locates the hopeful note in natural processes of regeneration, observing how "the spring is floating / to the canyon, / needles burst yellow / from the sugar pine; / the stories / have built / a new house."

Reclaiming and rebuilding that new narrative architecture is as much an exigency of survivance in a settler colonial era as it is, perhaps, a part of the continuous cycle of tradition itself, which is never static but breathes new life into itself with each separate telling and each new set of listeners. Still, the forced interruption is not one to be dismissed, and there is genuine, profound loss that must be grappled with and mourned. Rose cautions how

> The spirits
> should have noticed
> how our thoughts wandered
> those first days

how we closed our eyes against them
and forgot all the signs; the spirits were never
smart about this
but trusted us
to remember it right
and we were distracted,
we were
so new.

This gentle rebuke collapses the timeframe of the poem, reminding us that we are not just adrift in the recollections of a girl whose young mind wanders while her mother braids her hair, but that this is a deeper, more layered meditation on cultural loss and the ability to claim absolution. Rose apprehends in her poem that, regardless of the circumstances leading to such loss, the material traces of old stories remain where they have always been, rooted in the land and among the things that live and grow there, the rhythm and the movement of life that "make us dance / the old animal dances / that go a winding way / back and back / to the red clouds / of our first / Hopi morning." As Native peoples moved to reassert their sovereign identities in cultural, political, and literary spheres, they created space for tradition, narrative, song, dance, ceremony to come together in new forms that closely traced the shape and scaffolding of what remained of the old.

For all of these assertions and assurances, however, of crafting a new world from the narrative strands and traces that the storyteller's art might forge back into being, Rose acknowledges in the final stanza of "Story Keeper" just how precarious and uncertain are these pronouncements. To claim the mantle of story keeper in any culture, in any time and place, is to assume risk. There is risk in what we might reveal of ourselves in the offering, and there is the risk that we might get the particulars wrong, or fail to communicate in a manner that others can appreciate or hear, or that the things we cherish and hold sacred might appear to others to be small and without value. If these stakes may sound low to some, the fact remains that few are willing to open their inner worlds to public exposure. Although the compulsion towards poetry, the need to express the inner worlds that define for us the contours of our experience, may be universal, most people falter on the first word or quickly hide their endeavors in a dark drawer. One of the greatest risks each of us faces is the risk of revealing ourselves.

For Native writers who bear the burden of tragic wisdom, who have experienced firsthand how colonialism attempts to degrade and dismiss every expression of cultural legitimacy, the risks become exponentially higher. Native authors often find themselves held up as the public faces of their tribal communities—and sometimes even for the whole of indigenous peoples—placing enormous expectations and responsibilities upon their art. Being true to one's own personal experience might easily run afoul of what is perceived to be the greater collective experience of the tribe—or what the tribal community might prefer as its public face. The dominant settler culture enjoys such a narrative surplus that it can bear the burden of any number of poorly crafted, lowbrow, or misrepresentative texts. But Native people battle against a historical surplus of ill-informed or outright harmful representations, making it all the more imperative for Native writers to offer something ultimately positive or affirming as a corrective to the preponderance of negative myths and stereotypes. As Thomas King has observed, we "knew that stories were medicine, that a story told one way could cure, that the same story told another way could injure."[25]

Rose leaves us off in "Story Keeper" in the key moment of decision. She says, "I feel the stories / rattle under my hand / like sun-dried greasy / gambling bones." She is invoking tradition, the excavation of tradition, and the risk, pressing in from all sides, of preparing to launch these sacred materials into the world anew. In some indigenous stories, the world we know was created in just such a game of chance. Then, as now, everything remains at stake. There is a reason we blow on the dice before rolling them—endowing them with spirit, life. Wendy Rose's "Story Keeper" leaves us with the gambling bones still rattling in her cupped hands, in the precise moment before they are sent tumbling into the world—the moment of greatest hopefulness and greatest uncertainty. Her poem addresses so many of the challenges and concerns I want my students to appreciate when it comes to engaging with Native narratives, and does so in finely wrought aesthetic form. I have asked my students to read it aloud at the start of every semester of Native American Literature I have taught, and it always feels like the proper opening gambit.

Another poem that has been widely anthologized and has gained a kind of epic appreciation in Native literary circles is Joy Harjo's "She Had Some Horses," from the 1983 book of the same name. It is a poem that students, in particular, immediately relate to, as it conjures an almost reductive core set of images, yet is held together by something tough and sinuous, calling up a cascade of sometimes gorgeous, sometimes difficult, experiences that would seemingly have no outlet or articulation beyond the realm of poetic verse. As with "Story Keeper" and so many other Native works, Harjo's poem inhabits a space where tradition and lived experience intersect, a spiritual geography on a map "drawn of blood."[26]

Joy Harjo was made Poet Laureate of the U.S. in 2019, the first Native American poet to receive this honor. The title recognizes her long, illustrious career and the unlikely literary journey of her own life. In writing of her Indian boarding school days as a youth, Harjo recalled the "flat orange covers of those boring texts whose characters lived in the same white middle-class neighborhood of Dick and Jane." It was clear to her that these books offered no reflection of the world she knew and inhabited: "there was no magic, mystery, or paradox of the kind we [Native people] dealt with everyday in the strange worlds we navigated in the postcolonial tale," and, as she realizes, "we wrote poetry to speak of these things."[27]

The poem "She Had Some Horses" bursts upon the page with a stampede of language that is sensuous ("she had horses with full brown thighs"), tactile ("she had horses who were bodies of sand"), abstracted ("she had horses with eyes of trains"), full of life and laughter ("she had horses who waltzed nightly on the moon"), but also brutal ("she had horses who licked razor blades"), depleted ("she had horses who got down on their knees for any savior"), mired in traumatic loss ("she had horses who tried to save her, who climbed in her bed at night and prayed as they raped her"), exploding in color ("she had horses who were the blue air of sky") or draped in darkness ("she had horses who whispered in the dark, who were afraid to speak"), none of which could seemingly have any purchase in the staid universe of Dick and Jane. "She Had Some Horses" is a poem that powers its way through the pain and the silences, invoking the physical and spiritual embodiment of the horse in some way that remains indeterminate but immediately accessible and ultimately affirmative, even though the imagery trends darker and more desperate as the poem gallops forward. It concludes with a concession to the complexity of our natures, our lives, the universe itself, as Harjo claims, "She had some horses she loved. / She had some horses she hated // These were the same horses."

Harjo's poetic voice is lush and intimate, gritty at times as it chases the thread of culture and tradition down city streets and back alleys, but also lofty and elemental, as in her poem "Remember," in which she asks that we "Remember the sky that you were born under, / know each of the star's stories / Remember the moon, know who she is." Her plea is at once expansive and particular as it calls for one to hold tight to those elemental impulses that call us forth and give us identity. But Harjo has a way of always bringing us back down to earth as well and grounding her expansiveness in the most basic human drama, as she continues, "Remember your birth, how your mother struggled to give you form and breath, and her mother's and hers."[28] If Harjo's poetry does not have the traditional cadences of Ortiz's verse and is not as tightly constructed as Rose's poetry, there is an immediacy and power to her work that has successfully given voice to the inner experiences so many indigenous readers claim as their own. She reminds us that, "Every day is a reenactment of the creation story. We emerge from / dense unspeakable material, through the shimmering power of / dreaming stuff."[29]

Invocations of birth, of the processes of giving birth, of the births of songs and stories and stars and generations, all find a place in Harjo's poetic expression. And yet her ability to, once again, connect it to the domestic and the everyday allows Harjo to make powerful claims pertaining to the spiritual center radiating through our often mundane worlds. She opens one of her most oft-quoted poems, "Perhaps the World Ends Here," with the blunt observation that, "The world begins at the kitchen table," placing the traditional domain of women at the center of all things. "No matter what, we must eat to live," she reminds us. "The gifts of earth are brought and prepared, set on the table. So it has been since the creation, and it will go on." Not only is life created and sustained in this space, but it is where stories, and the culture manifested in stories, are given shape. "It is here that children are given instructions on what it means to be human. We make men at it, we make women / At this table we gossip, recall the enemies and the ghosts of lovers."[30]

Harjo, however, is always somehow larger than the spaces she defines. As much as she may evoke the woman's domain of the kitchen, the backseat of a Chevrolet, or the pressed-in perch of the 13th-floor window ledge of a Chicago skyscraper, she is never seemingly at risk of being pulled down into such cramped quarters herself. Nor are her domestic spaces in any way likened to those belonging to the mainstream icons of children's books, Dick and Jane. They remain unruly places, promiscuous and loud, with chickens running underneath the tables while "Our dreams … laugh with us at our poor falling-down selves." As she notes in her poem "The Flood," "her imagination was always larger than the small frame house at the north edge of town."[31] I have, at times, found it best to resist the act of interpretation or of teasing out a close reading of Harjo's poems in class. When I teach "She Had Some Horses," I have my students read it together, each student taking a line as we move around the circle and just letting it sit and breathe at its concluding utterance.

Louise Erdrich's book of poetry, *Jacklight*, appeared in 1984, the same year that her first published novel, *Love Medicine*, burst on the scene and catapulted her to the forefront of Native fiction writers, at least in terms of publishing industry success. Readers can apprehend the creative junctures in these two works, where inspiration crosses genres, the materials of her poems threading their way into her novel as well, even though her poems seem to draw such moments from a more intimate personal space. The poem "Family Reunion" bears resemblance to an event in the early passages of *Love Medicine* where a similar sense of unruly family tensions erupt into chaos. Certain poems from the section in *Jacklight* entitled "The Butcher's Wife" seem to draw inspiration from the materials Erdrich examined for her second novel, *The Beet Queen* (as well as *Tracks* and the later novel *The Master Butcher's Singing Club*), which focusses more on the German immigrant side of Erdrich's family.

Erdrich's poem "Walking in the Breakdown Lane" calls up the fierce, bleak isolation of the North Dakota plains beyond Fargo, where "Wind has stripped / the young plum trees / to a thin howl." There is torment here, evocative of the "low moaning" of the telegraph pole from Zitkala-Sa's "School Days of an Indian Girl" (see Chapter 3), as well as simple youthful angst churning beneath other wounds. "Everything around me is crying to be gone," she tells us as she makes her way down the "margin of gravel," that liminal space she occupies, on the side of the highway—the place where things break down. It is tempting to imagine this as a trace of some poignant episode from Erdrich's own life, and one that also, perhaps, sparked the opening passage of *Love Medicine*, where June Kashpaw abandons the margins and gives her body up to the elements between the highway and home. There is a familiar sense of almost desperate abandon here, as Erdrich writes, "Between the cut swaths and the road to Fargo, / I want to stop, to lie down / in standing wheat or standing water." And there is foreboding as well, a sense of dread that prowls this stretch of asphalt between the worlds of the settler culture and Erdrich's reservation home, the scene of countless ugly tragedies, particularly for Native women. Although these intimations of violence are not spoken outright, we hear the howl in the plum trees and feel the almost suffocating tension as she notes, "Behind me thunder mounts as trucks of cattle / roar over, faces pressed to slats for air. / They go on, they go on without me. / They pound, pound and bawl, / until the road closes over them farther on."[32]

Unlike June in *Love Medicine*, Erdrich will complete her journey home, but the snapshot of her, a young woman, alone on the highway, both tough and extremely vulnerable, speaks to many of the themes animating *Jacklight* as a whole. We aren't told how she arrived on that abandoned stretch of highway, but we might well imagine that, to make it home, she will need for someone to stop and offer her a ride (Fargo and Turtle Mountain are separated by 250 miles of mostly empty prairie), and this relates in subtle ways to the tensions between trust and betrayal, desire and fear, predator and prey that intermingle, erupt in violence, or are, at times, cagily subverted in Erdrich's poetry. In an epigraph to the title poem of the collection, we are told that, "the same Chippewa word is used for flirting and hunting game." "Jacklight" is a poem that explores this paradoxical attraction—how we are at times inexplicably drawn to things that have the potential to destroy us. It does not seek to condemn or condone that attraction (likened to the manner in which deer are drawn from their haven in the woods by the hunter's flashlight), but to inhabit it, accept it as something inescapably true. She concedes that, "Each of us took the beams like direct blows the heart answers. / Each of us moved forward alone," even though they could sense the threat, catch the scent of alcohol on the hunters' breath, and "smell the itch underneath the caked guts on their clothes. / Smell their minds like silver hammers / cocked back, held in readiness / for the first of us to step into the open."[33]

In this poem, as well as in other places in her vast oeuvre, Erdrich will not deny the attraction that pulls two peoples together, whether out of love, desire, violence, or some mix of all three. It is her family story, and the story of many of the Anishinaabe. Rather, she seeks to claim it and interrogate the wreckage caused by "this night sun, / this battery of polarized acids, / that outshines the moon." But she also seizes the moment, in the poem's concluding stanza, claiming that, in the long wake of colonization, with its forced dislocations, disease, destruction of culture, infiltration of Christian spirituality, it is nevertheless now "their turn to follow us. Listen, / they put down their equipment. / It is useless in the tall brush. / And now they take their first steps, not knowing / how deep the woods are and lightless."[34] This is, in fact, how the character Fleur, in the shape of a doe, lures the hunter Eli into the woods in the novel *Tracks*. It is Erdrich's observance that attraction works both ways, and, true to form, that attraction may stem from a flirtatious gesture of reconciliation or, conversely, suggest that the one-time hunted have now become the hunters, luring their prey into a "wilderness" space where they will be disoriented and defenseless. Erdrich does not say which result will ensue, because, perhaps, she knows it will be both.

Finally, both Erdrich's poetry and prose are predominantly situated in the space of her Turtle Mountain Ojibwe reservation in the northernmost reaches of North Dakota, or a fictionalized version of the same. Although she has at times faced internal criticism for hewing too closely to western literary conventions and for offering up representations that have struck some critics as advancing negative stereotypes concerning reservation life, nevertheless, her literary achievement, with few exceptions, is centered in this Native space and speaks to the complex world she internalized growing up there. As in her poem "Jacklight," it is a world where cultures either clash, merge, or embrace in uneven ways, and this can be seen in the last poem in the *Jacklight* collection, entitled "Turtle Mountain Reservation."

She opens the poem looking skyward, where "The heron makes a cross / flying low over the marsh. / It's heart is an old compass / pointing off in four directions. / It drags the world along, / the world it becomes."[35] These lines are typical, in some ways, of Erdrich's craft—the manner in which she places the image of a cross over the reservation, signaling, perhaps, that western religion hovers over this space in some intrusive, if ambiguous, way. But this symbol, as ephemeral as some summer contrail, is drawn into place by the heron, one of the clan totems of the Anishinaabe, and, as such, bears as much, or more, of a relation to Anishinaabe tradition and spirituality as it does to Catholicism. In Anishinaabe tradition, the creator called upon bird-like spirits to fashion the world, and each point of the compass marked an essential aspect of that fashioning. Most western readers will not know this, of course, and yet the language and images should be suggestive enough to the perceptive reader to cue us in to the juxtaposing markers that speak directly to the tensions between the Anishinaabe world and the Catholic church of the colonizer that intersect and cross over Erdrich's reservation space.

Such tensions continue to inform the poem as her Uncle Ray flails behind the "jagged window" of his H.U.D. house, referred to as "a new government box," drunk on the whiskey that French traders first introduced in the seventeenth century. In the throes of his 3-day bender he sees visions of the "beast"—perhaps "Misshepishu," the underwater serpent—glaring at him in the small hook and eye of the door latch. Disrupting that vision, however, are 20 nuns who fall from the clouds, catching themselves on the same latch so that he can see up their sleeves and count the hairs on their "frozen arm pits" like stars. The miraculous and the mundane compete for attention here and confuse the senses, as cultural icons displace one another in a hallucinatory haze. In another room, another stanza, Erdrich's grandfather spoons himself portions from a can of soup while listening to the scratch of owl claws upon the roof, as he utters to himself "a word / that belongs to a world / no one else can remember." Erdrich's reminiscence of Turtle Mountain, which is dedicated to her maternal Anishinaabe grandfather, is one that lingers upon juxtaposition, witnesses how the old and the new occupy the same space, and how the reeds of time and tradition that have passed across her grandfather's weathered hands also belong to her—"Hands of earth, of this clay / I'm also made from."[36]

Other poets, too many to reference here, have continued to track the journey of indigenous experience through the spaces that remain repositories of Native stories, belief, history, even though rendered palimpsestic by the endless endeavor of colonial culture to distort, erase, and deny Native presence. As Abenaki storyteller and author Joseph Bruchac notes in the introduction to Cheryl Savageau's collection *Dirt Road Home*, "Coming home is not easy. It is even harder when that homeland is no longer on any maps but kept in the memory of yourself and those few others who see beyond the road signs and beneath the concrete."[37] For Savageau, who is also Abenaki, these spaces are the "Trails of Ndakinna," and she remembers the words of her father, "who taught me to see no borders / to know the northeast as one land." Although the word *Ndakinna* itself was not known to Savageau's father, a casualty of that colonial palimpsest, he had nevertheless translated it for her "without knowing it / *our country, Abenaki country*."[38]

It is a country that, for Savageau, continues to define the contours of her world, both inner and outer, as she tracks the ancestral presence of "Grandmothers and grandfathers" roaming in her blood, "walking the land of my body / like the trails of Ndakinna / from shore to forest." Her poem "Trails of Ndakinna" is tinged with the knowledge of how the Abenaki were forced to bury their identities, to construct false fronts in the face of war, scalp bounties, and eugenics projects, all of which specifically targeted them as a people over the course of centuries. They were driven underground, dislodged from their foundation of culture, tradition, and unity as a people. As Wendy Rose noted in "Story Keeper," they became "distracted" from the knowledge of who they were and how they lived, although Savageau marks the trails that continue to form a path through the labyrinthine maze of her own body, catching glimpses of her Native past in the mirror even, where "the lines of nose and chin / startle me, then sink / behind the enemy's colors / You are walking the trails / that declare this body / Abenaki land / and like the dream man / you are speaking my true name / Ndakinna."[39]

The Monacan poet Karenne Wood begins her collection of poetry *Markings on Earth* by orienting herself in ceremonial space, plotting out the six directions as they correspond to the bearings of her indigenous identity, rather than how they might map out in settler colonial cartography. She opens by noting that, "East is a genesis, *house made of / dawn*, where streaked clouds in / lavender, red, orange, brush the / world's edge, where the dance / circle begins. Doors of domed / wigwams face morning." She similarly marks out the remaining cardinal points as well as gesturing toward the earth and sky, invoking in her opening verse the exhalation of pipe-smoke that precedes ceremony, while also incorporating the inhalation of sensory experiences accompanying these six points: "summer's white heat / without shade," the "bodies of lovers, clothes / peeled like fruit skins," "the elder men / crafting gourd rattles, singing / thin clouds into lightning for / corn," and "new snow / piled on boughs, ribs gnawed with / scrimshawed grooves." To know the world from this intimate decolonized perspective, however, is also to know its history in a way that slips beneath the radar of a dominant culture that has claimed and occupied this terrain. In "Site of a Massacre," Wood reflects upon the tragic wisdom of knowing a landscape in a way its occupiers do not, echoing Ortiz's lamentations on Sand Creek. She reminds us that, "Blessed are those who / do not hear the cries cut short / or gunshot or hooves, / who cannot feel lingering / grief. In the afternoon sun, / each rock flashes. In the wind, / each blade of grass is screaming."[40]

To know the land in this manner is to exist in a world where the past is still present, the names of ancient stones are remembered, the sites where ancestors lay buried under concrete or in unmarked fields, and centuries-old wounds still bleed in the grass. In the title poem for the collection, Wood observes how

> we locate our markings on earth.
> As the only descendants of a nation, we remain
> to find ancestors stored in warehouses, bagged, labeled, their spirits
> neglected, dust pressing over their bones in the spirit
> of historical research. We are left among ruins to save
> what we can.[41]

Wood maps out the western part of Virginia, her Monacan homeland, in a series of stories, histories, recollections that have been as long buried as her ancestors who encountered the first English colonists entering this region in the seventeenth century—but she is, of course, unable to mark those relations whose remains were pilfered, catalogued, and contained in the name of science.

To encounter Wood's poetry is to harvest a yield of personal and historical offerings rooted in the memory of her people, even as they flit along the verge of colonial consciousness, seemingly as ephemeral and fleeting as the signal of fireflies flickering in a summer's night. Fragments of this repressed and tamped down history are related in "Jamestown Revisited," where she writes,

> We are words of tongues
> no one dared speak. We are
> nameless, named by others:
> *mulattos* and *mongrel*
> *Virginians*. We are white flints
> and chips of bone, pottery
> sunk in red clay, black glass
>
> like spearpoints found here,
> of obsidian mined among tribes
> who lived a thousand miles

west. We are refrains of our
grandparents' songs that drift on
night winds with our dreams.[42]

Layered in these few lines alone are references to the little-known Virginia Eugenics Project, the attempts by bureaucrats to designate all Virginia Indians as "colored" or "mongrel," thereby (under colonial law) disenfranchising them of their lands. Wood references ancient indigenous trade routes that spanned the continent and the frayed ends of culture that her generation has so strenuously endeavored to maintain under the constant grind of colonial coercion, classification, and erasure. All this in a poem centered around the invitation, extended by that same settler colonial culture, to come speak at Jamestown and take part in an annual ritual of historical absolution without substance or sacrifice. The bones of her ancestors may be crated in museums in the nation's capital, yet Wood, herself, is routinely asked to offer absolution over the preserved and protected sites of settler remains.

A cluster of poems from Layli Long Soldier's collection *Whereas* grapple with the officious language of settler colonialism, taking as a launching-off point the apology issued by Barack Obama to indigenous peoples of the U.S. on Saturday, December 19, 2009. In Native poetry, language is so often a tool of survival and yet the very location where colonialism first insinuates itself, always already imposing its norms in the internal meanings of things that adhere to words, grammar, and thought itself. Acknowledging the difficulties created by this dynamic, Harjo has noted, "it is through writing in the colonizer's language that our lands have been stolen, children taken away. We have often been betrayed by those who first learned to write and to speak the language of the occupier of our land." Yet she also notes that, "to speak, at whatever cost, is to become empowered rather than victimized" and she embraces the potential for Native peoples to transform the "enemy's language" by appropriating it and bending it to their own usages.[43] Long Soldier locates her poems in the heart of this tension. She pulls at the language contained in the presidential apology and its context as an official statement buried among other official statements that was never publicly pronounced or presented in person to its proper audience. She tugs at the language of oppression and contrition in her book of poems and reworks it, shifts the order of things, breaks apart the words, and considers them from all angles, adding her own perceptions, her own string of *Where-ases* that have laid their impressions and continue to inform her life, until the official apology itself, although never precisely quoted, is finally exposed as the abstraction that it is, with no recourse to definition in visible deeds or compelling redress of past wrongs.

Long Soldier breaks down the conditions for us,

> Whereas the word *whereas* means it being the case that, or considering that, or while on the contrary; is a qualifying or introductory statement, a conjunction, a connector. Whereas sets the table. The cloth. The saltshakers and plates. Whereas calls me to the table.

But, even as the grammatical function of the term *whereas* is mapped out, Long Soldier begins its unraveling, pointing to her own dislocation within the speech act in question, proclaiming,

> Whereas, I have learned to exist and exist without your formality, saltshakers, plates, cloth. Without the slightest conjunctions to connect me. Without an exchange of questions, without the courtesy of answers ... so that with or without the setup, I can see the dish being served.[44]

By the time she is finished, the word "Whereas" has been hollowed of meaning, losing its ability to function in its originally intended form.

For me, this pageant of textual manipulations and contortions comes to a head when Long Soldier presents the letter of a 14-year-old school girl who, upon visiting a South Dakota Indian reservation, is touched by the conditions of poverty and deprivation there. She writes to Long Soldier, asking that the poet sign a well-meaning petition to the president demanding an apology to all Native peoples. Long Soldier can do little but admit that such an apology has already been issued, however half-heartedly, and yet failed to produce any visible changes in the ongoing conditions colonization brought into being.[45] Long Soldier later informs that, "in many Native languages, there is no word for 'apologize.'" This does not mean, she tells us, "there aren't definite actions for admitting and amending wrong doing." But the implication is this: the gesture that restores balance among relations and operates with the intention to set things right is contained in actions more than words, and she ponders what the elision of that word "apologize" from the officious language of U.S. Native diplomacy might affect.[46]

Long Soldier's book of poetry is well suited for a Native American Literature class, particularly one that takes the historical approaches recommended here. Her poems do not necessarily invite one in—they are elusive and even typographically challenging in the ways they provoke our levels of comfort with the printed word and the language of colonization. Yet she is also very much in conversation with the intellectual traditions of past Native writers, exploring the constraints of their speech, the elisions that slip from the pages of their textualized productions, and the history with which they grappled and endured. One encounters Zitkala-Sa, James Welch, and Charles Eastman in her poems. Her work, overall, provides a framework, perhaps, to interrogate and deconstruct the intrusions, the violence, of the written word itself on our comprehension of Native lives and cultures.

In her poem "38," which references the history of the 38 Lakota who were hanged at Mankato, Minnesota, on December 26, 1862, she recalls the history that led up to that infamous event. The Dakota people of Minnesota, who had, by treaty, agreed to confine themselves to ever smaller tracts of real estate, were unable to support themselves through traditional means and became reliant upon promised annuities. When those annuities were withheld, the people starved. This was brought to the attention of the colonial authorities, one of whom suggested that, "if they are hungry, let them eat grass." After the uprising, this individual was found slain, his mouth stuffed with grass. Long Soldier tells us, "I am inclined to call this act by the Dakota warriors a poem."[47] The grasses remain a constant symbol in Long Soldier's book, referent of beauty, violence, and maintained silences, the grass blowing in the wind urging her to "shhhhhh."[48] One might say that grief memorizes this grass, and, as in Ortiz, the ground itself is silent witness to the bloody deeds of the past. Long Soldier notes,

> As treaties were abrogated (broken) and new treaties were drafted, one after another, the new treaties often referenced the old defunct treaties, and it is a muddy, switchback trail to follow.
>
> Although I often feel lost on this trail, I know I am not alone.[49]

There are many others I would like to reference here, such as Allison Hedge Coke, Heid Erdrich, Margo Tamez, Gerald Vizenor, whose poetry can be so wonderfully provocative, Mihku Paul, who writes of "Lesson number one, / my body the geography, altered terrain, / illumined in the brilliant October Moon, / fading in the morning sun that rises / on Columbus Day," and others.[50] What I have referenced here are poems that are either personal favorites or have proven indispensable to my pedagogy when teaching Native literature classes. But the themes these poems touch upon can be encountered in a much wider range of Native poets and remain central to the experience Native poets are driven to relate. As poet Natalie Diaz has noted,

> In my Mojave culture, many of our songs are maps, but not in the sense of an American map. Mojave song-maps do not draw borders or boundaries, do not say this is knowable, or defined, or mine. Instead our maps use language to tell about our movements and wonderings (not wanderings) across a space, naming what has happened along the way while also compelling us toward what is waiting to be discovered.[51]

Notes

1 Jeanette Armstrong, "Land Speaking," *Speaking for the Generations: Native Writers on Writing*, Ed. Simon Ortiz (Tucson: University of Arizona Press, 1998), 175–194.
2 Layli Long Soldier, *Whereas* (Minneapolis: Graywolf Press, 2017), 6.
3 Kimberly M. Blaeser, "Sacred Journey, Poetic Journey: Ortiz Re-turning and Re-telling from the Colonized Spaces of America," *Simon J. Ortiz: A Poetic Legacy of Indigenous Continuance*, Eds. Susan Berry Brill de Ramirez and Evelina Zuni Lucero (Albuquerque: University of New Mexico Press, 2009), 213.
4 Simon Ortiz, *Woven Stone* (Tucson: University of Arizona Press, 1992), 110.
5 Ortiz, "Introduction," *Woven Stone*, 18.
6 Ortiz, *Woven Stone*, 37.
7 Ortiz, "Introduction," *Woven Stone*, 5.

8 Ortiz, *Woven Stone*, 41–42.
9 Ortiz, *Woven Stone*, 74.
10 Simon Ortiz, *from Sand Creek* (Tucson: University of Arizona Press, 1981), 9.
11 Ortiz, *Woven Stone*, 72.
12 Ortiz, *Woven Stone*, 73.
13 Ortiz, *Woven Stone*, 73.
14 Blaeser, 216.
15 Ortiz, *Woven Stone*, 116.
16 Ortiz, "Our Homeland, A National Sacrifice Area," *Woven Stone*, 351.
17 David L. Moore and Kathryn W. Shanley, "Native American Poetry: Loosening the Bonds of Representation," *The Routledge Companion to Native American Literature*, Ed. Deborah L. Madsen (New York: Routledge, 2016), 442. Ortiz, *Sand Creek*, 10.
18 Ortiz, *Sand Creek*, 11.
19 Ortiz, *Sand Creek*, 19.
20 Ortiz, *Sand Creek*, 14.
21 Ortiz, *Sand Creek*, 9.
22 Janice Gould, "Coyotismo," *Reinventing the Enemy's Language: Contemporary Native Women's Writings of North America*, Eds. Joy Harjo and Gloria Bird (New York: W.W. Norton, 1997), 52.
23 "White shamanism" is understood is an act of cultural appropriation practiced by non-indigenous peoples who assume roles of indigenous knowledge-keeping and mysticism, either for profit or their own gratification, often distorting or fabricating the traditions they pretend to emulate.
24 Wendy Rose, "Story Keeper," *The Halfbreed Chronicles* (Los Angeles: West End Press, 1985), 25–27.
25 Thomas King, *The Truth about Stories: A Native Narrative* (Minneapolis: University of Minnesota Press, 2203), 92.
26 Joy Harjo, "She Had Some Horses," *She Had Some Horses* (New York: Thunder's Mouth Press, 1983), 63.
27 Joy Harjo, *Reinventing the Enemy's Language*, 54.
28 Harjo, "Remember," *Horses*, 40.
29 Harjo, "A Postcolonial Tale," *The Woman Who Fell from the Sky* (New York: W.W. Norton, 1994), 18.
30 Harjo, "Perhaps the World Ends Here," *Woman Who Fell*, 68.
31 Harjo, "The Flood," *Woman Who Fell*, 16.
32 Louise Erdrich, "Walking in the Breakdown Lane," *Jacklight* (New York: Henry Holt, 1984), 19.
33 Erdrich, "Jacklight," *Jacklight*, 3–4.
34 Erdrich, "Jacklight," *Jacklight*, 4.
35 Erdrich, "Turtle Mountain Reservation," *Jacklight*, 82.
36 Erdrich, "Turtle Mountain Reservation," *Jacklight*, 85.
37 Joseph Bruchac, "Introduction," *Dirt Road Home* (Willimantic, CT: Curbstone Press, 1995), 7.
38 Cheryl Savageau, "Like the Trails of Ndakinna," *Dirt Road Home*, 90.
39 Savageau, 90–91.
40 Karenne Wood, *Markings on Earth* (Tucson: University of Arizona Press, 2001), 20.
41 Wood, 27–28.
42 Wood, 23.
43 Joy Harjo, "Introduction," *Reinventing the Enemy's Language*, 20–23.
44 Long Soldier, 79.
45 Long Soldier, 84.
46 Long Soldier, 92.
47 Long Soldier, 53.

48 Long Soldier, 32.
49 Long Soldier, 50.
50 Mihku Paul, *20th Century PowWow Playland* (Greenfield Center, NY: Bowman Books, 2012), 10.
51 Layli Long Soldier, "Women and Standing Rock: Introduction," *Orion Magazine* https://orionmagazine.org/article/women-standing-rock/ (accessed 3/12/2019).

6

"EVERY ONE OF THOSE STARS HAS A STORY"

Narrative and Nationhood

Nation to Nation

Abenaki scholar Lisa Brooks has written about what it means to think of oneself as belonging to a nation even when an external federal government refuses to acknowledge that such nationhood exists. In the case of the Abenaki, who battled the U.S. government in the 1980s, ostensibly over traditional fishing rights along the Missiquoi River in Vermont, there was no existing legal precedent to deny the reality of Abenaki persistence as a cohesive people or, for that matter, their aboriginal title to the river and the land. Therefore, one had to be invented. As Brooks notes, it was determined by the court that the "weight of history" had pressed the Abenaki people to the point of cultural irrelevance, or, in other words, it had resulted in their legal weightlessness. It was an almost poetic way of saying that centuries of colonial abuse had, in the final analysis, irrevocably legitimized the very abuse in question.

In some ways, Brooks is mapping out the same relationship with settler culture language that Long Soldier deconstructs in her poetry collection *Whereas*, discussed in the previous chapter—the elegant legalese by which Native peoples are continuously disenfranchised and put in harm's way in the name of democratic jurisprudence. Brooks notes that anyone wishing to witness firsthand what internalized oppression looks like need only have visited the Abenaki tribal offices at that time to see how such aesthetically crafted settler colonial jargon could work to crush the spirit of a people. In the end, however, Brooks observes that the court's ruling

> did not change the perception of the families from Missiquoi. In fact, if anything, that long, drawn-out legal battle only solidified the relationship between families and the land to which we belong. And what the stories that

outlast the papers say is that as long as families continue to gather in place, the nation will exist.[1]

The topic of nationhood can be a vexed one in Native Studies, if for no other reason than "nationhood" itself is a western-European concept projected upon Native space and used to describe relationships with identity, culture, and geography that, arguably, had little purchase on the North American continent prior to colonization. I have often heard the structure of indigenous community in precolonial times likened to a spider's web, where kinship relations and trade linked networks of villages together without demand for any central ruling authority. It may be that this wasn't always the case, and perhaps more densely populated hubs, resembling Cahokia in the tenth and eleventh centuries, were yet in place at the advent of colonization. But predominantly, Native America was a village world, and the kinship structures within these networks of villages were cemented by a system of clans that enabled and helped define extended relations from village to village. In most, if not all, cases, the practice was to marry outside of one's own clan, further interknitting kinship ties that spread out over Native space.

In his book *X-Marks*, Anishinaabe scholar Scott Lyons offers the provocative suggestion that indigenous "nationhood" was, in fact, inaugurated by the very act of signing treaties with Europeans, a transformative moment that immediately alchemized Native communities into nations. He writes,

> treaties compelled Indians to change how they lived. They addressed the parties who signed treaties in a new way, too—as "nations"—thus bringing to bear a platonic character that wasn't necessarily there before. Smaller groups became larger, more nominative, and more abstractly defined as political entities, assuming a "soul" or "spiritual principle" that in all likelihood did not exist—at least not in the way we think of such things now—prior to the arrival of the whites and their strange ways of doing things.[2]

What Lyons suggests is that, by signing the treaties, formerly loose affiliations of peoples connected by language, kinship, and shared tradition were compelled to restructure their collective identity to suit the demands of settler colonial diplomacy and control. They were born as nations the moment the treaties were signed.

At the same time, nationhood, regardless of the cultural baggage that adheres to the term, has its usefulness as a species of rhetoric, and there are those who fully embrace it as a viable vision of an indigenous past. Chief Irving Powless of the Onondaga writes that,

> we [the Onondaga] are a sovereign nation of people ... We have our own language. We have a government that has the process and protocol to put our leaders in place and remove them ... We have our own land base. This

then means that we have the right to make treaties with foreign nations. We have made treaties throughout our history.[3]

Powless unequivocally bases these claims in a continuum with a pre-Contact past, holding up, as example, the story of the Peacemaker who emerged in troubled times for the Haudenosaunee to put a stop to the endless cycles of war, establishing the clans, laws, ceremonies, and a system of government that Arthur Parker would later refer to as the "*Constitution* [italics mine] of the Five Nations." As Powless instructs, "we were also given a very precise process of protocol for us to meet foreign nations," and the first colonists to come to this land were incorporated into these protocols in a manner that might just as well have (to turn the tables on Lyons's claim) redefined who the colonists were as political entities rooting themselves in a new unfamiliar space in which they, in fact, were the aliens. As Brooks observes in her book *The Common Pot*, when European settlers first arrived to North America, "they entered into this Native space: a network of relations and waterways containing many different groups of people as well as animal, plant, and rock beings that was sustained through the constant transformative 'being' of its inhabitants."[4]

Nevertheless, scholars such as Brooks acknowledge being "wary" of talk of "nationalism" as it "calls to mind the setting of boundaries, both physical and cultural, and defending those boundaries with force. It calls to mind the sounds and images of patriotism and jingoism." Brooks is mindful of championing a different kind of nationalism, one not bound to binary oppositions or notions of self and other. And, along with a number of other Native scholars such as Jace Weaver, Robert Warrior, Craig Womack, and Elizabeth Cook-Lynn, she argues for an "American Indian Literary Nationalism"—one that "does not root itself in an idealization of any pre-Contact past, but rather relies on the multifaceted, lived experience of families who gather in particular places" and know themselves as much by the stories they tell as by the mutual commitments to the land upon which they live, sharing it with all the other beings that occupy it.[5]

The poet Simon Ortiz first called for a national Indian literature in 1981 in a seminal essay that many Native scholars continue to place at the forefront of their critical thinking. Responding to a number of scholarly claims being leveled at the time that Native literature had been effectively colonized, subjugated, and could only exist in a kind of compromised post-colonial state, Ortiz reflected upon ongoing traditions from his home at Acqumeh (more generally known as Acoma Pueblo). Some of those traditions—in the form of feast days and festivals—were surely introduced by Spanish Christians who entered into Pueblo space nearly 500 years ago, but, as Ortiz points out, they had taken on a character that was strictly Acqumeh, and he saw in this a kind of cultural "authenticity" (another vexed word in Native Studies) that bespoke of a national Pueblo identity, which he unabashedly claimed for himself and his own literary output. Speaking of one such "Saint's Day," Ortiz writes,

> this celebration speaks of the creative ability of Indian people to gather in many forms of the socio-political colonizing force which beset them and to make these forms meaningful in their own terms. In fact, it is a celebration of the human spirit and the Indian struggle for liberation.[6]

This notion of nationalism, or what Robert Warrior has subsequently labeled "intellectual sovereignty," began to inform a great deal of Native literature and criticism in the wake of Native literary regeneration. Sovereignty (which—we may as well say it—is also a vexed term), despite its practical roots in the charred cauldron of western-European nation-state formation, takes on a different connotation in Native space, where it asserts the notion of autonomy, the right of self-governance, and the need for Native peoples to understand and actively define themselves within their own cultural sphere of practices, stories, and traditions. To declare sovereignty is to position oneself in a political and practical posture of defiance against the assumptions of settler colonialism, to assert the legitimacy (what Ortiz calls the "authenticity") of one's culture, and to demand the nation-to-nation status of diplomacy that is inherent in global notions of treaty-making. As Lenape scholar Lisa King writes, "to be called sovereign was to be understood as on par with one's international peers, with and among other sovereigns."[7]

The turn to the rhetorics of sovereignty in the 1990s, once it came about, utterly transformed Native criticism and the ways we read and study indigenous works of literature. The practical implications were, perhaps, most directly articulated by Craig Womack, who claimed in his groundbreaking book *Red on Red* that,

> Native literature, and Native literary criticism, written by Native authors, is part of sovereignty: Indian people exercising the right to present images of themselves and to discuss those images. Tribes recognizing their own extant literatures, writing new ones, and asserting the right to explicate them constitute a move toward nationhood.[8]

Prior to this movement, it is worth remembering, Native people were certainly producers of literary and rhetorical expression, but they were typically drowned out by a flood of white critics, authorities, specialists, and culture cultists who had much greater access to print discourse and who exercised a 400-year-old prerogative of controlling the intellectual levers of how Native identity, history, and culture were to be interpreted, contained, and publicly reproduced. It was a process that literally submerged and unwitnessed all the dynamics that the assertion of Native intellectual sovereignty now makes possible.

Warrior's largest claim when he introduced the term "intellectual sovereignty," building on what Ortiz had called for almost 20 years earlier, was that Native writers (and, by extension, those who write and teach about Natives) should respect their own tribally specific literary and critical heritages and build their own sense of identity and expression from within those sources—a network of cultural productions and practices that most white intellectuals and critics simply had no idea even existed, being so far removed as they were from the subjects upon which they asserted their presumed authority. One thing I have learned about teaching Native authors and intellectuals of earlier centuries is that, when you present a long and lettered history of Native writing and resistance, it has the effect of helping to concretize Native presence in the here and now.

The practice of intellectual sovereignty, in some ways, went against the grain of how scholarship was being done. A great deal of literary analysis prior to the early 1990s still treated the literary text as a self-contained artifact, with all its merits, unities, allusions, tendencies, and flaws most perfectly expressed between the bound covers of the book itself. To seek additional context or desire some additional application of cultural/historical layering was regarded as superfluous to the project of interpreting the literary object in hand. This methodology was, perhaps, defensible when readers claimed a shared foundation of spiritual and historical allusions that needed no supplementation in order to be understood. The assumptive basis for such a school of criticism, however, was ever rooted in white privilege, or the presumption that western European standards, practices, and beliefs were self-evidently the accepted and foundational norm for all critique. Unfortunately, most critics were interpretively illiterate when it came to unpacking indigenous cultural references—more so than they were, even, at unpacking African American, Chicano/a, Asian American, or any other non-white, non-male, non-*normatively* gendered literary offering. Their frameworks were impoverished by the common round of false assumptions that even so-called experts continued to perpetuate concerning Native identity, and, as such, the layered and nuanced references to tribal life and community from which indigenous writers inevitably drew were lost upon these self-appointed experts—something that remains a problem to this day.

Another prominent school of dominant critical thought at the time had its roots in post-structuralism, which understood language itself to lack concrete signification and identity. Discrete cultures were deemed no more than "constructs" largely determined by the way that power is distributed, institutionalized, and enforced within a given milieu. In this framework, literature was not a profound expression of the private self, nor could it be seen as an expression of coherent cultural strains of thought and belief being carried forward through time. Rather, this avenue of critique sought to accentuate the artificial nature of literary/historical productions and proved a direct assault on the belief that discrete cultural identities or, for that matter, any kind of coherent meaning could travel uncorrupted through the channels of discourse. Literature appeared as a conjuration of prevailing discursive modes, incapable of pointing to anything absolute or authentic, but merely draping in costume jewelry the imaginary playthings permitted within a particular sphere of power relations. In other words, just as Native people were attempting to define who they were by recalling past expressions of nationhood, identity, and resistance, the whole idea of historical identities, and the archive of recoverable knowledge upon which they are founded, seemed to be disintegrating in an intellectual parlor game of postmodern deconstruction.

Some Native critics such as Gerald Vizenor embraced the turn to the postmodern, apprehending the useful means it opened up of interrogating western culture's construction of Native identity and how colonial "simulations of dominance" resulted in the persuasive narrative of the vanishing Indian, in ways historically utilized to unwitness systemic patterns of violence. To recognize the simulated nature of much of this history, the harm it inflicted, and the cultural biases that went into the formation of its archive is to take a step toward dismantling that history, decolonizing it, and building something new and more dynamic in its stead—what Vizenor refers to as "postindian simulations of survivance."[9] Vizenor's novels, such as the *Bearheart Chronicles*, a kind of post-apocalyptic indigenous *Canterbury Tales*, faults its characters who situate their identities in what he calls "terminal creeds," or convictions founded on the dead-end simulations produced within the stew of colonial appropriation and conquest. Vizenor champions the dynamic trickster figure who forges a makeshift identity from the cultural materials at hand—neither denying nor fetishizing tradition. Even for Vizenor, however, it is important that something of past tradition carries forward, even if it is simply the traces of stories that elude the containment of print discourse by continuing to travel through indigenous circuits of knowing, each story a unique creation of the moment, but carrying within some scent or resonance of the tribal past.

On the other hand, Craig Womack, who deftly twines in and out of postmodernism's epistemological basket-weaving, has asserted, "it is way too premature for Native scholars to deconstruct history when we haven't yet constructed it."[10] As Womack recognized, alongside Jace Weaver, Robert Warrior, and others, is that intellectual sovereignty retains its significance in the global marketplace of ideas concerning identity, history, and culture, given that such a marketplace persists and continues to influence social outcomes, with or without the interventions of literary postmodernism.

The result of this shift to "intellectual sovereignty" as the driving mechanism for understanding Native literary production did not suggest, as many might expect, a return to nostalgic ideas of representation, outdated practices, or attempts to reify traditions that had been presumably corrupted by the advent of modernity—any more than to reexamine the ideas and values of America's revolutionary founders would suggest that we all return to riding on horseback and wearing powdered white wigs. Intellectual sovereignty is forward-facing. Much of the intellectual work of the past, as the book you hold in your hands has attempted to outline, was produced within extremely self-conscious modes of struggle and resistance through periods of desperate engagement with settler colonial culture. Learning of those traditions and placing oneself within a framework that recognizes the intellectual rigor of those struggles and successes are forms of empowerment based in continuance and survivance. As Warrior acknowledged, his call for Native people to more fully examine their own traditions and literatures, within their own tribal contexts, "stands or falls on how well it removes American Indian discourse from what I consider its essentialist, parochializing strategies and prepares for such wide-ranging engagement."[11] It is a means of taking pride in one's culture based not on dress, appearance, or the outer trappings of identity (although such regalia are called for on special occasions), but in the intellectual accomplishments of one's forebears and recognizing how those accomplishments might be seen as working in tandem with long-standing indigenous epistemological structures, rooted in deep knowledge of the land, human nature, and the natures of all the other beings inhabiting Native space.

Which brings us back to Brooks, and her call for a national literature evocative of "the multifaceted, lived experience of families who gather in particular places." The "particular place" she had in mind at the time was the kitchen table where her Abenaki relatives gathered during, and in the devastating aftermath of, the "Weight of History" court decision. But the "kitchen table" pointed, as well, to the kitchen table of Joy Harjo's poem (see Chapter 5)—the place where the world begins, in all of its confusion, beauty, unruliness, and passion, in Native space. Get ye to the kitchen table—it is there that Native nationalism, Native stories, and any responsible Native criticism must begin. That is where Native literature seems to have located itself in this period as well, no longer reliant on the outlier returning home in a state of ruin and alienation, but already more confidently centered in Native space, inviting the reader to come experience it from within, making of the white reader the stranger in a space that most Natives understand as home.

The expectation is that those who study and teach Native literature will do the same. That they will make every attempt to learn something of that space and that history, as understood and processed by Native scholars, writers, and critics, before making any assumptions or presuming to speak on a subject they are otherwise quite likely to misrepresent. Not everyone can make it to the kitchen table, so to speak, but we can make conscientious efforts to find out what Native scholars are saying and writing about a particular author and about a particular community. We can turn to Native scholars from a particular tribe or nation to acquire a feel for their interpretive strategies. We can go to official tribal websites to see what the current concerns of a specific community might be, and how those concerns are reflected in their cultural practices, their legal battles, their history, and their literature. We can remind our students (and ourselves) that the most qualified experts on Native literature and culture are, generally speaking, Native peoples themselves, and that we shouldn't feel put out or alienated from their discourse if it turns out, as Thomas King once opined, that they are not the Indians we had in mind.

Beyond the Native American Literary Renaissance

The change, at first, is subtle, but it's there all the same, well before Warrior and others began posting their interpretative claims. Native writers began situating their works more firmly in Native spaces, wherever those spaces might be, with characters who, despite their inner conflicts and struggles with outside social forces, are nevertheless comfortable with being Indian and are not possessed by an incessant grappling with their Native identities. As Dakota critic Elizabeth Cook-Lynn noted of Leslie Marmon Silko's second novel, *Almanac of the Dead*, "it is not the mystical story of alienation" white readers had come to expect, nor would it provide "the poetic resolution of conflict so compelling in her first novel."[12] *Almanac*, in fact, remains a difficult novel for white audiences as it makes no apologies for its vision of a resurgent Red Power that lays bare the historic violence of colonialism.

Cook-Lynn felt that the important question for Native writers was not, "Who am I?" as a Dakota, Laguna Pueblo, Acoma, Kiowa, or Anishinaabe writer, but rather, "Who are we?"—a question that, in its decentralization of the literary "I," was a more "self-less" and therefore more tribal question.[13] Many Native writers were moving in a similar direction and began populating their stories with Native people who, despite whatever difficulties or conflicts they faced, were, at the very least, comfortable in their own skins. In Linda Hogan's 1990 novel *Mean Spirit*, characters with names such as Michael Horse can drive to church in a gold Cadillac while still living in his "tepee." Listening in on a sermon one Sunday morning, Horse hears the Reverend Joe Billy declare that the "Indian world is on a collision course with the white world," to which Horse inwardly muses, "isn't that the truth ... it didn't even need to be said."[14] Such acknowledgments and seeming paradoxes do not make these characters any more or less "Indian," nor does it mean that their lives will not be, or haven't already been, struck by the thunderclap of settler colonial violence in profound ways. But the struggles the Osage characters face in Hogan's novel are more about socio-economic forces that seek to violently disenfranchise the Osage from their lands than any tortured state of identity. The main Native characters in *Mean Spirit* are possessed of an almost extreme self-assuredness and negotiate the modern world with alacrity and poise.

In the novels and short stories of Thomas King, we typically find characters who wear their First Nation status with a kind of detached irony. One work I love to teach is his short story entitled "Borders," found in the collection *One Good Story, That One*. The plot involves a boy in his early teens who sets out on an excursion with his mother to cross the border from Canada into the U.S. in order to visit the boy's older sister, Latetia, who has recently moved to Salt Lake City. There is nothing in the representation of the characters that strongly identifies either as Native. The mother packs bag lunches with sandwiches, chips, and fruit for the ride and insists they both dress properly for the occasion because she doesn't want them "crossing the border looking like Americans." The boy is self-conscious about traveling with his over-protective mother, but still would very much like to stop at "one of those restaurants" where the promise of a cheeseburger, shake, and fries still holds some magical allure, like the sugar-infused icing atop the cake of settler colonialism.[15] The indicators early on in the story are of a certain class consciousness more than anything innately "Indian," and the mother can be heard bragging to her inquiring neighbors on the reserve how her daughter did "real good" by leaving on her own terms and not because she was chasing some man or had gotten pregnant.

The characters' First Nation orientation emerges almost exclusively in points of reference, such as when the boy recalls how his sister had "left the reserve, moved across the line," but even the phrase "across the line" is suggestive of the historical ambivalence with which indigenous people relate to the border.[16] That ambivalence is furthermore suggested when the mother and son, on their way to the border, pull up alongside a run-down museum, "mostly blown away," with boards up over the windows and the roof.[17] The scene is suggestive of the way that the very history of that border remains in neglect and disrepair.

But "Borders" reveals itself as a story of sovereignty and nationhood when these ostensibly apolitical characters are stopped at the checkpoint and the mother politely refuses to declare citizenship to either the U.S. or Canada. When pressed on the issue by the patient guards, she only responds "Blackfoot," an answer that will not open up the gates of settler colonial nationhood. When asked where she is from, she truthfully answers "Standoff," the name of the town on the Blood First Nation Reserve where she lives—but also an apt descriptor of her situation. Her act of passive resistance freezes the well-oiled gears of border security, and mother and son are repeatedly denied access, ping-ponged from one border checkpoint to the other. They are finally forced to park in the liminal space between the U.S. and Canadian lines and left to roam the duty-free shop with its aisles of "cigarettes, and liquor, and flags" until nightfall.[18] The next day offers an exact repetition of the first, and, on the second night of sleeping in their car in the parking lot, the boy steps out to find his mother leaning against the hood and looking up at the stars. "Every one of those stars has a story," she tells him, and, although the boy is still dreaming about burgers and fries, she begins to recount the stories, noting how it all began when "coyote went fishing one day."[19]

King's story, as understated as it is, is movingly told and ultimately brings into relief the nature of borders themselves, which are also fantastical constructs, exercises in power seeking to impose national identities upon us by plotting imaginary lines of demarcation over the landscape, whether we accept those identities or not. The story is only made more compelling by King's gently ironic, unassuming tone. He lulls us into a kind of complacency, so that we are as taken aback by the mother's refusal to surrender her Native identity as is her unsuspecting son, who, nevertheless, is taught a vital lesson about who he is and where he comes from.

Often, the characters who populate more recent Native fiction are acutely self-aware of the tropes and stereotypes that have traditionally been trotted out by settler and, to a lesser extent, indigenous writers, and they are eager to preempt or defuse them. Blake M. Hausman begins his 2011 novel *Riding the Trail of Tears* with the declaration, "Talulah Wilson never dies in her sleep." This seems to suggest that Talulah, whose name literally translates as tumbling or leaping waters, refuses to play the role of the tragic or vanishing Native. And yet Talulah's job, in this deeply ironic, postmodern, sci-fi experiment of a novel, is as supervisor of a virtual reality Trail of Tears theme park that invites tourists to "ride the trail." The novel sets up some excruciating scenarios designed to skewer the ceaseless cascade of presumptions and stereotypes that persist among non-Natives and are frequently given voice in a presumably safe environment created for white tourist consumption. But it also asks a number of tough questions about the line between history and entertainment, and what happens when Native peoples attempt to market aspects of their culture for monetary gain, as happens to some extent on the Eastern Cherokee reservation today, as well as in many other Native spaces where casinos, craft tables, and curio shops line the main concourses. One could argue, as does Elizabeth Cook-Lynn, that the Native novel itself is an attempt to capitalize on the exotic otherness of indigenous culture.

Hausman's novel brings up questions that not only hold true to Native spaces, but are equally relevant to other sites that attempt to monetize history in the public sphere (in my own neighborhood, Colonial Williamsburg and Historic Jamestowne come to mind). When history is marketed to tourists, complete with gift shops, restaurants, book stores, and small theater troupes of period reenactors, there is inevitable pressure to water down those passages that members of affluent society (those most likely to part with their tourist dollars) are unwilling to hear—particularly those parts having to do with the tormented racial history that inevitably haunts these sites. History becomes a consumer-driven investment and must determine what the market will bear. Print history, too, is often an unruly reflection of those same market forces, although the opportunities for exploitation and intellectual compromise are not as blatant. The result, however, is that, even at well-meaning historical sites that seek the input and participation of local indigenous communities, there remain vexing problems of representation and commodification. In Hausman's novel, it is Talulah who, despite being a savvy and self-aware negotiator of these cultural spaces, ends up the one most burdened by the traumatic weight of the compromised history (in this case, the simulated Trail of Tears) she has walked more than 1,100 times in her career. In a sense, she is caught in a historical loop effect that perfectly mimics the way that trauma survivors experience the violent events at the heart of their condition. The problem is not that Talulah is caught between worlds, but that she has spent too much time serving as the tourist-friendly reservoir from which others siphon their fast-food fix of Cherokee culture and history.

An antidote, perhaps, to Hausman's darkly humorous adventure is Diane Glancy's more earnest, powerful, and equally troubling 1996 novel *Pushing the Bear*. Also about events pertaining to the Trail of Tears, *Pushing the Bear* could be thought of as a Cherokee version of Puritan author Mary Rowlandson's famous 1682 captivity narrative about King Philip's War. Rowlandson's colonial narrative came right out of the gate with her depiction of the attack on her unsuspecting village of Lancaster by a force of invading Narragansett. She and her surviving neighbors are forced at gunpoint to leave behind the lives they knew and join a community of Native refugees who are themselves on the run from the colonial army. In Glancy's novel, however, it is a Cherokee village being invaded by the Georgia militia in the opening pages, and the reader is forced to play catch-up as the story tracks their harrowing journey along the several "removes," as they are marched at bayonet-point some 900 miles from the Cherokee agency in North Carolina to Fort Gibson in Indian Territory.

The novel, written with an informed sensitivity and compassion by Glancy who is, herself, Cherokee, is presented in the form of numerous testimonies, a mix of invented and real-life figures whose voices push against the historical silences that continue to encompass the Cherokee experience of their forced removal. Rowlandson's seventeenth-century captivity narrative, in the way it was framed, immediately brought the reader's sympathies in line with the harried captives and served as powerful propaganda for the settler colonial endeavor of eliminating Native presence from the land. Glancy uses this strategy to similar effect, forcing readers to comprehend this poorly understood historical moment from the perspective of the Cherokees. In the opening passages, Maritole, whose testimony is most prominent throughout the novel and who, like Rowlandson, is forced from her home with an infant child in her arms, gives witness to her forced removal. She notes,

> a soldier with white eyes spoke and gestured to me to take the baby. He dismounted, put his bayonet to my side, and poked ... I couldn't leave the farm. The cabin in the yellow leaves. My grandmother's spinning wheel and cotton cards. The baby screamed and Knobowtee [the child's father] picked her up. The soldier lifted me to my feet, and I knew he said "March."[20]

For a number of years, I have alternated between teaching either *Pushing the Bear* or *Riding the Trail of Tears*. They are two completely different experiences and will provoke a completely different set of responses and questions from students. Both novels, however, seem to suggest the fluidity of tradition, the ability of Native peoples to adapt and survive under extraordinary circumstances, and the necessity of carrying something forward as well. As an aged basketmaker along the trail states in Glancy's novel,

> "you know the rim around the top of the baskets—the hickory withe.
> That's the edge of hills that used to surround us. I'll still rim my baskets with the hills in the new territory."

"What if there are no hills there?" Maritole asked.
"Then the rims will be clouds so my baskets will have new stories to tell."[21]

Baskets stand as a shifting metaphor for culture, geography, and stories in Glancy's novel—a material manifestation of the traditional skills and artistry that are creatively marshalled, with each new basket, into something new and useful and enduring. Like stories themselves, the baskets are carefully crafted vessels for culture and they are designed to hold all that must be taken along on the journey.

This history is difficult to teach and must be done with care and respect. I recommend Glancy's novel as the more appropriate entry for those who have not worked with these materials before. Hausmann's novel, though less accomplished in my opinion, is highly readable, and students are readily engaged by the host of fascinating questions it raises, making of it a very useful teaching tool, albeit one that requires more skilled interventions on the part of the instructor. In order to supplement both of these texts, I include selections from Theda Purdue and Michael D. Green's edited collection on *The Cherokee Removal: A Brief History with Documents* and I tend to include, as well, excerpts from the journal of Daniel Butrick, a missionary who walked the trail with the Cherokees and who provides an illuminating firsthand account of this moment in history. Ultimately, as is true of so much of the literature of Native Studies, the "Trail of Tears" is a trauma narrative—one that has been effectively contained, defanged, and sentimentalized in mainstream history, but the materials mentioned above put human faces on these stories and help us perceive these events as narratives of continuance and survivance for Cherokee people, even as they force non-Native readers to confront the ongoing violence of colonialism.

Confronting the atrocities of the past and finding dynamic literary strategies by which to convey how these events continue to play out in the present have been the object of a great many Native authors. In the 1988 novel *Ghost Singer* by Pawnee/Otoe author Anna Lee Walters, two of the main characters, Russell Tallman and George Daylight, are, respectively, an independent researcher and a tribal representative who chance to meet in an airport in Oklahoma City on their way to D.C. Tallman has a university education, reads *Time* magazine, regularly checks his wristwatch, and occasionally enjoys bagels and lox. Daylight also holds a university degree and has been married three times, once to a white woman who he claims made excellent fry bread. As acclimated as they are to the modern world, however, neither blinks an eye when their ensuing discussion turns to the matter of spirits that Daylight believes are haunting the Natural History Museum at the Smithsonian, knocking off its curators one by one. Both men are firmly situated within a tribal identity that is accepting of this reality and they apprehend the underlying causes that prompt Daylight to suggest, "something big and powerful done had a hold of that place."[22] Despite their advanced degrees, they instinctively know they will need to seek beyond their western educations to properly understand how to approach this problem.

Although NAGPRA (the 1990 Native Graves Protection and Repatriation Act) had yet to be signed into law when Walters was writing her novel, *Ghost Singer* narrativizes the concerns of Native communities who have seen their ancestors' regalia, funerary objects, and even their human remains either on display, kept as objects of study, or simply filed away in dusty shelves of the Smithsonian archive. The "ghosts" in Walters's story may be considered manifestations of Navajo belief, their anguish directly linked to the little-known history of nineteenth-century slavers who preyed upon Navajo families and desecrated their bodies, but these spirits are also, in a sense, a metaphor for the anguish of Native communities who have seen their graves dug up, their funerary objects traded on the open market, and the remains of their ancestors treated as objects of fascination for white museum-goers. As Daylight observes,

> maybe the time has come to rethink this whole process of buying Indian artifacts and materials for collections like this, along with the *need* for a collection like this at all. Who does it benefit—American society? Indian people? American society don't even pretend to know what all these objects here are by name or use ... this collection is going to be a sore spot between groups of people as long as it exists.[23]

The characters in the novel are tasked with trying to set matters right from a tribal perspective, but they remain hard-pressed to persuade the settler curators of the spiritual and cultural violence inflicted by such collections. This, in effect, is what NAGPRA was designed to perform, although, as Nipmuc anthropologist Rae Gould has observed, many museums and universities still lack the "institutional will" to make good on their legal obligations. There are some, like the Smithsonian itself, that seem to regard the relinquishing of their possessions as the equivalent of book-burning, as though whatever knowledge might be gleaned from these remains outweighs the basic human respect owed to tribal nations who wish to see their ancestors properly taken care of.[24]

Another novel that imaginatively confronts the traumas of the past is James Welch's indigenous epic, *Fools Crow*. A 1986 American Book Award winner, *Fool's Crow* has largely been forgotten by non-Native scholars and critics, although it remains one of the more poignant literary productions of the last half-century. *Fool's Crow* is a novel that centers itself in Native space, defining the parameters of that space in its opening passages as the main character, White Man's Dog, scans the flats of the Two Medicine River where the "lodges of the Lone Eaters were illuminated by cooking fires within." He then turns his gaze along the "Backbone of the World from south to north until he could pick out Chief Mountain ... its square granite face a landmark for all who passed." It is here, we are told, that the "blackhorn skull pillows of the great warriors still lay" and where forebears of the Pikunis, one of the three bands of the Blackfeet Tribe, had "dreamed their visions in the long-ago, and the animal helpers had made them strong in spirit and fortunate in war."[25] As the novel progresses, White Man's Dog will not only interact with this physical landscape in intimate ways, but he will enter into the circle of tradition that informs the land and imbues it with the spirit and memory of his people.

Louis Owens has noted how *Fool's Crow* "inverts" the framework of the classic western genre, where it is the Blackfeet who are situated within a sphere of domestic normativity, and it is the white intruders, referred to as *Napikwans* in Blackfeet, who pose an indeterminate threat to their settled way of life, always lurking just over the rim of the known world, waiting to pounce.[26] Although the Napikwans emerge as little more than a rumor in the early phases of the novel, a small assortment of traders and military detachments, their presence will become more pronounced as they begin to exert compounding pressure on the Blackfeet to surrender their lands and reorganize themselves as "nations" within prescribed reservation boundaries.

Welch's novel tells the tale of the Lone Eaters, a sub-band of the Pakunis, in the waning days of supremacy for nineteenth-century plains Indian culture. The narrative tracks the development of a Pakuni youth, White Man's Dog, who progresses into adulthood amidst the sweeping changes that are overtaking his community. By situating his novel in the Blackfeet world, with characters epistemologically rooted in values and beliefs that stand in opposition to the consensual terms upon which western discourse constructs its reality, Welch at once disorients his readers and yet is able to slowly legitimize that perspective, carefully disentangling his literary creations from enduring forced binaries of savagery and civilization.

Part of what makes the novel persuasive is its attention to detail, the intricacies of nineteenth-century camp life, and how Blackfeet material culture, tradition, and ceremony all come together to define the relationships between the characters, their attachments, obligations, concerns, joys, strengths, and weaknesses. White Man's Dog, who will take on the name of Fools' Crow as the story progresses, is unsure of his place in the community as the novel begins and defers to his bolder, more confident friend Fast Horse. But it is Fool's Crow's commitment to the ideals of his community and his ability to personify those ideals that make of him the heroic vehicle for the novel, surpassing the more impetuous Fast Horse in his ability to gain the respect of the band and the larger Blackfeet community. It is not in warfare that Fool's Crow makes his mark, although he fulfills his obligations in battle as well, but as someone who observes the kinship obligations binding the people together and who consistently chooses to act in the best interest of the tribe.

Welch's novel owes a literary debt to an earlier work about life on the plains, Ella Deloria's novel *Waterlily*, which was completed in 1947 but wasn't published until 1988, 2 years after *Fool's Crow*. Still, Welch must have known of Deloria's accomplishment, and their narratives follow similar trajectories as characters who feel themselves on the outer pale of camp circle life make their way to the center through deliberate correct action. Deloria, whose novel draws heavily from the years of ethnographic work she performed working with figures such as Franz Boas and Ruth Benedict, emphasized the importance of the *tiyospaye*, which literally translates as "group of tipis," in Lakota, Dakota, and Nakota life. She wrote,

> any family could maintain itself adequately as long as the father was a good hunter and the mother an industrious woman. But socially that was not enough; ideally it must be part of a larger family, constituted of related households ... In their closeness lay such strength and social importance as no single family, however able, could or wished to achieve entirely by its own efforts.
>
> In the atmosphere of that larger group, all adults were responsible for the safety and happiness of their collective children.[27]

Although many writers, photographers, historians, and artists within the dominant culture have been fascinated by plains Indian life and attempted to reproduce this culture in their various productions, they have almost entirely misconstrued male-gendered societal value as residing solely in the prowess of its warriors—as though this were the only measure of masculinity, the only capsule of male indigenous identity, that carried any standing (perhaps the role of orator has been similarly privileged, although it is typically imagined as being played by those too advanced in years to continue on the so-called "warpath"). But writers such as Deloria and Welch, drawing from deep wells of knowledge about the cultural lives of their people, understood that warfare was not something taken lightly or some natural inclination that Native men rushed to fulfill. When White Man's Dog is forced to kill a Crow youth early on in *Fool's Crow*, he inwardly deliberates over his options, before recognizing necessity and acting accordingly. He nevertheless experiences lingering remorse over his deed and, later in the novel, when he takes the scalp of a famed Crow enemy, an act that will ultimately earn him the name Fool's Crow, his reaction is ambiguous—in the heat of battle, he observes a young Crow girl wailing over her dead relative and he vomits at the site of the bloody scalp in his hand. He registers both grief and horror, but he also absorbs the praise of his father, Rides at the Door, who has witnessed his valor in combat, and the validation he receives from the larger community that celebrates his act. But, when Fool's Crow himself attempts to participate in the glory conferred upon him, waving the scalp before his father-in-law Yellow Kidney whom he has avenged, he feels inwardly shamed by his boastfulness. Welch communicates a sophisticated impression of how even culturally sanctioned violence operates on the human psyche and, like Deloria, he forwards a notion of indigenous identity that does not revel in warfare, but accepts it as a necessary part of life.

As recounted in Chapter 3, the turn-of-the-century Lakota writer Charles Eastman had also claimed of the "warrior" that he was trained to be, "in the broadest sense, a public servant." The works of Welch and Deloria are unique in their emphasis on domestic camp life and the small, mindful acts that worked to raise the esteem of certain individuals in the eyes of the community. Fool's Crow, when he returns from the hunt, leaves food for Heavy Shield Woman, who has lost her husband to the conflict with the Crows. He respects his elders, does not speak out of turn in council, and worries about his friend, Fast Horse, who has failed to fulfill a promise made unto Cold Maker, the powerful spirit-being who brings the winter in from the north. Fool's Crow also fulfills his obligations to the animal world, performing services for Raven and Wolverine who will later reciprocate, serving as spirit helpers in his endeavors. Although his engagements with the spirit world will strike western readers as a form of magical realism and, perhaps, intrude upon their sense of the novel's historical credibility, Welch apprehends these moments as commensurate with Blackfeet epistemology and as existing within the network of relationships Pikuni men would have earnestly maintained at this time, through fasting, dreaming, ceremony, and other acts incomprehensible to western spirituality. The careful maintenance of relationships is essential to the overall well-being of the *tiyospaye*, to use the Lakota term, and it is in the role of providers, mothers, fathers, healers, diplomats, thoughtful community-minded speakers, that the characters in *Waterlily* and *Fool's Crow* earn the regard and respect of their peers.

But Welch's novel also adheres closely to historical events that are coalescing around the world of Fool's Crow's small band of Pikunis, and Welch deftly threads his domestic drama of Blackfeet life with these encroaching outer forces. Welch introduces the treaty agreements that the Blackfeet have made with the whites, narrating these arrangements from the Pakuni perspective, who initially understood they had "given the Napikwans some land in return for promises that we would be left alone to hunt on our ranges. We were satisfied, for our ranges still extended beyond where sky touches the earth."[28] But the Napikwans are always greedy for more, and the crisis of the novel comes about with the realization that the Pakuni way of life is existentially threatened by the relentless demands of the colonizer. The manner in which the lives of the main characters ultimately intersect with the larger historical narrative of treaties, concessions, disease, devastation, and ultimately the January 23, 1870 event known as the Marias Massacre is almost unbearable, although it is told with great compassion and complexity.

Toward the close of the novel, Fool's Crow is given a vision of a handful of malnourished children in poor-fitting white man's clothes, fenced in on the periphery of some large institutional grounds that we must take to be the Indian boarding school. It is a heart-wrenching prediction of the fate of his people and the once-vibrant community of families, warriors, lovers, and kin that defined the early sections of the novel. But there is survivance as well, and Welch offers the thread of regeneration that is maintained through stories and ceremonies, passed from one generation to the next, like the woven baskets that are vessels for the items that sustain life.

Sherman Alexie and a Little Drum That Might Fill Up the Whole World

Novelist Stephen Graham Jones has reminded his generation of Native writers that, "This isn't the Native American Renaissance." He acknowledges,

> that was a great and essential and transformative movement without even meaning to be a movement, but … if you still stand up and try to fight for the same things those Native American Renaissance writers were fighting for, then you're pretty much saying that they didn't make any headway, that American Indian literature hasn't made any progress.[29]

One writer who very purposefully attempts to distance himself from that tradition is Sherman Alexie. Although Alexie's reputation in the Native community has been severely compromised of late by the irresponsible manner in which he is said to have wielded his influence and celebrity over aspiring Native women authors, his contribution remains unmistakably part of the history of Native literature in this period. Alexie gained acclaim in the 1990s as a poet, short-story writer, novelist, filmmaker, and public intellectual. Prior to the recent collapse of his reputation, Rebecca Tillett noted of the Spokane/Coeur d'Alene author that his public persona took on "aggressive forms of expression," making of him a kind of "enfant terrible of Native American Literature."[30] David Moore and Kathryn Shanley also comment upon the fact that, "anger, to Alexie, is a positive, freeing force."[31] And Lakota author Elizabeth Cook-Lynn singled Alexie out in particular in 1993 as one of the "new angry warriors" emerging on the scene.[32] These critics, though not uncomplimentary about Alexie's work, were responding to something unavoidable in his personal style—his apparent need to provoke, not only white audiences, but those in the Native establishment as well.

At times, there has been an immaturity in Alexie—he could reliably be counted upon to take the bait and strike back against his critics, especially female critics such as Cook-Lynn or Gloria Bird, a member of Alexie's own Spokane/Coeur d'Alene Indian tribe who questioned the fidelity of Alexie's reservation fiction.[33] Often he struck back in very personal ways, with stinging wit but, perhaps, less substance. In his poem "Tuxedo with Eagle Feathers," he verbally assaults Cook-Lynn on account of her critique, calling out the "Sioux Indian writer / And scholar" as one who has written,

> That Skins shouldn't write autobiography.
> She believes that "tribal sovereignty"
> Should be our ethos. But I call bullshit!
>
> My tribe tried to murder me—and I don't
> mean that metaphorically. I have been
> to dozens of funerals and wakes;

I've poured dirt into one hundred graves;
And if you study what separates me,
the survivor, from the dead and car-wrecked,
then you'll learn that my literacy
saved my ass. It was all those goddamned texts

by those damn dead white male and female
writers that first taught me how to be
a fighter.

So let me slap Cook-Lynn upside her head
with the right hand of John Kennedy
and the left hand of Emily Dickinson.
Let me kick her in the shins with the
left toe of Marianne Moore, and the right toe
of John Donne. I wasn't saved by the
separation of cultures; I was "reborn"
inside the collision of cultures; So
fuck Cook-Lynn and her swarm of professional
locusts.

To reductively frame a Native author as "angry" is, perhaps, the most tired cliché in the colonial critic's arsenal, and this is not my intention here. If Alexie has moments of rage that express themselves in his art, he is certainly not the first among indigenous authors to vent this emotion. In his short story "The First Annual All-Indian Horseshoe Pitch and Barbecue," he maps out how this reality might be boiled down to a simple mathematical equation: "Survival = Anger × Imagination," which he refers to as "the only weapon for survival on the reservation."[34] Alexie sees himself as a product of the settler colonial violence that destroyed so many lives around him, and yet he paradoxically attributes his own tenacity to the imaginative aesthetics he gleaned from his exposure to western literature at a young age. But he has demonstrated a need to lash out defensively, wielding his impressive wit and imagination in a manner that has wounded those around him. This tendency reveals itself in his novels as well, where he too often opts for the provocative jab, at the expense, perhaps, of a more sustained layering of narrative materials upon which the construction of a long-form world depends. Bird, in fact, suggests that much of Alexie's prose reads like bare-bone movie scripts with just a little bit of stage-costuming thrown over them. Poetry and the short story form, however (and arguably the Y.A. novel genre that benefits from his pared-down exposition), have proven far more successful vehicles for Alexie's style of hit-and-run aesthetics.

Alexie's poetic voice rarely strives for lyricism or any kind of rarefied synthesizing of landscape and language. He does not seek out the cadences of traditional song as we have seen in earlier poets, nor even reach for transcendent moments of inner revelation. His poems can often come across as undifferentiated from his prose, though constructed in stanza form, and his metaphors are so transparently packaged at times that they can occasionally be found hiding in plain sight. Alexie traffics in irony, sometimes couched in hyperbole, at times understated, and frequently delivered with the power of a prize fighter's punch, although just as often designed to seductively lure us in with humor, keep us interested, amused, entertained enough to stick around for the unexpected uppercut that will surely follow. Because, as he writes in "The Powwow at the End of the World," he has been "told by many of you that I must forgive and so I shall," he claims, but only "after an Indian woman puts her shoulder to the Grand Coulee Dam/ and topples it" and only after each successive dam downriver is toppled, and the salmon (traditional food staple of the Spokane) are freed to return once more on their upstream journey, and the work of colonialism is effectively dismantled. Only after a returning salmon "leaps into the night air above the water, throws / a lightning bolt at the brush near my feet, and starts the fire / which will lead all the lost Indians home," then and only then will he forgive, when he is dancing around that fire at the "powwow at the end of the world."[35]

"Powwow" is an unexpectedly poignant poem, invoking the history of colonial dam projects that have been detrimental to so many Native communities (including the Spokane) and extending the metaphor of their imagined dismantling to the resurgence of indigenous lives, traditions, foodways, all returning in a rejuvenating flood just as prophesized by Native spiritual leaders of the revitalization movements of the eighteenth and nineteenth centuries. As with Erdrich's "Turtle Mountain Reservation," there is the juxtaposition of indigenous and Christian spirituality in Alexie's poem—the apocalyptic flood that washes away our sins, the burning bush ignited by a lightning bolt-hurling deity. The imagery flirts with over-the-top parody, and yet the power of this poem is well earned and speaks to the unattainable wish struggling against the current in so much of Alexie's work, which is the wish, the need, to be made whole.

Alexie writes along the fault lines of his fractured sense of identity, acknowledging in many of his works the constructed postmodern state of Native identity in which he dwells. And yet, he is always attuned to the power of storytelling, the activated materials of tradition that could possibly address the wounds of history. Such wounds rip through his life like a raging storm in stories such as "Every Little Hurricane" or fall like spiders from the sky in his poem "The Summer of Black Widows."

In "The Summer of Black Widows," spiders, having materialized with the rain one season, suddenly turn up everywhere one looks: in window sills, lampshades, and cereal boxes. As the elders knew, the spiders "carried stories in their stomach," and, in the poem's unfurling, the metaphor becomes explicit, spiders and stories becoming interchangeable, provoking alarm and caution—you might accidentally step on one but, then again, you might open a cabinet and have one suddenly fall in your hair. There were stories everywhere one looked, springing unexpectedly from dark places, dropping in on the most domestic of scenes, until, at once, "the spiders disappeared suddenly / after that summer lightning storm. // Some people insist the spiders were burned to ash / while others believe the spiders climbed the lightning bolts and / became a new constellation." [36]

Alexie is referencing traditional stories of *Iktomi*, referred to by Zitkala-Sa as "a spider fairy"—a being who descended from the heavens on a web. He invokes the stars and constellations, which are the heavenly mnemonic map of indigenous storytelling.[37] But more importantly, perhaps, he is signaling his precarious ongoing relationship with stories and tradition—one with which he engages with utmost caution. The poem literally wonders whether Native tradition was irrevocably blasted apart in that long-ago lightning bolt of colonization, or if it was preserved in some remote, perhaps even inaccessible, form, having rescued itself by ascending the very lightning bolt that sought to obliterate it. These are issues that strike to the very core of cultural identity and ones that Alexie has habitually kept at arm's length, even as he returns again and again to the question itself. He concludes by noting,

> The elders knew the spiders
> had left behind bundles of stories.
>
> Up in the corner of our old houses
> We still find those small, white bundles
> and nothing, neither fire
> nor water, neither rock nor wind,
> can bring them down.[38]

Like these spiders, the material remains of tradition can still be discovered carefully stowed away in closets and attics, visceral reminders of designs and belief-systems that continue to spin their gossamer webs and attach themselves unseen in the dark neglected corners of Alexie's imagination. But the reverence in which he holds these beings also keeps him from getting too close, from seeking their authority or power. It is almost as though he fears the level of commitment and transformation that might arise from any direct engagement, knowing, as he does, that with great spider power comes great spider responsibility.

Alexie again signals this tentative relationship with the power of stories in his short story "A Drug Called Tradition." In this story, from the 1993 collection, *The Lone Ranger and Tonto Fistfight in Heaven*, his staple characters Victor, Junior, and Thomas Builds-the-Fire abandon a party to experiment with a "new drug" Victor has procured. As the drug takes effect, each character is transported, with the help of Thomas's storytelling embellishment, into a moment of self-actualized indigenous identity that can only reach fruition under the hallucinogenic powers of the mind-altering substance. In the dream visions that follow, Victor appears before the others on horseback, racing under the moonlight, having successfully emerged from a pony raid against an enemy camp. Junior realizes his potential as a rock-star performer, singing anthems of Indian empowerment and nationhood to an adoring, mostly Indian audience. And Thomas is seen dancing in the wake of epic devastation, his family and tribe decimated by disease, but, even as he dances, buffalo begin to rain down from the sky, and he is ghost-dancing the world whole again, so that soon his nation has sprung back up around him, dancing in ever larger circles, until they dance the white men to the furthest shores and set them on ships and watch them sail off to Europe, the weight of colonization lifted from the shoulders of the land.

But, as the three young men come down from their high, they return also to the emotional weight of their true lived experiences, and they slowly uncouple from the best idea of themselves encountered in their collective vision. Only Thomas, the quintessential outsider, still holds a portion of it in his being, but Victor, the story's narrator, scoffs, asking, "You don't really believe that shit?"[39] Later the next day, Victor runs into the spiritual leader and medicine woman of the tribe, known as Big Mom, who has somehow intuited Victor's nighttime experiment with tradition. She hands him a small drum, telling him "this is my pager. Just give it a tap and I'll be right over." But Victor is not prepared to accept that invitation or invite such forces into his life. As he relates at the story's end,

> I keep it really close to me, like Big Mom said, just in case. I guess you could call it the only religion I have, one drum that can fit in my hand, but I think if I played it a little, it might fill up the whole world.[40]

And that is a prospect that seems to exhilarate and terrify the young man, as though to open up the door a crack would release the floodgates in a manner that could not be called back. It is the difficulty, perhaps even impossibility, of imagining a world unbowed by colonization.

In the story "The Trial of Thomas Builds-the-Fire," Thomas is actually placed on trial and sentenced to two concurrent life sentences for the crime of revisiting the past in stories. On the witness stand, sworn in to tell the truth and nothing but, Thomas commits the unforgivable sin of reminding his white accusers of the deeds of their ancestors—how on September 8, 1858, in an attempt to crush the Spokane economy, Colonel George Wright ordered the slaughter of 800 Spokane ponies. Assuming the voice and perspective of one of the ponies that managed to escape the massacre, Builds-the-Fire recalls how they "were rounded into a corral and then lassoed, one by one, and all that dark night mothers cried for their dead children. The next day, the survivors were rounded into a single mass and slaughtered by continuous rifle fire."[41] The horrific scene serves as a prelude to Build-the Fire's next story, which is of Qualchan, a Spokane man who is forced out of hiding when he learns his father is being held hostage by Colonel Wright. Although promised fair treatment should he "come in," Qualchan is put in chains and "dragged to the noose," where he is hanged with six other compatriots.[42] The relevance of this brutal and unwanted history lesson is lost on Build-the-Fire's uncomfortable audience until he informs them that the location of this massacre is now the site of a proposed golf course in the modern-day city of Spokane, Washington. As with the poets Ortiz and Wood, Alexie is relating the tragic awareness of the history of his region—a history that white settler culture had safely contained within a fog of neglect and amnesia.

Qualchan golf course was, in fact, built, and a July 30, 2018, Spokane "Trip Advisor" post boasts "this is a great course. There are some really unique holes such as # 1 where you tee off from a cliff, hole # 13 where there is a video feed to see the landing zone, # 18 that goes across a ravine and back up a hill and so many more great spots."[43] Few golfers will be aware of the grief memorized by the grass at this space, but for the Spokane this is, indeed, a sacred spot memorialized by the tragic wisdom of the tribe.

Thomas and Victor get another opportunity to consider past traumas and what can be salvaged from the flames in the short story "This Is What It Means to Say Phoenix, Arizona," which, in 1998, was reworked into the major full-length feature film *Smoke Signals*, the first such film to be written, produced, and directed by Natives and to boast a Native cast in the starring roles. Although many Native Literature instructors have determined to take Alexie off their syllabi to make room for up-and-coming authors who have been squeezed out in the past by Alexie's immense popularity, it seems inappropriate to diminish the accomplishment of the talented team of players who collaborated so successfully on *Smoke Signals*. The film, directed by Chris Eyre, remains a poignant and often hilarious window into the world of Native American experience in the late twentieth century, capturing both the violent disruption of colonialism on a multigenerational level for the characters in the film, and also the cohesiveness of a tribal community in which the characters come to realize that no one individual owns a story—in this case, the story of Victor's father—but that its truths must be shared and acknowledged from multiple angles, regardless of the pain this must cause.

Smoke Signals has wonderful, engaging performances from the two main actors, Adam Beech and Evan Adams, and great supporting roles from Tantoo Cardinal, Irene Bedard, Gary Farmer, and others—a veteran cast that has long made the rounds in films calling for Native performers. It follows the genre of the classic road movie, as Victor and Thomas must journey to collect the ashes of Victor's recently deceased father and return them home, but applies an indigenous twist, capturing, in one particularly poignant moment, the look of anxiousness and uncertainty on both of the lead characters' faces when they are reminded that they are leaving the reservation behind and headed into a foreign country, the United States of America. Throughout it all, Thomas tenaciously adheres to his self-appointed role as tribal storyteller, even though no one wishes to hear his stories which at times cut too close to the truth. Both the movie and the short story conclude, however, with the possibility of redemption, for Victor's father who will rise from the ashes "like a salmon," and for Victor, too, who promises

Thomas that on some undetermined day in the future, he will stop and listen to at least one of Thomas's stories.[44]

Many other Native writers, including Leslie Marmon Silko, Diane Glancy, Louise Erdrich, and Gerald Vizenor, have, like Alexie, effectively crossed over genres and written poetry, novels, and short stories to wonderful and varied effect. Emerging artists such as Tommy Orange, Stephen Graham Jones, Toni Jensen, Therese Mailhot, Brandon Hobson, and others are continuing to stretch the bounds of Native literature and are already being heralded as members of a new Native Literary Renaissance. There has also been a renewed interest in making feature films that tell their story from Native space, using Native actors and artists. In the last 10 years, James Welch's novel *Winter in the Blood* was offered a very faithful (given its difficult form and subject matter) adaptation into film, as was Richard Van Camp's *Lesser Blessed* and, most recently, Richard Wagamese's hauntingly beautiful *Indian Horse*, which has received wide release and a great deal of critical acclaim, perhaps because Clint Eastwood was a producer and supporter of the project. Artists will continue to redefine the boundaries of Native literature, but, however that realm is enlarged, I imagine it will continue to explore relationships with the land that stand at the heart of what it means to be indigenous. Still, it must also negotiate the contorted pathways of cultural negotiation with a settler state that casts its shadow over and across the boundaries that seek to define and contain Native experience.

Notes

1 Lisa Brooks, "At the Gathering Place," American Indian Literary Nationalism (Albuquerque: University of New Mexico Press, 2006), 230.
2 Scott Lyons, *X-Marks: Native Signatures of Assent* (Minneapolis: University of Minnesota Press, 2010), 2.
3 Chief Powless Jr., "Treaty Making," *Treaty of Canandaigua, 1794: 200 Years of Treaty Relations Between the Iroquois Confederacy and the United States*, Eds. G. Peter Jemison and Anna M. Shein (Santa Fe: Clear Light, 2000), 34.
4 Lisa Brooks, *The Common Pot: The Recovery of Native Space in the Northeast* (Minnesota: University of Minneapolis Press, 2008), 3.
5 Brooks, "Gathering Place," 244.
6 Simon Ortiz, "Towards a National Indian Literature," *American Indian Literary Nationalism* (Albuquerque: University of New Mexico Press, 2006), 254.
7 Lisa King, "Sovereignty, Rhetorical Sovereignty, and Representation: Key Words for Teaching Indigenous Texts," *Survivance, Sovereignty, and Story: Teaching American Indian Rhetorics*, Eds. Lisa King, Rose Gubele, and Joyce Rain Anderson (Logan: Utah State University Press, 2015), 19.
8 Craig Womack, *Red on Red: Native American Literary Separatism* (Minneapolis: University of Minnesota Press, 1999), 14.
9 Gerald Vizenor, *Manifest Manners: Postindian Warriors of Survivance* (Hanover: University Press of New England, 1994), 1–44.
10 Womack, 3.
11 Robert Allen Warrior, *Tribal Secrets: Recovering American Indian Intellectual Traditions* (Minneapolis: University of Minnesota Press, 1995), xxiii.

12 Elizabeth Cook-Lynn, "Who Gets to Tell the Stories," *Wicazo Sa Review*, 9:1 (Spring 1993), pp. 60–64.
13 Cook-Lynn, 63.
14 Linda Hogan, *Mean Spirit* (New York: Ivy Books, 1990), 13–14.
15 Thomas King, "Borders," *One Good Story, That One* (Toronto: Harper Perennial, 1993), 133.
16 King, "Borders" 131.
17 King, "Borders," 132.
18 King, "Borders," 134.
19 King, "Borders," 142.
20 Diane Glancy, *Pushing the Bear: A Novel of the Trail of Tears* (San Diego: Harcourt, 1996), 2.
21 Glancy, 154.
22 Anna Lee Walters, *Ghost Singer* (Albuquerque, University of New Mexico Press, 1988), 17.
23 Walters, 126.
24 D. Rae Gould, "NAGPRA, CUI, and Institutional Will," *The Routledge Companion to Cultural Property*, Eds. Jane Anderson and Haidy Geismar (New York: Routledge, 2017), 137.
25 James Welch, *Fool's Crow* (New York, Penguin Books, 1986), 3.
26 Louis Owens, *Other Destinies: Understanding the American Indian Novel* (Norman: University of Oklahoma Press, 1992), 157.
27 Ella Deloria, *Waterlily* (Lincoln: University of Nebraska Press, 1988), 20.
28 Welch, 174.
29 Stephen Graham Jones, "Letter to a Just-Starting-Out Indian Writer—and Maybe to Myself," *Transmotion* 2:182 (2016).
30 Rebecca Tillet, *Contemporary Native American Literature* (Edinburgh: Edinburg University Press, 2007), 137.
31 David L. Moore and Kathryn W. Shanley, "Native American Poetry: Loosening the Bonds of Representation," *The Routledge Companion to Native American Literature*, Ed. Deborah L. Madsen (New York: Routledge, 2016), 445.
32 Cook-Lynn, 60.
33 Cook-Lynn. See also Gloria Bird, "The Exaggeration of Despair in Sherman Alexie's 'Reservation Blues,'" *Wicazo Sa Review*, 11:2 (Autumn 1995), pp. 47–52.
34 Sherman Alexie, "The First Annual All-Indian Horseshoe Throw and Barbecue," *The Lone Ranger and Tonto Fistfight in Heaven* (New York: Grove Press, 1993), 150.
35 Sherman Alexie, *The Summer of Black Widows* (New York: Hanging Loose Press, 1996), 98.
36 Alexie, *Summer*, 12–13.
37 Zitkala-Sa, "Iktomi and the Ducks," *American Indian Stories, Legends and Other Writings* (New York: Penguin Books, 2003), 7.
38 Alexie, *Summer*, 13.
39 Alexie, "A Drug Called Tradition," *Lone Ranger*, 21
40 Alexie, "A Drug Called Tradition," *Lone Ranger*, 23.
41 Alexie, "The Trial of Thomas Builds-the-Fire," *Lone Ranger*, 97.
42 Alexie, "The Trial of Thomas Builds-the-Fire," *Lone Ranger*, 99.
43 Qulachan Golf Course website. https://www.tripadvisor.com/Attraction_Review-g58759-d4509307-Reviews-The_Creek_at_Qualchan_Golf_Course-Spokane_Washington.html
44 Alexie, "Phoenix, Arizona," *Lone Ranger*, 74–75.

7

TEACHING LOUISE ERDRICH'S *TRACKS*

A Case Study

The Absent Presence of History

This *Introduction to Native American Literature* began by recognizing the levels of "sexual violence and outright predation that persist to this day on Indian reservations and First Nation reserves across the North American continent" (see Introduction). With the idea of confronting this ongoing injustice, Louise Erdrich wrote her novel *The Round House*, which won the National Book Award in 2012, bringing national attention to this crisis. I will close off this chapter with a brief discussion of Erdrich's much-praised book, but I begin with her 1988 novel *Tracks*, which, although not first among her published works, was Erdrich's earliest attempt at a book-length manuscript and remains among her most compelling and teachable creations. In many ways, it already begins to trace the lines of how commercial exploitation of the land is inextricable from the exploitation of women's bodies—how, when the natural world is broken down into commoditized parts, the indigenous body becomes one more resource to strip-mine, clear-cut, or despoil for profit.

Tracks tells the story of how the Anishinaabe people, or Chippewa (Erdrich is an enrolled member of the Turtle Mountain Band of Chippewa in present-day North Dakota), were dispossessed of the greater portion of their lands at the turn of the twentieth century. By opening its perspective up to alternating narrators, Nanapush and Pauline Puyat, *Tracks* presents to its reader two often competing accounts of events taking place on an unnamed Ojibwe reservation between the years 1912 and 1924. Despite the tensions engendered by the pairing of their stories, neither narrator is situated in a position affording them a comprehensive view of the historical storm tearing through their lives and the lives of their people. In many ways, this is the genius of the novel. *Tracks* is a tightly constructed work of historical recovery, but the history is expertly baked into the narrative structure. On its surface, the novel functions as an indigenous domestic drama, telling the intimate stories of two or three families whose long-standing histories and feuds come into conflict with one another on the reservation. At the core of the novel, however, is how these richly rendered characters struggle to maintain their lands, their traditions, and the very fabric of their kinship ties amid the violent transformations taking place all around them.

I was a fan of Erdrich's novel long before I became a graduate student or had any idea that I would be a professor of English specializing in Native American literature. But Erdrich's writing played a definitive role in sparking my interest in Native culture and ultimately encouraging me along in this direction. When I first read *Tracks*, however, as much as I was moved by Erdrich's prose and her ability to make me care deeply about the lives of her characters, I remained largely unaware of the novel's historical dynamics, for which the fates of her characters essentially serve as microcosm. I didn't really think of it as a historical novel at the time, but merely regarded *Tracks* as a poignant character study, set in a remote place and time, reflecting upon the generalized "tragic" plight of Native peoples. In other words, it was impossible for me to connect the narrative in any concrete way to the systemic series of actions, historical events, legal manipulations, and environmental depredations about which I knew so very little, but which precisely inform the narrative trajectory, making *Tracks* not only a very localized study, but representative of tales of indigenous dispossession and survivance occurring throughout the continent at the turn of the century. I was equally unaware of how Erdrich carefully threads Anishinaabe worldviews and traditions into the novel, making of it a richly layered, indigenous masterpiece.

The kinds of details that inform western notions of history-keeping are rarely given explicit articulation in Erdrich's novel. As Nancy J. Peterson writes,

> the tension and conflict at the heart of *Tracks* come into focus only when the readers have some knowledge of the Dawes Allotment Act of 1887, but the text does not refer to the act directly. The documentary history of dispossession that the novel uses and resists functions as an absent presence; the text acknowledges the way in which this historical script has impinged on the Anishinabeg but opposes allowing this history to function as the only story that can be told.[1]

Erdrich has chosen instead to foreground the lives of her characters and their epistemological perspectives, keeping the extent of her archival research muted— an invisible thread that holds all the other various strands in place. Major events, such as World War I, that were demanding the attention of the rest of the nation at the time in which the novel is set are glimpsed only on the periphery and have fleeting impact. Conventional dates and seasons are provided as part of the chapter headings, such as "Winter 1912," which opens the novel, but they are paired with what Erdrich offers as their Anishinaabeg equivalents—in this case "*Manitou-geezisohns*: Little Spirit Sun."[2] These pairings work to situate the reader in the space between two epistemological frameworks, two culturally separate ways of comprehending the marking and movement of time.

Erdrich's sense of Anishinaabe history and culture is informed by her own upbringing and stories she gathered from family members and members of her community. But she also draws from archival materials to help her construct an Anishinaabe world at the turn of the century. Those materials consist of early Jesuit relations and the eighteenth-century narrative of John Tanner, "The Falcon," who was adopted into an Anishinaabe family as a child and left a stirring account of his life. She also draws from the writings of nineteenth-century Ojibwe historian William Warren and a host of other nineteenth- and twentieth-century ethnographical compilations, including works by Frances Densmore, Irving Hallowell, Ruth Landes, Basil Johnston, and others. It isn't necessary to read all of these works to appreciate the layered manner in which Erdrich pulls from historical sources, but it is helpful to understand that these connections are mined for deep metaphorical effects, some of which will be more fully explicated here. *Tracks* invites mainstream audiences into a remote, foreign, narrowly conscripted world, while remaining an accessible and mesmerizing work of fiction, providing the general reader access through Erdrich's gifted story-telling ability and layered characterizations.

Nanapush

The history that most explicitly comes into play in the novel is that related by Nanapush, one of the two narrators and a Native elder of some 50 years who has lived through many of the great transitions come sweeping through Anishinaabe space. Nanapush tells us in the novel's opening passage how,

> We started dying before the snow, and like the snow, we continued to fall ... For those who survived the spotted sickness from the south, our long flight west to Nadouissioux land where we signed the treaty, and then a wind from the east, bringing exile in a storm of government papers, what descended from the north in 1912 seemed impossible.[3]

As is the case with many oral narratives, Nanapush offers a compressed history, invoking the significant, indelible moments almost like verbally rendered winter counts and binding them in a form that also serves as invocation of the four directions, an orientation in space situating us in his Anishinaabe world and, in a sense, inviting us into the ceremony. But behind that compressed history is Erdrich's awareness of when the treaty creating the Turtle Mountain Reservation was signed and the wave of epidemics that followed in the wake of white encroachment.[4]

That these events are all in some way related, a series of contingencies that remain largely invisible to western history, though experienced firsthand by the Anishinaabe, can be seen in Melissa Myers's illuminating essay "We Can Not Get a Living as We Used To" on the dispossession of the White Earth Agency between 1889 and 1920. Myers demonstrates how the legal machinations that chipped away at Anishinaabe lands were designed both to enable settler encroachment and for the lumber companies to despoil the land of its resources, resulting in the upending of the "seasonal rounds" by which the Anishinaabe had historically survived. The loss of land and the wanton destruction of flora and fauna forced Anishinaabe people to live in more compressed, densely populated spaces than they previously had known and made them that much more vulnerable to disease when the coughing sickness—tuberculosis—made its way through their villages.[5] Although Native people are often depicted as victims of blameless pandemics to which they had no immunity, this simplified narrative easily elides the forced conditions of congestion, the lack of social distancing, and deprivation that rendered Natives ever more susceptible to these outbreaks. Nanapush recognizes this as well, observing,

> this disease was different from the pox and fever, for it came on slow. The outcome, however, was just as certain. Whole families ... lay ill and helpless in its breath. On the reservation, where we were forced close together, the clans dwindled.[6]

Nanapush has attained the tragic wisdom that allows him to connect these events together. As he relates, in a monologue directed at his adopted daughter, Lulu,

> My girl, I saw the passing of times you will never know. I guided the last buffalo hunt. I saw the last bear shot. I trapped the last beaver with a pelt of more than two years' growth. I spoke aloud the words of the government treaty, and refused to sign the settlement papers that would take away our woods and lake. I axed the last birch that was older than I, and I saved the last Pillager.[7]

Nanapush has not only witnessed these transformations, but he has survived them, along with a handful of others, and bears the burden of having to preserve the culture and pass what he knows on to the next generation.

Erdrich has been criticized for perpetuating stereotypes of the vanishing Indian in this and other passages, creating in the character of Nanapush a romanticized nostalgia that renders traditional Native culture as static.[8] One can see how the critique might apply if we view the portrayal of Nanapush as locked in this particular mode of pining away for the past, standing in as the last, and soon to be vanished, hold-out for Anishinaabe tradition. Students, and instructors too, will be tempted to see Nanapush in this narrow light, as purely representative of former lifeways (standing in direct contrast to Pauline, who appears to fully embrace dominant white Christian values). I would argue, however, that Erdrich, as a rule, deftly avoids such one-dimensional characterization, and that her rendering of Nanapush offers layers of complexity that defy any attempt to freeze him in a bygone age. In fact, he is the very embodiment of the flexibility of tradition and the ability to adapt to changing circumstances in proactive ways. More than simply typifying the past, Nanapush is most often a proponent of the good way of doing things, proper action, drawing from what is usable in both Anishinaabe and settler tradition to divine a path forward. Although he naturally maintains certain practices and beliefs that are central to his cultural upbringing, he is also the least likely of the novel's characters—Christian, Native, or otherwise—to fall prey to rumor or ascribe supernatural explanations to events that can be explained through human agency. He maintains a friendship with Father Damien, the priest assigned to the reservation, goes to church on occasion, and even attends confession at least once. These are tensions that can be usefully teased out in reading the novel, as they actually help to subvert internalized notions of what it means to be both "traditional" and "Indian."

An early task I set for students is to have them identify the ways in which Nanapush is an upholder of tradition in the novel and then, conversely, the more difficult challenge of identifying how he defies the perceived traditional mode. I try to emphasize through this line of questioning how, when Nanapush frequently does uphold tradition, it is most often in a "good way," or with a good mind, to borrow a term we have already seen from Haudenosaunee history. Erdrich herself has referred to this as *mino bimaadiziwin*, an Ojibwe term suggesting adherence to a "good life" characterized by knowledge seasoned with "generosity and kindness."[9] And, when Nanapush seems to depart from tradition, it is in keeping with the goals of continuance—or actions designed to preserve cohesion within his Anishinaabe community.

Nanapush's name references the great culture hero of Anishinaabe tradition, Naanabozho, described by Gerald Vizenor as the "compassionate woodland trickster" who is "teacher and healer," bringing to the Anishinaabe people special knowledge relating to "healing plants, wild rice, maple sugar," and other necessities of survival on Turtle Island.[10] John Tanner, who was adopted into an Ojibwe family in the 1780s, grew up within these traditions and describes "Nanabush" as the "ever benevolent intercessor between the Supreme Being and mankind [who] procured for their benefit the animals whose flesh should be their food, and whose skins were for their clothing."[11] In stories, it is Naanabozho who reconstitutes the world during the great flood, drawing from a collop of earth retrieved by a muskrat to allow for solid land to rematerialize, just as it had in earlier times when Sky Woman first fell from her home in the clouds. By drawing upon tradition and doing things in a good way, Naanabozho is able to maintain the balance of earthly forces and create a place for the Anishinaabe and all other beings of the planet to live and thrive.[12]

As Erdrich acknowledges, however, the name also references the radical instability associated with trickster tales. In *Tracks*, Nanapush recalls the words of his father, who told him his name "has got to do with trickery and living in the bush. Because it's got to do with something a girl can't resist. The first Nanapush stole fire. You will steal hearts."[13] This kind of sexual braggadocio is part of Nanapush's character, too, and results in some of the comical exchanges that inform Erdrich's authorial sensibility. But even this is in keeping with Erdrich's sense of traditional culture, a kind of bawdy teasing that Anishinaabe religious scholar Lawrence W. Gross describes as "a long-time character trait of the Anishinaabe."[14] Folded into these trickster encounters is the awareness that, as with mere mortals, the designs of gods and first beings do not always succeed as planned.

As such, Nanapush *does* represent tradition in ways that are very deliberately marked out for the reader, but, just as Naanabozho will be responsible for finding strategies to reconstitute the earth in time of deluge, so must Nanapush find ways to reconstitute life as he knows it on the dwindling lands belonging to the Anishinaabe. It is no coincidence that Nanapush tells us his humble little cabin is located "overlooking the crossroads."[15] Nanapush has situated himself at the intersection of Anishinaabe and settler culture, where tradition and change inevitably meet. He is one of the few Native characters in the novel who has acquired western literacy, having survived a stint at the Jesuit boarding school as a child, and he is the only one who keeps abreast of events happening in the world outside the reservation. Nanapush receives the newspaper once a week from Grand Forks and even though, as he notes, "a system of post was still a new and different thing to Indians," nevertheless it is he who "was marked out by the agent to receive words in envelopes." Among these are official government notices, catalogues, and "letters from the land court," all of which he preserves in a skin "tied and stowed beneath my bed,"[16] making of his home a kind of tribal archive (as is the case with many Native people involved in the affairs of their tribe today). Enveloping these details into our understanding of Nanapush helps to fill out his character and poses a challenge to the static representation it is so tempting to project upon him.

Because of his skill in deciphering signs and written words, Nanapush comprehends the designs laid to cheat his small band of their holdings. We are informed that he had "already given Father Damien testimony on this Anishinaabe land," but, as he admits, "There were so few of us who even understood the writing on the papers" and too many unwittingly "signed their land away with thumbs and crosses."[17] Ultimately, there is little Nanapush can do to stem the tide of dispossession that has swept over his home, but, as he tries to caution Lulu, the wayward granddaughter to whom his tale is told, their troubles have nothing to do with the past or traditional lifeways once cherished by the Anishinaabe. Rather, he tells her, "our trouble came from the living, from liquor and the dollar bill. We stumbled toward the government bait, never looking down, never noticing how the land was snatched from under us at every step."[18] Land, as Nanapush knows, "is the only thing that lasts life to life. Money burns like tinder, flows off like water. And as for government promises, the wind is steadier."[19]

When we first encounter Nanapush in the novel, he is telling the story of how he saved Lulu's mother, Fleur Pillager. Nanapush has accompanied the tribal police officer, Edgar Pukwan, deep into the woods on the far side of Lake Machimanito to see if any of the Pillager family, the tribal inheritors of this lot, had survived the recent epidemic. Pukwan, whose official position implicates him in the dynamics of settler power and authority on the reservation, is nevertheless frightened to trespass upon these lands, fearing it may be cursed by the ghosts of Pillagers swept off by disease. His anxiety is so overwhelming that he abdicates his responsibility to investigate the cabin when they come upon it. It is Nanapush, although apprehensive himself, who must break through the frozen skin of the window and crawl down into the "stinking silence," where he discovers the young Fleur, still alive among the remains of her relations. Before extracting the young girl from this de facto crypt, Nanapush "touched each bundle [the dead bodies of the Pillagers] in the gloom of the cabin, and wished each spirit a good journey on the four-day road, the old time road, so well-trampled by our people this deadly season."[20]

Fleur herself is wild with grief and needs to be forcibly dragged from the cabin and strapped to the sled that had been brought along in case of survivors. Pukwan, driven by his fear of Pillager spirits, will not assist in any of this, but manages to fulfill at least one official role by hammering a quarantine sign on the cabin. Later, when, owing to legal considerations, Pukwan must return to the cabin to bury the bodies, Nanapush once again accompanies him to ensure all is done properly. It is Nanapush who carves out the clan markers on the burial boards, says a small prayer, and offers tobacco for the departing spirits. If not for his intervention, none of these rites would be honored or fulfilled.[21]

Erdrich is not succumbing to stereotypes of vanishing in her portrayal of Nanapush, but she is offering a poignant, imaginative, and dynamic reminder of what Anishinaabe and other Native people suffered in this period of compulsory transition. Nanapush, too, has just recently survived the disease that took his wives and children. Both Nanapush and Fleur are connected by unspeakable grief. Both witnessed the deaths of their loved ones and both maintain their ties to traditional ways. Fleur only survives the epidemic because Nanapush rescues her, and Nanapush survives, as we later learn, by telling stories, stringing together words and histories and old tales so that, "death could not get in a word edgewise, grew discouraged, and traveled on."[22] Nevertheless, as the two pass the remainder of the winter together, they become ossified in their loss, too apathetic to eat or to even desire to draw breath. "I learned later that this was common," Nanapush recalls, "that there were many of our people who died in this manner, of the invisible sickness."[23] Gross, offering an Anishinaabe reading of the novel, refers to this phenomenon as "postapocalyptic stress syndrome," as individuals coped with the devastating loss of entire family groups and the disruption of traditional custom and knowledge that accompanied it.[24] Clearly, Erdrich has recalled such stories as well. Through the perspective of Nanapush, she offers profound insight into this larger cultural trauma, a world of loss and grief but also survivance, as she suggests the way out, the way to cheat this premature death, is through the perpetuation of stories.

Fleur

Although Nanapush has the first and last word in the novel, the story itself belongs to Fleur Pillager, the interest of all the major characters and the power at the center of all the various plot threads. As with Nanapush, Fleur's name has cultural relevance beyond the world created by the novel. The Pillagers were an actual band of Ojibwe who, according to the nineteenth-century Ojibway historian William W. Warren, were noted as being "the bravest band of the tribe," a characteristic, he assures us, "they have retained ever since." Their name in Anishinabeg is *Muk-im-dua-win-in-e-wug*, or "men who take by force." Warren goes on to say that the Pillagers were "filled with a daring and independent spirit, and no act was so wild, but that they were ready and disposed to achieve it."[25] Although Warren does not appear to be referencing the Pillager women in his description, Erdrich has no hesitation in transferring these characteristics directly to Fleur.

Fleur's story begins to take shape in the novel when she enters the town of Argus, North Dakota, in 1913, seeking employment at the local butcher shop (a locale Erdrich visited previously in her 1986 novel *The Beet Queen*). It is here that Fleur encounters Pauline Puyat, the novel's other narrator, who, although only 15 at the onset, has turned her back on her mixed-blood family on the reservation and cast her lot in with these distant white relations in Argus. Pauline is a homely and awkward child, unloved and overlooked by all those in her sphere. Like a moth to a flame, she is drawn to power—it is her way of coping with the traumatic losses of the recent past, of seeking security, and of latching on to something stronger and more substantive than herself. As such, Pauline is immediately drawn to Fleur, a woman whose power and raw beauty exert a magnetic hold on all those she encounters.

When Fleur insinuates herself into the nightly poker game held by the men in the butcher shop, they too prove unable to resist her pull, even as they are incapable of perceiving a Native woman as a worthy adversary. The ensuing scene, which spools out slowly over a number of pages, is expertly crafted and demonstrates Erdrich's ability to build tension through small, acutely observed details such as the texture of the greasy playing cards, a small lap dog springing to attention at the game's tensest moments, the tremble of a freshly drawn card in a player's hand, or the oppressive smell of smoked meats from the butcher shop that clings to Fleur's flimsy dress as well as to the skin of the poker players. Believing they hold all the cards, the men allow Fleur to string them along over a series of evenings at the poker table on the assumption that "the squaw can't bluff." As such, they are hardly amused when Fleur, with a wolfish smile, finally lays down the winning hand and divests them of their money.[26]

Having lost their wages to Fleur, the men are quick to retaliate. When Fleur is subsequently raped, the reader is shielded from the full brutality of the act by Pauline's equivocating perspective. Nevertheless, Pauline is witness to it all. She might have run to Fleur's aid or called out for help, but instead she remains silent throughout, paralyzed by her warring impulses. Fleur has shown Pauline flashes of tenderness—cared for her in a disinterested manner that was nevertheless greater comfort than Pauline had previously known. But the white men, to whom Pauline was all but invisible, were the ones who, in her calculation, held all the real power. Fleur is left to fend for herself, and Pauline is left to dangle in her conflicting allegiance, even as a tornado rips through the town, as though in fury over Fleur's violation, destroying the butcher shop and claiming the lives of Fleur's assailants. For the remainder of the novel, Pauline wrestles with her complicity in Fleur's assault. It becomes a disruptive metonym for her rejection of her own people. She is equally tormented, however, by the spirits of the three assailants who, having taken shelter from the tornado in the meat locker, become trapped inside and subsequently freeze to death when no one comes to look for them. The memory of Pauline's agency in this event is replayed and repurposed in her mind throughout the novel, as she attempts to reconcile the divided parts of her psyche.

When Fleur returns to the reservation, she is able to pay the fees for her allotments with her poker winnings and reestablish herself on Pillager lands on the far side of the lake, even though, as Nanapush notes, "a young girl had never done such a thing before."[27] Although her return sparks malicious rumors concerning how she acquired the money, she is still full enough in her power to attract the attention of young Eli Kashpaw who, with the help of some sexual counseling from Nanapush, becomes Fleur's lover. The ensuing revelation that Fleur is pregnant stirs even greater controversy as the town speculates over the child's paternity. Pauline, who has also returned to the reservation, adds fuel to the fire by playing into local belief-systems, asserting,

> it was clear that Misshepeshu, the water man, the monster, wanted her for himself. He's a devil, that one, love hungry with desire and maddened for the touch of young girls, the strong and daring especially, the ones like Fleur.[28]

Misshepeshu, the lake spirit, is a presence invoked throughout the novel, representing traditional belief and the source of Fleur's power. Its presence is a complicated one that should be teased out carefully in classroom conversation. Although Misshepeshu is often referred to as a "monster" or even a "devil" in the novel, these terms tend to be forwarded by Pauline or others who share her allegiance to dominant white belief systems. To refer to Misshepeshu as a "devil" or to imply that its essence is evil or malevolent is in keeping with age-old strategies of the Christian church to denigrate and dismiss Native spirituality. The Jesuits, in their relations, equated manitous with the great deceiver and referred to indigenous spiritual leaders as "conjurors," "jugglers," and "frauds." Traditional practices such as the shaking tent ceremony, a custom practiced by members of the powerful *midéwiwin* or medicine society throughout the Great Lakes region, were routinely represented as attempts to communicate with the devil. These rhetorical strategies of the Jesuits, whether sincerely believed or not, largely succeeded in making indigenous practices seem, at best, strange and barbaric and, at worst, demonic to those who read the accounts published by these early Christian evangelists.[29]

Misshepeshu, Misshipishi, Michibizhi, the horned serpent, also referred to as the underwater lynx or panther, is a being referenced in a great many indigenous traditions. French explorers, as they first passed through in the eighteenth century, recounted being awestruck by great paintings of Misshepeshu high on the cliffs of the Mississippi River, and the horned serpent can still be seen today in petroglyphs carved on rocks in Lake Superior and elsewhere. Erdrich writes of encountering such rock art in her collection of essays *Books and Islands from Ojibwe Country* and concludes that the horns depicted on serpents and other supernatural beings "connote intellectual and spiritual activity."[30] Misshepeshu and water spirits in general were seen to be in contention with the Thunderers, or sky spirits, and their cosmic battles are threaded throughout Anishinaabe lore. Anthropologist Michael Angel suggests that, "Thunderers and Underwater Panthers represented the two sides of the whole, both of whom had to be placated so that things could be kept in balance."[31] Like water itself, Misshepeshu's agency cannot be properly viewed as good or evil, but, rather, as life-sustaining and unpredictable, a force difficult to harness and capable of great destruction but also capable of granting gifts. Misshepeshu was often invoked in regards to romantic obsession, as well. The water spirit was believed to attract human mates or present itself as "an alluring person of opposite sex."[32] In her poem "The Flood," Joy Harjo makes reference to this, asking "how could I resist the watersnake, who appeared as the most handsome man in the tribe, or any band whose visits I'd been witness to since a child?"[33] Erdrich draws on these interpretations in multiple ways throughout the novel, although the spirit itself is never encountered in its tangible form.

In *Tracks*, it is Old Man Pillager, Fleur's father, who first drew the lake spirit to the lake Matchimanito, as the band was pressured to relocate from their homes in the east. As Nanapush later observes, there were those who were glad Fleur had returned to the reservation because they felt "she kept the thing controlled."[34] Whatever we are to make of Fleur's relationship to the lake being, she is feared as a result of it, and the perception of her ties to it are furthered by Pauline's gossip. Nanapush, on the other hand, observes how Pauline's gift for "wagging" her tongue was worse than his own, "for while I was careful with my known facts, she was given to improving the truth."[35] It is an early indication that Pauline is not the most reliable of narrators. In her speculation over the child Fleur carries, Pauline wonders whether it was "fathered in a smokehouse, or by a man with

FIGURE 7.1 Illustration of "The Woman Who Loved a Serpent Who Lived in a Lake" by Passamaquoddy artist Joseph Tomah. The Algonquin Legends of New England or Myths and Folk Lore of the Micmac, Passamaquoddy, and Penobscot Tribes by Charles G. Leland (1884). Courtesy of the Maine historical Society

brass scales."[36] For his part, Nanapush respects the power of the lake spirit, but remains more skeptical in relation to the rumors of paternity and carefully observes Fleur's progress from a distance, hoping to better comprehend what has happened to the young woman formerly under his protection.

Fleur's power is registered in other ways as well. The implication is that it was she who summoned the tornado responsible for killing her assailants in Argus. Men who attempt to intrude on Fleur's lands meet mysterious ends, and even Edgar Pukwan, the tribal policeman who refused to assist Nanapush in her rescue, eventually dies of the disease he had hoped, through his cowardly actions, to avoid. Fleur is believed to be able to shapeshift, take animal form, or call upon the manitous to assist her in hunting. Some critics have even referred to her as a "bear walker," known as "one of the most feared types of shamans."[37] But her power should not be regarded as intrinsically malevolent. Fleur cultivates a mystique about her that leads others to attribute their ill luck to her power. In this manner, she protects herself from a world in which she is, in fact, utterly vulnerable to the violent, dominant white-male power structures encircling her world, and many of the deaths attributed to Fleur are, in fact, brought about by the careless or malignant acts of the victims themselves.

When Fleur's child, Lulu, is born, however, the forest itself seems to come alive in response, "as if the Manitous all through the woods spoke through Fleur, loose, arguing ... Turtle's quavering scratch, the Eagle's high shriek, Loon's crazy bitterness, Otter, the howl of Wolf, Bear's low rasp."[38] The precise moment of Lulu's birth is marked by the appearance of a bear that, having broken into Nanapush's secret stash of wine, becomes inebriated and stumbles through the door of the birth cabin. The passage brings to mind stories, preserved on sacred Ojibwe birchbark scrolls, of the first bear manitou who broke through four medicine lodges to carry the message of Gitche-manidoo pertaining to the rules of life into the world.[39] Understanding this facet of Anishinaabe culture provides an extra layer of meaning to this moment of birth, hope, and renewal. "It could have been a spirit bear," Nanapush muses, as he springs up on a pile of logs to avoid the bear's approach. Eli's mother, Margaret Kashpaw, must chase the bear from the cabin, and Pauline, soon after, emerges with a rifle to shoot it. Although the bear is observed rushing off wounded into the woods, it is not seen again.[40] All these events speak to Fleur's affiliations with manitou and spirit-helpers, which assist her in the height of her power and contribute to Lulu's entry into the world. But it also suggests a ceremony gone awry in a world turned upside down for the Anishinaabe people.

Important to keep in mind is that Fleur, for all her presumed power, is still human—a strong human woman, albeit with limited agency in the world. Her power and resolve cannot prevent her from being raped, it cannot prevent her from being a victim of physical and economic colonial violence, it cannot help her keep her land, nor, can it, in the end, help her save or preserve those she loves. Following Lulu's birth, the young priest, Father Damien, arrives to administer baptism. Margaret, who has adopted Christianity herself, allows for this additional brief ceremony to occur, unbeknownst to Fleur who lies recovering in the cabin. At that moment, because Eli is not present and because the child's paternity is uncertain, Nanapush offers his own surname for the baptismal record. Nanapush's trickster impulse guides him in this act. As he rationalizes it, "there were so many tales, so many possibilities, so many lies. The waters were so muddy I thought I'd give them another stir."[41]

Pauline

Pauline provides the counterpoint to Nanapush in *Tracks*, often seen as representing the dominant worldview of white settler Christian culture. But this, too, is inadequate. It would be more accurate to suggest that Pauline represents the post-colonial condition—a tormented and twisted self-loathing that is brought about by the imposition of colonial norms, colonial violence, and domination. Although Pauline lacks self-awareness, and many of her convictions are self-serving, she is still able to conclude of herself that, "I was cleft down the middle by my sin ... scored like a lightning struck tree."[42] This self-representation evokes the claim of Latina scholar and poet Gloria Anzaldua who, reflecting upon the tensions engendered by identity politics at the U.S.–Mexican border, cried, it "splits me splits me."[43]

A good exercise is to have students first describe Pauline's relationship to Christianity—how it develops and where it leads. Is her faith clearly established at the onset of the novel, or does it progress in stages? And how does it transition from ambivalent to fanatical? In my own reading of *Tracks*, I see Pauline first turning to Christ for protection after she uses Anishinaabe love medicine to entrap Eli in a sexual liaison. It is Fleur's wrath that she fears, and the Virgin Mary appears before her in this moment as a spirit helper, offering secret assurance of Christ's protection. In this sense, Pauline's version of Christianity is steeped in indigenous notions of spirituality in which Christ is viewed as a kind of power-broker, one spirit among many, who must be appealed to and appeased. Even the Virgin Mary, in the form of a plaster statue kept in the reservation church, is regarded by Pauline as nothing more than a vessel of God's power, her small, delicately crafted, bare white foot crushing its weight down upon the back of a serpent. The figurative relationship between the snake, the devil, Mishepeshu, and Native culture in general is apparent, but for Pauline the light brown eyes of the virgin also "held the same lively curious suspension as the snake's." The forces that animate God and manitou are indistinguishable, except that one must ultimately prove more powerful than the other. By the novel's end, however, Pauline, in her growing derangement, arrives at the startling conclusion that Christ himself "was weak," and that it is *she* who must serve as *his* champion against the devil-worshipping pagans on the reservation.[44]

Pauline's character, although indisputably a destructive force in the novel, is treated with a great deal of sympathy by Erdrich. A mark of Erdrich's style is that she rarely creates pure villains, but is able to find a common core of humanity in all her characters. As is true in regard to the lake spirit in Machimanito, sustained life on Earth depends on maintaining a balance of forces, and nothing is all dark or all light. Even Linden Lark, the character responsible for the destructive acts that drive the narrative of *The Round House*, is rendered with complexity and granted his human moments. Pauline's character is arguably capable of equal or greater violence, although her agency is nearly always diffused and obfuscated by her tormented psyche. She is at least partly responsible for the deaths of the three men in Argus who raped Fleur. She murders at least one man outright. Her actions bring about the dissolution of Fleur and Eli's partnership, and her willful ineptitude is to blame for the passing of Fleur's second child and the near death of Lulu. Pauline also bears a child out of wedlock, a "sin" she will refuse to acknowledge, placing her at odds with her eventual vows to God when she enters the convent. In the hands of a lesser novelist, Pauline would be a caricature, perhaps, of colonial evil. And yet we never lose sight of the fact that Pauline, too, is a victim of forces beyond her control.

It is Pauline's own sexual awakening and need for human attention that prompts her to get between Fleur and Eli, to try to "warm my hands at the fire between them."[45] When these tactics prove fruitless, however, she turns her attentions on Napoleon Morrisey, the rough-hewn mixed-blood brother of Bernadette Morrisey who has taken Pauline in upon her return to the reservation. Bernadette is the self-appointed care-giver for the dead and dying on the reservation and she begins to include Pauline on her rounds. It is here that Pauline discovers a kind of aptitude in helping the dying along on their journey, easing for them the turbulent passageway between life and death. Death is another form of power, and Pauline appoints herself its "midwife," so that, "now when people saw me walking down the road, they wondered who was being taken, man, woman, or child."[46]

Napoleon has no interest in Pauline beyond base lust, but even he prophetically looks down upon her during an attempted seduction, "like a dog sensing the presence of a tasteless poison in its food."[47] Nevertheless, the two manage to conceive, and, upon discovering she is pregnant, Pauline does all in her power to prevent this life, too, from coming forward. But the child, Marie, proves the greater life force of the two and pushes free of Pauline, much like the spirit bear breaking through the wall of the lodge to open a passage to the greater world. With the birth of the bastard child Marie, Pauline is sent away to the convent. Here, in the presence of Christ, whom she conjures on the convent stove, she secretly renounces all connection to her bloodlines. She tells herself, "I was not one speck Indian but wholly white."[48]

Apart from interrogating Pauline's relationship to Christianity, it is worth observing how the other characters in the novel interact with her. Even after entering the convent, her magnetic attraction to Fleur persists, and she is drawn obsessively to the cabin on the far side of the lake. Lulu's birth initially restores a semblance of life to the Pillager lands, and the cabin becomes the center of a growing family circle, with Margaret, her younger son, Nector, and Nanapush all visiting or residing there on a regular basis. Pauline observes how "they formed a kind of clan, the new made up of bits of the old, some religious in the old way and some in the new." Although she intuits, "that the Kashpaws and the Pillagers didn't like to have me around," Pauline nevertheless knows the traditions of hospitality mandating that she be cared for, and she is willing to intrude, even in times of hunger, and eat of their last bowl of broth.[49] Despite all the disruption she initiates, Pauline is always accepted back into the fold. She is fed and cared for and never held fully accountable for what happens—always treated with a modicum of pity.

As such, Pauline is present at the birth of Fleur's second child. The scene that follows once again testifies to Erdrich's ability to create moments of supreme tension—to draw from life's quotidian scenarios moments of impossible emotional and psychological impact. Pauline, unsurprisingly, proves no assistance when Fleur's pregnancy goes awry. Unable to move for fear of precipitating the birth, Fleur tasks Pauline with gathering herbs from the root shack to mix for medicine to stop the hemorrhaging. Pauline gathers the wrong materials, however, contaminating the winter stores in the process, and, despite her seeming desire to help, only renders the situation more dire. When Lulu announces she will run off for assistance, Pauline disregards the fact that the girl wears only store-bought red plastic shoes that are insufficient in the snow and frigid temperatures. Fleur, herself, has to cut the birth cord with a hunting knife when the child, grey and lifeless, spills out of her. She tries to breathe life into its lungs and must stumble across the room in an attempt to prepare the medicine that Pauline has failed to produce.

When none of these efforts prove successful, however, Fleur gathers her child in a bundle and is soon walking the 4-day road, the Ojibwe road of the dead, with Pauline at her heels, on a journey that will once again expose the limits of Fleur's power. Prior to embarking along this liminal path, Fleur has pinned Pauline's skirts to the cabin floor with her hunting knife, and so it is their spirits alone that can travel this road. Erdrich, in interviews, has asserted that she does not employ the device of "magical realism" in her work. She maintains that the narrative possibilities raised in her fiction conform to the lived experiences of those in her community. As such, we can interpret the passage that follows as a vision, a dream, or an out-of-body experience. For an indigenous epistemology, these rationalizations may not matter—we are being asked to engage with an Aninshinaabe consciousness where the world of dream stands in balanced relation to waking life. Erdrich, however, has rendered moments of ecstatic Christian visions as well and brings to the fore the understanding that miracles and otherworldly experiences are not simply the domain of Native "superstition." All cultures allow for, and build their spiritual lives around, belief in supernatural events. For Fleur and Pauline, it places them upon this path of hungry ghosts, at the end of which they find the three men from Argus, seated at their poker table, still waiting to play out one last hand with Fleur. This time, however, the stakes are higher, and, when the men produce Lulu's red plastic shoes and place them in the pot, Fleur understands the game is no longer in her control, nor can she bluff her way out of it. Pauline, too, discovers that she is no longer invisible to the men in this space, and their eyes track her accusingly.

However we choose to interpret this moment, Erdrich weaves an abundance of Anishinaabe tradition, belief, medicine, and consciousness into its narrative structure. Gambling itself plays an important role in Anishinaabe tradition, with Nanabhozo, at the dawn of time, playing for cosmic stakes. Fleur's poker game is a microcosm of the game played in mythic time, and, for her, the stakes are just as high. Although nobody leaves the table a true winner, she does escape with her life and the life of one of her children.

The Song Sang Itself

Fleur's power in *Tracks* is self-willed, whether she draws it from her relationship with the man in the lake or it is an illusion she creates, playing upon the fears and superstitions of weaker minds around her. According to Gross, when Fleur's circumstances begin to unravel, it is a result of her having used her powers irresponsibly. He writes that Fleur "chose to use her power to inspire fear and intimidation, and it did not work. As a strategy for survival, using her blessings to do harm proved to be a losing gamble."[50] This claim is complicated by the fact that Fleur is, in fact, a compassionate character. Even after Pauline "bewitches" Eli, using love medicine to entice him into a torrid romance with the character Sophia Morrisey, Fleur does not ultimately blame Pauline. She still allows Pauline into her home and even bathes the wretched creature at one point, in a moment powerfully suggestive of how traditional Native hospitality is at least the equal of Christian kindness. Fleur holds Eli to a higher account, however, and knows it is his own weakness that betrayed him. Such is the nature of power. It operates especially on those who do not rise up with an equal power of their own to meet it.

As for Nanapush, he confides,

> I never made the mistake of thinking that I owned my own strength ... and so I never was alone in my failures. I was never to blame entirely when all was lost, when my desperate cures had no effect on the suffering of those I loved. For who can blame a man waiting, the doors open, the windows open, food offered, arms stretched wide? Who can blame him if the visitor does not arrive?[51]

Nanapush is a survivor. He survives the coughing sickness by telling stories, not allowing death a word in edgewise. He survives that first season of post-apocalyptic grief by conserving energy in his cabin until the priest, Father Damien, arrives with treaty rations. And, when he and Eli spend a hungry winter together, he guides Eli on the hunt, erasing the distance between them with the song he has been given by his spirit helpers, alone in his cabin, maintaining the heartbeat with his drum, until, in the trance that comes over him, the song sings itself and directs Eli to the place deep in the forest where a moose has stopped to feed.

Dream hunting was an important component of Algonquian woodland culture. Spiritual leaders called upon the manitous to help them in their hunt, and often the location of moose, deer, or other beings would be made known to them in their dreams, enabling them to guide the hunters to their prey. Fleur, too, can be seen using this power in the novel, and her dreams of game also guide Eli in his hunting and help feed the family. The assistance of the manitous was not a given, however, and so it was important to maintain balance with one's spirit helpers and understand the reciprocal nature of the relationship. John

Tanner, in his eighteenth-century memoir, spoke often of his adopted mother's visions. He wrote how he would be wakened from a deep sleep to hear her say, "My son, last night I sung and prayed to the Great Spirit, and when I slept there came to me one like a man, and said to me … tomorrow you shall eat bear."[52] She would then proceed to give specific directions as to where the bear would be waiting. Tanner did not question her power and does not attempt to offer any kind of rationalization when her predictions prove true. This manner of relationship with the spirit and animal world was simply a given of the Anishinaabe space in which he was raised.

Erdrich notes how, as a young girl, she came upon Tanner's memoir in her grandfather's home on the Turtle Mountain reservation and, between herself and her sister, Lise, managed to read the book until the binding wore off and the pages broke loose.[53] Here Erdrich gleaned what she calls the "terrible fixity of purpose" attending survival and how "starvation haunted Ojibwa winters." Details that appear in *Tracks*, such as dream hunting or the necessity in lean times to boil and eat one's own moccasins, can be found here. We also learn of Tanner's adopted mother, Net-no-kwas, and how she wielded great authority among both whites and Indians. Tanner speculates that, "she could accomplish whatever she pleased … in some measure, because she never attempted to do anything which was not right and just."[54] Net-no-kwa's power is similar to Fleur's, although her moral authority also evokes that of Nanapush who, despite mischievous tendencies, has never killed a man and seeks to influence his world through healing and persuasion. In this way, both Nanapush and Net-no-kwa represent *mino bimaadiziwin*, the good life characterized by proper action, and this is the aspect of tradition that most sustains them.

The passage in which Eli hunts moose, guided by Nanapush's vision, is beautifully rendered, evoking the manner in which traditional Anishinaabe life and custom are fixed to the rhythms of survival, of enduring extreme hardship to procure food for one's family, and the practical and spiritual expertise this requires. When Eli finishes butchering the moose, he must bind the warm slabs of meat to his body, using the moose's own sinew to secure it to him. It is a basic, almost primal, moment of regeneration as,

> he pressed to himself a new body, red and steaming, swung a roast to his back and knotted its ligaments around his chest. He bound a rack of ribs across his hat, jutting over his face, and tied them on beneath his chin. Last of all he wrapped new muscles, wide and thick, around each forearm.

Eli recreates himself in this moment, and Nanapush leads him cautiously back home, beating

> out footsteps for Eli to hear and follow. Each time he speeded I slowed him. I strengthened the rhythm whenever he faltered beneath the weight he bore.

> In that way, he returned, and when I could hear the echo of his pounding breath, I went outside to help him, still in my song.⁵⁵

When Lulu arrives at Nanapush's doorstep, during the delivery of Fleur's second child, her feet frozen in their red plastic shoes, Nanapush has to again call upon all of his resources to save her. He recounts,

> In the terrible times, the evils I do not speak of, when the earth swallowed back all it had given me to love, I gave birth in loss. I was like a woman in my suffering, but my children were all delivered into death. It was contrary, backward, but now I had a chance to put things into a proper order.

He sings, cradling Lulu's feet in his armpits while the fevers and tremors crash through her body. He tells her stories, talking endlessly, "until you entered the swell and ebb and were sustained."⁵⁶ When the priest brings the town doctor to the cabin, Nanapush must decide whether to abandon Lulu to their care or trust in his own power, knowing that western medicine, though it might save her life, will lead to amputation and the crushing of Lulu's spirit. But, despite his doubts about his own ability, Nanapush will not relinquish his daughter in name to the careless white physician, and ultimately his own medicine prevails.

It is never precisely clear until the final chapters of the novel how land lies at the heart of the story. The reader is absorbed in the drama of love, hunger, birth, and survival, even though the threat of displacement is always there, in the sounding of axes in the distance, the far-off crashing of trees in the forest, the newly acquired wealth of the mixed-blood Morriseys and Lazarres, the need for Fleur to have traveled to Argus in the first place to acquire money to pay the fees on her allotments. The desperate state of things is only clarified, however, when, after yet another lean winter, Father Damien arrives once more with rations and news.

It might have been the easiest thing for Erdrich to treat the priest assigned to the reservation as yet another quasi-villainous character, but Father Damien proves an ally, actually taking up the struggle of the traditionalist Pillagers and Kashpaws by pointing out to them the color-coded map showing the advance of the lumber company and the tightening ring around reservation lands, including their own. Nanapush, upon hearing this news, observes, "I was taught by the Jesuits … I know about law. I know that 'trust' means they can't tax our parcels."⁵⁷ But the law, more often than not, is created to serve those in power. Excess tribal lands created by the passing of the Dawes Act and its successors were leased out to the lumber companies, who were able to extract the valuable resources of the land for virtually no money down. The 1906 Burke Act made it possible to eliminate the 25-year "trust" period meant to protect Native people from having their land swindled out from under them. The Anishinaabe lands presumably in trust were transformed into "force-fee patents," which required that taxes be paid, often unbeknownst to the allotment holders. By 1920, on the

Turtle Mountain Reservation, nearly 90 percent of the original Native allotments were either sold off or put up for auction owing to the inability of the residents to pay taxes they didn't even know they owed.[58]

Although the Kashpaw and Pillager families bond together once more to try to prevent this outcome by harvesting and selling the bark used to prepare popular commercial remedies of the time, their efforts in the end are insufficient, the system already rigged against them from the start, regardless of their efforts. It is Nector Kashpaw, Eli's younger brother, who brings the money they earned to the Indian agent's office, but, as we later learn, an additional late fee was tacked on to the total, and Nector only has the money to secure one allotment—that belonging to his mother, Margaret. As Deborah Madsen observes, it is the demands made by the corrupt Indian agent that force Nector to "choose between paying the taxes on Pillager or Kashpaw land. Thus, the action by the corrupt representative of the U.S. government fractures family relationships and, with them, alliances within the tribal community."[59] Fleur is forced off her land, Eli ends up working for the lumber company, and Lulu is sent to the Indian boarding school, where her repeated attempts to run away result in humiliating punishments designed to break her spirit.

Nanapush, who only gave out his name in writing the one time in his life, on Lulu's baptismal record, decides to run for tribal chairmanship in the end, wryly observing that,

> we were becoming ... a tribe of filing cabinets and triplicates, a tribe of single-space documents, directives, policy. A tribe of pressed trees. A tribe of chicken-scratch that can be scattered by a wind, diminished to ashes by one struck match.[60]

He is, of course, referring to the manner in which settler bureaucracy has reduced the tribe to its laws, decrees, and paper surveillance. There is a greater irony, however, in that the paper that now contains and controls their identity is produced from the very lifeblood of the forest, the pulp of the trees that have been harvested from Anishinaabe lands. And the people are now mere marks on paper, tracks in a blizzard of white. And yet, as a result of the tracks Nanapush surreptitiously left on the priest's baptismal record, Nanapush and Margaret are able to reclaim Lulu from the boarding school at the end. It turns out that, on occasion, the x-marks made under coercive circumstances can witness in favor of indigenous peoples, and it is just Nanapush's luck that the tracks he left, the signing of his name, works to reunite at least part of his fractured family and leave hope for generations to follow.

The Round House

Erdrich explores the lives of those future generations of Anishinaabe in many of her later novels, including her 2012 novel *The Round House*. Different family lines are plotted out, but the lives of characters continue to intersect in surprising ways and, although the story takes place at the end of the twentieth century, Nanapush makes an appearance in the narrative in a compelling manner that proves central to the concerns of the novel. *The Round House*, as already stated, is meant to shed light on the systemic injustices that have left Native women vulnerable to sexual predation, largely by white males—a dynamic that has prevailed over centuries, with no serious attempt to repair the social imbalances allowing these violations to recur. Although the historical circumstances have changed somewhat since the timeframe of *Tracks*, the underlying doctrine is the same, as articulated by Traci Brynne Voyles, who claims that, "the study of environmental injustice is the study of race, resources, and power and their intersections with gender and sexuality."[61] Muscogee/Creek legal scholar Sarah Deer draws similar parallels, noting,

> there has been a significant increase in crime committed against Native people in North Dakota since 2008, likely attributable at least in part to the man camps associated with the oil boom. Journalists and tribal leaders have described a higher-than-usual rate of prostitution, drug use, and crime.

She concludes that the harm

> Native women are experiencing as a result of the exploding fracking business has parallels with the harm being done to the planet—the land and water are being poisoned as the hearts and spirits of native women break. Thus another generation experiences displacement and abuse.[62]

Erdrich already anticipated as much when she wrote *Tracks* some 30 years earlier. She explicitly linked the despoliation of Anishinaabe woodlands for commercial gain with the rape of Fleur and the ensuing discourse surrounding control of the narrative of Fleur's body—a discourse claiming either monstrous paternity or placing the blame on her own promiscuity, founded in the presumed availability and exploitability of racialized bodies. Just as the law will bend to power in the claiming of Native land, so will it bend to power in the claiming of Native women.

The plot of *The Round House* is meant to flesh out the legal ambiguities that allow this violent exploitation to continue, exposing the structures of jurisprudence that make it so difficult to prosecute cases of sexual assault on Indian reservations. In this case, Linden Lark, the perpetrator, has carefully exploited existing law so that, even though his guilt is not in question, there is no legal statute under which he can be brought to justice for his horrible crime. Perhaps to further drive this point home, Erdrich has made the victim's husband, Antone Bazil Coutts, a reservation judge who has spent his career trying to carefully build up indigenous case law, one small decision at a time. In attempting to explain this over dinner to his 13-year-old son Joe, the novel's narrator, he constructs an absurd edifice of kitchen utensils piled one atop the other, all of them mired in burnt casserole noodles. Looking over his impossible and precarious construction, he says,

> Everything we do, no matter how trivial, must be crafted keenly. We are trying to build a solid base here for our sovereignty. We try to press against the boundary of what we are allowed, walk a step past the edge. Our records will be scrutinized by Congress one day and decisions on whether to enlarge our jurisdiction will be made. Some day. *We want the right to prosecute criminals of all races on all lands within our original boundaries.* [63]

Judge Antone Coutts is an honorable man who has placed his hope in the possibility of colonial justice, as broken as it is, and this proves insufficient in the end to bring his wife's rapist to account or to heal his family's wounds. This conflict will be clear to most readers, but what might not be as evident is the subtle comparison Erdrich is making to traditional indigenous law. Couts himself is all too aware of it, observing that once, in keeping with Anishinaabe justice, "we would have sat down to decide his [Lark's] fate. Our present system though …"[64] and here his voice trails off, for there is nothing left to add. Western justice is impersonal and inflexible, save for where it bends to power. It seemingly does not allow for improvisation, nor does it adjust for circumstances—at least not indigenous circumstances.

Materializing around the edges of Erdrich's narrative is the awareness of indigenous legal custom and how it operates even within the superstructure of western jurisprudence. When Joe's mother, Geraldine, retreats to her bed, refusing for weeks to come out, his father, the judge, decides they must at least eat together and attempt to keep the ceremony of the family gathering in place. When Geraldine simply turns her back to them, he ignores this and, like Nanapush, keeps up a one-sided monologue night after night, "a lone paddler on an endless lake of silence."[65] In one of these monologues, he seems to recall that,

> of course an Ojibwe person's clan meant everything at one time and no one didn't have a clan, thus you knew your place in the world and your relationship to all other beings. The crane, the bear, the loon, the catfish, lynx, kingfisher, caribou, muskrat—all of these animals and others in various tribal divisions, including the eagle, the marten, the dear, the wolf—people were part of these clans and were thus governed by special relationships with one another and with the animals. This was in fact … the first system of Ojibwe law. The clan system punished and rewarded; it dictated marriages and regulated commerce, it told which animals a person could hunt and which to appease, which would have pity on the doodem or a fellow being of that clan, which would carry messages up to the Creator over to the spirit world, down through the layers of the earth or across the lodge to a sleeping relative.[66]

At a later moment in the novel we are offered a narrative of indigenous justice gone awry. Joe's grandfather, Mooshum, apparently talking in his sleep, tells the story of a traditional Anishinaabe wife and mother, Akii. During a time of starvation, Akii is falsely accused of turning *wiindigoo*, or being possessed of a spirit that makes a person behave like an animal, perceiving other humans as prey. Tribal justice demands that Akii be killed, but, to avoid the probability of revenge, it has to be done by someone from her own family, a blood relative of her own clan. This rules out her accuser husband, Mirage, who is, by custom, of a different clan than his wife. And so the task falls to her eldest son.

> The boy was given a knife and told to kill his mother. He was twelve years old. The men would hold her. He should cut her neck. The boy began to weep, but he was told that he must do it anyway. His name was Nanapush.[67]

Because he knows his mother is not truly *wiindigoo*, Nanapush resists, thrusting the knife at one of the men instead. The men finally determine that they will drown her instead, everyone participating in the act, so they bring Akii to the lake and thrust her down into a hole in the ice. When she doesn't resurface, the men depart, but Nanapush returns and is able to pull his mother out, she having sustained herself by breathing in the thin sliver of space between the water and the ice. Akii tells her son how a fish spoke to her while she was in the water and sang for her a buffalo song. Here, Erdrich signals her understanding of the kind of deep ecological knowledge that traditional peoples routinely incorporate into their generational understanding of Native space, and how settler encroachment already plays a role in the disruption of that system. The fish tells Akii that it misses the buffalo who, in days past, would come to the water to drink and shed their tasty fat ticks for the fish to eat. But, with the buffalo hunted to near extinction, the fish no longer benefit from the buffalo's presence. The rabbit too, we discover, longs for the return of the buffalo who once churned up the earth with their massive hooves, making the grass grow better for rabbits to eat. Akii tells Nanapush "all the animals miss the buffalo, but they miss the real Anishinaabeg too."

And so Nanapush is sent by his mother to find the buffalo, the last buffalo as it turns out, one that he claimed to have hunted in the early passages of *Tracks*. When he discovers her, "a hide draped loosely over rickety bones," he sings the song his mother has taught him—the song she learned from the fish. "Old Buffalo woman, I hate to kill you," he says, "but then again, as you are the only hope for my family, perhaps you were waiting for me." As he is butchering the beast, taking care in all the ways Eli had when he hunted the moose, a snow storm blows out of nowhere, and Nanapush must enter the cavity of the buffalo's body to keep himself alive. And, "with his belly full and with the warmth pressing around him ... this buffalo adopted Nanapush and told him all she knew."[68] Nanapush is ultimately able to bring the buffalo meat home to his mother, and so they survive by listening to their animal helpers and conducting themselves in a good way.

Nanapush knew that his mother was falsely accused, and that his father and the other members of the band had not followed the good traditional way when they accused her. We are told how, when he was ordered to kill his mother "a great rift opened in his heart ... a crack so deep it went down forever."[69] And this is why, in later years he seeks to understand and uphold traditional justice. It is why he ultimately seeks to become tribal chairman, and it is why, on the instruction of the buffalo women spirit, he has the round house built. She tells him

> your people were brought together by us buffalo once. You knew how to hunt and use us. Your clan gave you laws. You had many rules by which you operated. Rules that respected us and forced you to work together. Now we are gone, but as you have once sheltered in my body, so now you understand. The round house will be my body, the poles my ribs, the fire my heart. It will be the body of your mother and it must be respected the same way.[70]

This is the story that beats at the heart of Erdrich's book in its quiet yet insistent suggestion that traditional Anishinaabe values provided a kind of glue that, prior to colonization, kept all the occupants of Native space together in a good way. Perhaps, she seems to suggest, this is the way out of the cycles of violence and degradation that have so severely wounded the Earth and its occupants in this era of settler colonial dominance.

Some Sources for *Tracks*

Maze of Injustice: The Failure to Protect Indigenous Women from Sexual Violence in the USA (New York: Amnesty International, 2007).
Selwyn Dewdney, *The Sacred Scrolls of the Southern Ojibway* (Toronto: University of Toronto Press, 1975).
Louise Erdrich, *Books and Islands in Ojibwe Country* (Washington, D.C.: National Geographic, 2003).
Basil Johnston, *The Manitous: The Spiritual World of the Ojibway* (St. Paul: Minnesota Historical Society Press, 1995).
Ruth Landes, *Ojibwa Religion and the Midéwiwin* (Madison: University of Wisconsin Press, 1968).
Melissa L. Meyer, "'We Can Not Get a Living as We Used To': Dispossession and the White Earth Anishinaabeg, 1889–1920," *The American Historical Review* 96:2 (1991).
John Tanner, *The Falcon: A Narrative of the Captivity and Adventures of John Tanner* (New York: Penguin Books, 1994).
Christopher Vecsey, *Traditional Ojibwa Religion and its Historical Changes* (Philadelphia: The American Philosophical Society, 1983).

Gerald Vizenor, *The People Named the Chippewa: Narrative Histories* (Minneapolis: University of Minnesota Press, 1884).
William W. Warren, *History of the Ojibway People* (St. Paul: Minnesota Historical Society Press, 1984).

Notes

1. Nancy J. Peterson, "History, Postmodernism, and Louise Erdrich's *Tracks*," *Publication of the Modern Language Association* 109:5 (1994), pp. 982–994, 986–987.
2. I qualify this statement in recognition that Anishinaabe author David Treuer has challenged the authenticity of the language Erdrich uses here. Erdrich herself has taken to preemptively stating, as she does in the afterword to *The Round House*, that "any mistakes in the Ojibwe language are mine and do not reflect on my patient teachers." David Treuer, *Native American Fiction: A User's Manual* (Saint Paul: Graywolf Press, 2006), 62–64. Louise Erdrich, *The Round House* (New York: Harper Perennial, 2013), 321.
3. Louise Erdrich, *Tracks* (New York: Perennial, 1988), 1.
4. Erdrich never refers precisely to the reservation in her novels as the Turtle Mountain Reservation, and we can assume it is meant to be a composite of Anishinaabe spaces, to which she gives the name Little No Horse in a later novel. The Beauchamp Treaty of 1863, referenced in *Tracks*, was important in creating the bounds of the White Lake reservation and carving out territory for the Pembina Band in North Dakota, but, according to Connie Jacobs, the actual Turtle Mountain Reservation was not bounded until 1882. See Connie A. Jacobs, "A History of the Turtle Mountain Band of Chippewas," *Approaches to Teaching the Works of Louise Erdrich*, Eds. Greg Sarris, Connie A. Jacobs, and James R. Giles (New York: Modern Language Association, 2004), 29.
5. See Melissa L. Meyer, "'We Can Not Get a Living as We Used To': Dispossession and the White Earth Anishinaabeg, 1889–1920," *The American Historical Review* 96:2 (1991) pp. 368–394.
6. Erdrich, *Tracks*, 2.
7. Erdrich, *Tracks*, 2.
8. See Gloria Bird "Searching for Evidence of Colonialism at Work: A Reading of Louise Erdrich's *Tracks*," *Wicazo Sa Review* 8:2 (1992), pp. 40–47.
9. See Deborah L. Madsen, "Louise Erdrich: The Aesthetics of *Mino Bimaadiziwin*," *Louise Erdrich: Tracks, The Last Report on the Miracle at Little No Horse, The Plague of Doves*, Ed. Deborah L. Madsen (New York: Continuum International, 2011), 6.
10. Gerald Vizenor, *The People Named the Chippewa: Narrative Histories* (Minneapolis: University of Minnesota Press, 1884), 2–3.
11. John Tanner, *The Falcon: A Narrative of the Captivity and Adventures of John Tanner* (New York: Penguin Books, 1994), 184.
12. See Basil Johnston, *The Manitous: The Spiritual World of the Ojibway* (St. Paul: Minnesota Historical Society Press, 1995), 11–13.
13. Erdrich, *Tracks*, 33.
14. Lawrence W. Gross, "The Trickster and World Maintenance: An Anishinaabe Reading of Louise Erdrich's *Tracks*," *Studies in American Indian Literature* 17:3 (2005), pp. 48–66.
15. Erdrich, *Tracks*, 4.
16. Erdrich, *Tracks*, 97.
17. Erdrich, *Tracks*, 99.
18. Erdrich, *Tracks*, 4.
19. Erdrich, *Tracks*, 33.
20. Erdrich, *Tracks* 3.
21. Erdrich, *Tracks*, 6.

22 Erdrich, *Tracks*, 46.
23 Erdrich, *Tracks*, 6.
24 Gross, 50.
25 William W. Warren, *History of the Ojibway People* (St. Paul: Minnesota Historical Society Press, 1984), 256.
26 Erdrich, *Tracks*, 20.
27 Erdrich, *Tracks*, 8.
28 Erdrich, *Tracks*, 11.
29 See Drew Lopenzina, "Le Jeune Dreams of Moose: Altered States Among the Montgnais in the Jesuit Relations of 1634," *Early American Studies* 13:1 (2015), pp. 3–37.
30 Louise Erdrich, *Books and Islands in Ojibwe Country* (Washington, D.C.: National Geographic, 2003), 55.
31 Michael Angel, *Preserving the Sacred: Historical Perspectives on the Ojibwa Midewiwin* (Winnipeg: University of Manitoba Press, 2002), 23.
32 Ruth Landes, *Ojibwa Religion and the Midéwiwin* (Madison: University of Wisconsin Press, 1968), 31.
33 Joy Harjo, "The Flood," *The Women Who Fell from the Sky* (New York: W.W. Norton, 1994), 14.
34 Erdrich, *Tracks*, 35
35 Erdrich, *Tracks*, 39.
36 Erdrich, *Tracks*, 31.
37 Quoted in Gross, 52.
38 Erdrich, *Tracks*, 59.
39 See Selwyn Dewdney, *The Sacred Scrolls of the Southern Ojibway* (Toronto: University of Toronto Press, 1975), 31–32. The story of the spirit bear's four "breakthroughs" stands at the beginning of a 103-foot-long migration scroll made on birchbark, in the possession of James Red Sky, and is an important part of the rites pertaining to the sacred Midewiwin society.
40 Erdrich, *Tracks*, 58–60.
41 Erdrich, *Tracks*, 61.
42 Erdrich, *Tracks*, 195.
43 Gloria Anzaldua, *Borderlands/La Frontera: The New Mestiza* (San Francisco: Aunt Lute Books, 1987), 24.
44 Erdrich, *Tracks*, 192–195.
45 Erdrich, *Tracks*, 75.
46 Erdrich, *Tracks*, 75.
47 Erdrich, *Tracks*, 73.
48 Erdrich, *Tracks*, 137.
49 Erdrich, *Tracks*, 70–71.
50 Gross, 54.
51 Erdrich, *Tracks*, 177.
52 Tanner, 32.
53 Erdrich, "Introduction," *The Falcon: A Narrative of the Captivity and Adventures of John Tanner* (New York: Penguin Books, 1994), xi–xiii.
54 Tanner, 27.
55 Erdrich, *Tracks*, 103–104.
56 Erdrich, *Tracks*, 167.
57 Erdrich, *Tracks*, 174.
58 Amelia V. Katanski, "Ojibwe Roots of Erdrich's Novels," *Approaches to Teaching the Works of Louise Erdrich*, Eds. Greg Sarris, Connie A. Jacobs, and James R. Giles (New York: Modern Language Association, 2004), 68.
59 Madsen, 7.
60 Erdrich, *Tracks*, 225.

61 Traci Brynne Voyles, *Wastelanding: Legacies of Uranium Mining in Navajo Country* (Minneapolis: University of Minnesota Press, 2015), 23–24.
62 Sarah Deer, *The Beginning and End of Rape: Confronting Sexual Violence in Native America* (Minneapolis: University of Minnesota Press, 2015), 78.
63 Erdrich, *The Round House*, 227–230; italics in original.
64 Erdrich, *Round House*, 196.
65 Erdrich, *Round House*, 152.
66 Erdrich, *Round House*, 153–154.
67 Erdrich, *Round House*, 181.
68 Erdrich, *Round House*, 186.
69 Erdrich, *Round House*, 213.
70 Erdrich, *Round House*, 214–215.

CONCLUSION
Greetings from Standing Rock

In August of 1846, Henry David Thoreau travelled from his home in Concord, Massachusetts, to the town of Indian Island, Maine, in search of a Native guide to lead him on a planned expedition to the summit of Mt. Ktaadn. Believing himself to be something of an expert on the character and traditions of the "red man," Thoreau was, nevertheless, disenchanted with the apparent squalor of the living conditions of the Penobscot, observing somewhat glumly that, "these were once a powerful tribe. Politics is all the rage with them now."[1] Thoreau does not let on why "politics" should be considered a negative thing, but clearly he believed that Indians and politics did not mix. What had Native people to do with politics anyway? It seemed to diminish them in his eyes—to compromise their once noble bearing and displace them from the pure state of nature to which he presumed they belonged.

Fast forward to November 2016, when I found myself stuffing my backpack full with a week's worth of clothing and gear and catching a plane to Bismarck, North Dakota, and taking a rental car from there to the Standing Rock Sioux Reservation. I had come to participate in the ongoing NoDAPL movement, a large-scale indigenous-centered action attempting to halt the construction of the Dakota Access Pipeline. Energy Transfer Partners, the corporation responsible for the project, was at that moment preparing to drill under the Missouri River in order to connect some 1,700 miles of oil pipeline running from the Bakkan shale oil fields (located on the Fort Berthold Reservation of the Mandan, Hidatsa, and Arikara Nation near the Canadian border) all the way to Illinois, where it would hitch up with existing infrastructure to distribute oil to refineries in Texas and Louisiana. I didn't know anybody at Standing Rock when I went and had little notion of what I would be getting into, but I felt something transformative and exciting was taking place. Politics was all the rage there. As someone who has worked to be both an ally to Native people and a proponent of social and environmental justice, it seemed important that I be there too, to help out, to back up my declared commitments, and to be a witness to history. Unlike Thoreau, I came to Native space specifically for the politics and was not disappointed by what I found.

Oceti Sakowin, or the Seven Council Fires camp, where most newcomers to the movement camped, was positioned at the confluence of the Missouri and the Cannonball Rivers, both of which coursed like brilliant glittering ribbons of blue through the golden rolling prairieland on the verge of the Standing Rock Reservation. There were roughly 8,000 people living there when I arrived, and the camp sprawled out like a picturesque, anachronistic fantasy of multicolored dome tents, tipis, yurts, campers, portapotties, people on horseback riding beside cars, trucks, and vans, and, improbably, a large white geodesic dome seated near the center of all the activity. Raised along the main road entering the camp were dozens of flags snapping in the persistent breeze, representing the many visiting indigenous nations who had thrown in their support with the Standing Rock tribe.

For a week, I was away from everyone I knew, unplugged from the rest of the world and all its conveniences, shivering in my one-person tent at night in single-digit temperatures, and yet aware of feeling completely connected and centered in my purpose and the collective purpose of all those gathered. The camp was a ceremony, the goal of which was peaceful resolution to a historically intractable problem—not just the pipeline, but the determined despoliation of the Earth's resources urged along by the insatiable demands of settler colonial culture. And most everyone who came to visit and pitch in observed these same rites,

FIGURE C.1 November 2016 view of the Oceti Sakowin campsite and the Missouri River at Standing Rock (author's photo)

foregoing the comforts of home, turning off cameras and cell phones, swearing off alcohol and firearms, sharing food and resources, and working as a community toward a shared vision. The spirit of the movement was effectively captured by a single phrase, *mni wiconi*—water is life.

Water is life.

It was not simply some New Age, feel-good catchphrase born of the political moment to splash over posters, t-shirts, and bumper-stickers. It was a claim that lay at the spiritual, ceremonial, and practical center of lived Native experience on this North American continent. The world itself began, in many indigenous stories, with a woman falling from the sky into a realm covered in water. With the help of the other beings of this realm, she initiated the ceremony that would bring forth everything needed for life to thrive. In her book *Braiding Sweetgrass*, published in 2013, 3 years before events at Standing Rock erupted, Robin Wall Kimmerer related a Haudenosaunee Thanksgiving address that evokes the spirit of this understanding:

> we give thanks to the waters of the world, we are grateful that the waters are still here and doing their duty of sustaining life on mother earth. Water is life, quenching our thirst and providing us with strength, making the plants grow and sustaining us all. Let us gather our minds together and with one mind, we send greetings and thanks to the water."[2]

The "water protectors" (as we were called) at Standing Rock were carrying this simple, sacred idea forward, with one mind, in hopes of preventing the almost inevitable contamination of the upper Missouri's near-pristine waters and reaffirming the value of all the Earth's water sources.

The action at Standing Rock was ultimately unsuccessful in preventing Energy Transfer Partners from drilling beneath the river and laying their pipeline. But the action cannot be labeled a failure. Native people have been fighting these types of projects on their lands for generations. The violations taking place at Standing Rock were happening, and had been happening, to some degree at virtually every other Native reservation across the country, whether in the form of oil extraction, uranium mining, the construction of hydro-electric dams flooding Native people off their lands, the clear-cutting of forests, the laying down of intercontinental railroad tracks—the list goes on. How different, in fact, were events at Standing Rock from the circumstances faced by the nineteenth-century Pequot preacher, William Apess, when he formed a peaceful movement to stop local overseers from harvesting wood and other resources from the Mashpee reservation on Cape Cod in 1833. How different was it from the circumstances faced by the Kiowa warrior Satanta when he declared to U.S. officials at the Medicine Lodge Treaty of 1867 that,

> A long time ago this land belonged to our fathers; but when I go up to the [Arkansas] river I see a camp of soldiers, and they are cutting my wood down, or killing my buffalo ... and when I see it my heart feels like bursting with sorrow.[3]

And it was certainly nothing new for the Lakota, Nakota, and Dakota people. As Lower Brule Sioux historian Nick Estes writes, "what happened at Standing Rock was the most recent iteration of an Indian War that never ends."[4] What made events at Standing Rock unusual, however, was the national attention it ultimately received and the sheer number of Native nations that banded together to show their support for the Lakota people. It was an unprecedented display of indigenous solidarity, necessitated, perhaps, by a growing realization in Indian country that the Earth is at a tipping point—there was no more time to put one's own concerns ahead of others. Our minds must be gathered together as one.

It should come as little surprise, then, that this effort toward encouraging ecologically sustainable models of development, agriculture, and energy should begin in Native space. Native people have been bearing the brunt of western culture's irresponsible intrusions for centuries. But Standing Rock gave us a blueprint for how to resist, and, for once, a portion of the white world took notice. As Dina Gilio-Whitaker observes, even in the settler community, there was a growing recognition

> that the assaults on the environment committed by relentless corporate "extractivism" and development are assaults on the possibility for humans to sustain themselves in the future. They recognize that in some ways, what happened to the Indians is now happening to everybody not in the 1 percent.[5]

Since Standing Rock, a new federal administration with a bent toward protecting and promoting extractive industries has attempted to ramrod its policies through all legal and cultural barriers, but this has only engendered a renewed sense of purpose and resistance. There are more large-scale environmental protests gearing up. Native peoples across the continent are organizing like never before. In 2018, for the first time in the 230-year history of the United States government, not just one, but two Native women were elected to Congress, representing the states of Kansas and New Mexico. In Canada, protests against the Coastal Gas Link Pipeline through Wet'suwet'en lands brought the rail lines to a standstill for a week in the winter of 2020, and new truth and reconciliation policies are at least attempting to shed new light on past national abuses. In the U.S., tribal enrollments are up, as are overall population totals for indigenous peoples. Language reclamation projects have taken hold across the continent, and, for some tribes, courses for language instruction are even being offered online. Native scholarly organizations such as NAISA (Native American and Indigenous Studies) and SAIL (Society of American Indian Literature) have strong memberships and backing. As the reservation DJ announces at the start of the movie *Smoke Signals*, "it's a good day to be indigenous." Or at least there is hope.

Nevertheless, it can still be intimidating, for both Natives and non-Natives alike, to decide to bring the kinds of issues discussed in this book into the classroom. Whether the current trajectory in Native space remains forward-moving or the struggle falls back into old familiar battlegrounds, students will continue to come into class expecting James Fenimore Cooper-type Indians, locked in the past, in the throes of vanishing, speaking in clipped noble cadences, and serving as spirit warriors commissioned to weep over western civilization's continued bad behavior. Our students are not necessarily to blame. It is what most of them have been taught throughout their lives, both in and out of the classroom, and you will mostly discover that this programming cannot be completely undone in the course of a single semester. This is, in fact, what makes the project, which should be so positive, so truly daunting at times. Settler colonial culture has a way of constantly pushing back. It doesn't want to hear the news of indigenous resurgence you've come to tell or confront the violent legacies of colonialism. So, it has planted a myriad of pseudo-intellectual defenses in place to keep people from absorbing this knowledge. Like Thoreau, students will automatically wonder why the class has to be so "political." Why can't we just study the "nice" Indian literature and talk about nature, vision-quests, spirit animals, teepees, and buffalo hunts.

But the literature *is* political—even when it doesn't want to be. Denying the political nature of the history and the literature is just another way of making Native people vanish, of dismissing their concerns and refusing to be witness to the catalogue of wrongs committed against them by settler colonial nation-states. It is a way of denying the vitality of Native cultures. When we deny the political, the only remaining recourse is to feel sorry for all those things that happened in "the past," without having to do anything about it or to feel responsible or complicit in the ongoing abuses of sovereign rights. But, to acknowledge this complex history, to call up the traditional aspects of the literature and forefront the ways that writers of Native literature continue to engage with all this history and culture, is to meet Native peoples in the present, to recognize them where they are now, and to seek equity and fair treatment in all things moving forward. Along the way, you will also find that Native literature easily holds its own against the most rewarding and beautifully crafted works being produced in our era.

So, this is a challenge—to embrace the difficulty, to understand that you will make mistakes, you will pronounce things incorrectly, you will get some of the history wrong, there are things you just won't know, can't know, and must not pretend to know—you will have to proceed with the unsettling knowledge that you may not be the "expert" that your professional training and your positionality in front of a class of eager students suggest you should be. But, if you are willing to learn from the literature (and from the excellent body of Native-centered scholarship that exists today and even, quite often, from your own students) and do the necessary groundwork, you can commit to a process that will allow you to grow into these materials and teach them with the respect and tribal specificity they deserve.

I didn't know what to expect at Standing Rock. I had very real concerns that I might be arrested, beaten, sprayed with tear gas, attacked by dogs. But those fears quickly peeled away once I fell into the rhythm of camp life at Oceti Sakowin and was welcomed by the people I met there, both Native and non-Native. There were certainly hangers-on at camp—people who were simply there for "the scene," using up valuable space and resources while contributing nothing. But, once people saw that you were committed, willing to pitch in and be a protector—then you were regarded with kindness, hospitality, and respect. The chance of getting arrested, sprayed, or attacked remained just as real—but so much easier to face when you feel part of a community and a cause. And that has been true with my journey teaching Native American literature as well. It requires commitment. I began with a great deal of anxiety, worried that I hadn't the authority to teach these materials, and that I would be rejected by people in the indigenous community who would view me as an imposter. But I also learned that the onus was on me to build trust and demonstrate that I wasn't just a hanger-on, someone in it for "the scene" but not the "politics."

It shouldn't be easy. There is a lot at stake. But I think of Wendy Rose's "Story-teller," the "sun-dried greasy gambling bones" in her hand, preparing to loose those stories into the world, knowing that there can be no continuance, no survivance, without risk.

Notes

1 Henry David Thoreau, "Ktaadn," *The Maine Woods* (New York: Penguin Books, 1988), 8.
2 Robin Wall Kimmerer, *Braiding Sweet Grass: Indigenous Wisdom, Scientific Knowledge, and the Teachings of Plants* (Canada: Milkweed Editions, 2013), 311.
3 Quoted in Henry Morton Stanley, *My Early Travels and Adventures in America and Asia*, Vol. 1 (Cambridge: Cambridge University Press, 2011), 249.
4 Nick Estes, *Our History is Our Future: Standing Rock versus the Dakota Access Pipeline, and the Long Tradition of Indigenous Resistance* (New York: Verso, 2019), 10.
5 Dina Gilio-Whitaker, *As Long as Grass Grows: The Indigenous Fight for Environmental Justice from Colonization to Standing Rock* (Boston: Beacon Press, 2019), 12.

APPENDIX: SAMPLE SYLLABUS FOR NATIVE AMERICAN LITERATURE

Texts

William Apess, *A Son of the Forest*, University of Massachusetts Press
Louise Erdrich, *Tracks*, Harper Perennial
Ernestine Hayes, *Blonde Indian*, University of Arizona Press
John Joseph Mathews, *Sundown*, University of Oklahoma Press
Cheryl Savageau, *Dirt Road Home*, Curbstone Books
Blake Hausman, *Riding the Trail of Tears*, Bison Books
The Cherokee Removal: A Brief History with Documents, Ed. Theda Perdue, Bedford/St. Martins

Digital Readings Available from Web Sources

Zitkala-Sa, *American Indian Stories*, http://digital.library.upenn.edu/women/zitkala-sa/stories/stories.html
"Woman and Standing Rock," https://orionmagazine.org/article/women-standing-rock/
Molly of Denali, www.youtube.com/watch?v=27kWBgJGYpA&feature=youtu.be&fbclid=IwAR2Q2EyXNAxzG_WOExYg-a7Sgrp_1lJaj01XiKM8fzcP5lKNLGoo0BPJosY
On the Wampum Trail, www.penn.museum/blog/museum/wampum-field-report-part-2-kaianeraserekowa-stephanie-mach/

> We knew that stories were like medicine, that a story told one way could cure, that the same story told another way could injure.
>
> *Thomas King*

But spring is floating
to the canyon,
needles burst yellow
from the sugar pine;
the stories have built a new house.
Wendy Rose

Course Objectives

- Gain knowledge of the rich tradition of Native American cultures and literatures.
- Encourage an appreciation for literary and cultural encounters.
- Foster improvements in writing techniques, focusing on grammar, style, form, and content.
- Develop strategies for critical independent thinking.
- Encourage ability to confidently voice opinions and participate in substantive discussions based on demonstrably informed perspectives about culture, tradition, and the discourse of race in America.

Schedule

Week 1-T   **Introductions: Entering Native Space**
Wendy Rose (Hopi), "Story Keeper"
Source: Wendy Rose, *The Halfbreed Chronicles* (Los Angeles: West End Press, 1985).

Week 1-Tr   **Start Where You Are**
Pocahontas, Washington R*dsk*ns, and Other Virginia Indians

Week 2-T   **In the Beginning**
Arthur Parker (Seneca), "How the World Was Made" and "The Origin of the Longhouse" (handout)
Source: Arthur C. Parker, Seneca Myths and Folk Tales (Lincoln: University of Nebraska Press, 1989).

Week 2-Tr   Chief Irving Powless Jr. (Onondaga), "Treaty Making" (handout)
On the Wampum Trail (see Digital Readings)
Source: Treaty of Canandaigua, 1794: 200 Years of Treaty Relations Between the Iroquois Confederacy and the United States, Eds. G. Peter Jemison and Anna M. Shein (Santa Fe: Clear Light, 2000).

Week 3-T   **Earth Divers**
Thomas King (Cherokee), "You'll Never Guess What Happened" (handout)
Source: Thomas King, The Truth about Stories: A Native Narrative (Minneapolis: University of Minnesota Press, 2003).

Week 3-Tr	Joy Harjo (Creek), "The Woman Who Fell from the Sky" (in class) **Source:** Joy Harjo, *The Woman Who Fell from the Sky* (New York: W.W. Norton, 1994) **Suggested Reading:** Craig Womack (Creek), "In the Story Way," from *Red on Red: Native American Literary Separatism* (Minneapolis: University of Minnesota Press, 1999).
Week 4-T	**Lasting of the Mohegans** Samson Occom (Mohegan), "A Short Narrative of My Life" (handout) **Source:** *The Collected Writings of Samson Occom, Mohegan: Leadership and Literature in Eighteenth-Century Native America* (New York: Oxford University Press, 2006).
Week 4-Tr	Chapter on Mohegan writers, from *Dawnland Voices* (handout) **Source:** *Dawnland Voices: An Anthology of Indigenous Writing from New England*, Ed. Siobhan Senier (Lincoln: University of Nebraska Press, 2014).
Week 5-T	**A Light in the Forest** 2–3-page response paper due on Apess William Apess (Pequot), "A Son of the Forest," from *A Son of the Forest* (1–52) **Source:** Barry O'Connell, *On Our Own Ground: The Complete Writings of William Apess, a Pequot* (Amherst: University of Massachusetts Press, 1992). **Suggested Reading:** Scott Lyons (Anishinaabe), *X-Marks: Native Signatures of Assent* (Minneapolis: University of Minnesota Press, 2010).
Week 5-Tr	William Apess (adopted into Mashpee Wampanoag), "An Indian's Looking-Glass for the White Man," from *A Son of the Forest* **Source:** Barry O'Connell, *On Our Own Ground: The Complete Writings of William Apess, a Pequot* (Amherst: University of Massachusetts Press, 1992). **Suggested Reading:** Drew Lopenzina (Sicilian), "Letter from Barnstable Jail," *Journal of Native American and Indigenous Studies* 3:2 (2016), pp. 105–127.
Week 6-T	**Unhappy Trails** Marilou Awiakta (Eastern Cherokee), "The Origin of Corn" **Source:** Marilou Awaikta, *Selu: Seeking the Corn-Mother's Wisdom* (Golden, CO: Fulcrum, 1993). **Suggested Reading:** Daniel Heath Justice, *Our Fires Survive the Storm: A Cherokee Literary History* (Minneapolis: University of Minnesota Press, 2006).
Week 6-Tr	**Assignment due: Write a letter to the Editor of the *Cherokee Phoenix***

	Documents related to the Cherokee Removal from *The Cherokee Removal: A Brief History with Documents*
Week 7-T	Blake Hausman, *Riding the Trail of Tears*
Week 7-Tr	Blake Hausman, *Riding the Trail of Tears*
Week 8-T	**East of Eden**
	Zitkala-Sa (Lakota), *American Indian Stories*, Sections 1–4 (see Digital Readings)
	Suggested Reading: P. Jane Hafen, "'Help the Indians Help Themselves': Gertrude Bonnin, the SAI, and the NCAI," *American Indian Quarterly*, 25:2 (Summer 2013), pp. 189–213.
Week 8-Tr	**The Closing of the Frontier**
	Charles Eastman (Lakota), "Wounded Knee," from *The Deep Woods to Civilization* (handout)
	Layli Long Soldier, "38" (handout)
	Source: Charles Eastman, *From the Deep Woods to Civilization* (Boston: Little, Brown, 1916) and Layli Long Soldier, *Whereas* (Minneapolis: Graywolf Press, 2017).
	Suggested Reading: See last two chapters of Dee Brown, Bury My Heart at Wounded Knee: An Indian History of the American West (New York: Bantam Books, 1970) and Nick Estes, "Origins," Our History Is Our Future: Standing Rock versus the Dakota Access Pipeline, and the Long Tradition of Indigenous Resistance (New York: Verso, 2019).
Week 9-T	Louise Erdrich (Turtle Mountain Ojibwe), *Tracks*
	Suggested Reading:www.amnestyusa.org/pdfs/MazeOfInjustice.pdf
Week 9-Tr	Louise Erdrich (Turtle Mountain Ojibwe), *Tracks*
Week Ten-1	**Sunset, Sunrise**
	John Joseph Mathews, *Sundown*
	Suggested Reading: Gertrude Bonnin, Charles H. Fabens, and Matthew K. Sniffen, *Oklahoma's Poor Rich Indians: An Orgy of Graft and Exploitation of the Five Civilized Tribes—Legalized Robbery* (Philadelphia: Office of the Indian Rights Association, 1924).
Week 10-Tr	John Joseph Mathews, *Sundown*
Week 11-T	**2–3-page response paper due**
	John Joseph Mathews, *Sundown*
Week 11-Tr	**Native American Repatriation Day (Thanksgiving)—No Class**
Week 12-T	**This Is Indian Country**
	Cheryl Savageau (Abenaki), *Dirt Road Home*
	Suggested Reading: Margaret M. Bruchac (Abenaki), "Earthshapers and

	Placemakers: Algonkian Indian Stories and the Landscape," *Indigenous Archaeologies: Decolonizing Theories and Practice*, Eds. Claire Smith and H. Martin Wobst (New York: Routledge, 2005).
Week 12-Tr	**Red on Blonde**
	Ernestine Hayes (Tlingit), *Blonde Indian*
Week 13-T	Ernestine Hayes (Tlingit), *Blonde Indian*
Week 13-Tr	**Pipe Dreams**
	"Women and Standing Rock" (see Digital Readings)
Week 14-T	Joy Harjo (Muskogee/Creek), "She Had Some Horses" and "Perhaps the World Ends Here" (handout)
	Source: Joy Harjo, *She Had Some Horses* (New York: Thunder's Mouth Press, 1983) and Harjo, *The Woman Who Fell from the Sky* (New York: W.W. Norton, 1994).
Week 14-Tr	**Final Projects Due**
	Lisa Brooks (Abenaki), "At the Gathering Place"
	Watch *Molly of Denali* (see Digital Readings)
	Source: *American Indian Literary Nationalism* (Albuquerque: University of New Mexico Press, 2006).

INDEX

Abel 104–6
Abenaki 5, 49, 97, 127, 134, 140, 193, 194
Acoma 114; Pueblo 114, 136, 141
Akwesasne Notes 114
Alexie, Robert 84
Alexie, Sherman 2, 108, 150–6
Allen, Chadwick 32
Allotment Act 69, 71–73, 76, 77, 90, 92, 95, 101, 159, 176
Anishinaabe 1, 4, 11, 37, 58, 93, 108, 114, 125, 126, 135, 141, 158–64, 167, 169–78; Anishinaabeg 160, 179, 180
Apess, William 11, 12, 51–8, 63, 65, 66, 69, 90, 186, 190, 192
Arapahoe 117
Armstrong, Jeanette C. 114
Awiakta, Marilou 27, 192
awikhigan 37
Aztec 30, 31, 37

Baca, Damien 37
Baum, Frank L. 82
Bauerkemper, Joseph 95
Bernardin, Susan 66
Big Foot 68
Bird, Gloria 150–151
birchbark scrolls 29, 30, 37, 169, 182n.39
Blackfeet 9, 146, 147, 149; Blackfoot 10, 142
Blaeser, Kimberly 115, 117

Boas, Franz 148
Bonnin, Gertrude Simmons, 24, 65, 82–86, 96, 97, 193; as Zitkala-sa 11, 66, 67, 74–76, 103, 125, 130, 153, 190
Boudinot, Elias 59, 60
Brander Rasmussen, Birgit 30, 37
Brant, Beth 94
Brant, Joseph 58
Brill de Ramirez, Susan Berry, 27
Brooks, Joanna 41
Brooks, Lisa 5, 11, 30, 49, 55, 134, 136, 140, 194
Brothertown 47, 50
Brown, David 59
Brown, Dee 114, 193
Bruchac, Joseph 127
Bruchac, Margaret 85, 194
Butrick, Daniel 61, 62, 145

Caddo 88, 116, 117
Cahokia 32, 135
Callahan, Alice S. 66, 90, 91
Carlisle School 73, 75–7, 83, 84
Carlson, David J. 14
Ceremony 106, 107, 109, 115
Cheeshateaumauk, Caleb 20–22, 38, 41–43
Cherokee 27, 57–63, 72, 74, 88, 89, 92, 99, 143–145, 192 ; authors 15, 18, 25, 29, 46, 59, 89, 90, 93, 94, 96, 110, 191, 192; Eastern Cherokee 143; removal 60–63, 145, 190, 193; syllabary 59, 88; Cherokee vs. the State of Georgia 60

Cherokee Night 101
Cherokee Phoenix 59, 60, 89, 192
Cheyenne 74, 77, 93, 102, 111n14, 117
Chickasaw 92
Choctaw 92, 94
Cody, Buffalo Bill 93
Collier Act 101
Collier, John 101, 102
Coke, Alice Hedge 131
Comanche 74, 88, 116
Common Pot 136
communitism 15, 46
Conley, Robert 61, 89
continuance 13, 27, 67, 69, 78, 101, 140, 145, 162, 189
Cook-Lynn, Elizabeth 136, 141, 143, 150, 151
Cooper, James Fenimore 8, 56, 62, 67, 188
Copway, George 59
Cortes, Hernan 30, 31
Coushatta 116
Coutts, Antone Bazil 177, 178
Coutts, Joe 1, 177, 178
Coyote 26, 28, 115–117, 142
Crazy Horse 77
Curtis Act 92, 95
Curtis, Edward 69
Cusick, David 59

Dakota 37, 38, 130, 131, 141, 148, 187; North Dakota 1, 108, 124, 126, 158, 165, 177, 181n.4, 184; South 65, 90, 130
Dakota Access Pipeline 57, 185, 193
Darley, Felix Octavia Carr 44
Dawes Act *see* Allotment Act
Dawes, Henry 69
Deer, Sarah 177
Deloria, Ella 104, 147, 148
Deloria, Philip 87n.8, 110
Deloria Jr., Vine 69, 114
Densmore, Frances 160
Diaz, Natalie 131
Douglass, Frederick 57
Driskel, Quo-Li 29

Eastman, Charles 24, 66, 74, 78–81, 93, 94, 130, 148, 193
Eastman, Elaine Goodale 80
Eliot, John 9, 21, 43, 44, 53, 73
Erdrich, Heid 131
Erdrich, Louise 1, 2, 4, 108, 124–126, 152, 156, 158–180, 190, 193

Estes, Nick 187, 193
Eulogy on King Philip 57, 58
Eyre, Chris 155

Flathead 102
Fleur Pillager 125, 164–177
Fools Crow 9, 146–149; Fools Crow 147–149
Fort Laramie Treaty 72
Fort Marion 74, 75
Fowler, David 50
Fowler, Jacob 50
Fowler, Mary 48, 50
from Sand Creek 116, 117

Garret, Katherine 3, 4, 12, 41, 42, 48
Garrison, William Lloyd 57
George, Sally 54, 55
Gilio-Whitaker, Dina 187
ghost dance 77–81
Ghost Singer 145, 146
Glancy, Diane 61, 144, 145, 156
Goode, Batiste 36, 37
Gould, Janice 119
Gould, Rae 146
Great Law of Peace 33
Great Sioux Reservation 72
Great Sioux Uprising 78, 79, 131
Green, Michael D. 60, 145
Gross, Lawrence W. 163, 164, 173

Harjo, Joy 2, 9, 108, 113, 122–24, 129, 140, 167, 192, 194
Harvard Indian College 21, 73
Haudenosaunee 24–27, 33, 39n.23, 50, 85, 93, 136, 162, 186
Hausman, Blake 61, 143–145, 190, 193
Hayonwhatha *see* Hiawatha
Hayes, Ernestine 28, 38, 190, 194
Hieroglyphs 30
Hiacooms, Joel 21
Hiawatha 33, 58, 93; *Song of* 93
Hidatsa 185
Hobson, Brandon 156
Hogan, Linda 108, 109, 141
Hopi 119, 121. 191
Horned Serpent *see* Mishepeshu
House Made of Dawn 94, 104, 106, 107

Iagen"tci *see* Sky Woman
Indian Horse 156
Indian Nullification 57, 63
Indian Removal 57, 59, 60, 67
Indian Reorganization Act (I.R.A.) 101

"Indian's Looking-Glass for the White Man" 55–7, 192
Indian Territory 74, 88, 92, 109, 144; I.T. 90–93, 95

Jackson, Andrew 57, 59, 60–62, 90
Jackson, Helen Hunt 68
Jamestown 6, 7, 15, 129; Historic 5, 143; "Revisited" 128
Jensen, Toni 156
Johnson, Joseph 50
Johnson, E. Pauline 66, 93, 94, 114
Johnston, Basil 84, 160, 180
Jones, Peter 59
Jones, Stephen Graham 150, 156
Justice, Daniel Heath 11, 59, 61, 63, 192

Kelsey, Penelope Myrtle 37
Kimmerer, Robin Wall 186
Kiowa 28, 75, 88, 106, 116, 141, 186
King, Lisa 5, 137
King Philip's War 144
King, Thomas 18, 25, 26, 28, 122, 140–142, 191
Kinship 6, 8, 10, 13, 42, 44, 50, 58, 74, 102, 103, 135, 147, 159
Klammath 102

Lakota 36, 38, 57, 66, 68, 69, 70, 72, 77–80, 84, 93, 113, 114, 130, 148–150, 187, 193
Landes, Ruth 160, 180
Last of the Mohicans 8, 12, 67
Lenape 5, 137
Leon-Portilla, Miguel 30, 31
Life and Adventures of Joaquin Murieta 89
Little Big Horn 77, 93
Little Crow's War *see* Great Sioux Uprising
Longfellow 58, 93
Long Soldier, Layli 113, 129–131, 134, 193
Lookinghill, Brad 75
Love Medicine 108, 124, 125; love medicine 170, 173
Lyons, Scott 14, 135, 136, 192

Maddox, Lucy 81
Madsen, Deborah 176
Maidue 119
Mailhot, Theresa 156
Mandan 184
Mankato, Minnesota 78; "38" 78, 130
Many Lightnings 78
Marshall, John 60

Mashpee 56, 57, 186, 192
Mason Land Case 45, 47
Massasoit 14
Mathews, John Joseph 94–101, 190, 193
Mattaponi 8, 15
Mayan 30, 31
Maze of Injustice 4, 180
Mean Spirit 109, 141
McNickle, Darcy 101, 102, 112n.56, 114; Center 102
medicine lodge 169; Treaty of 74, 186
Menominee 102
Midiwiwin 37, 167, 180, 182n.39
Misshepeshu 166, 167, 170
Mississippian Culture 32, 33
Miwok 119
Mojave 131
Mohawk 58, 93, 94, 114
Mohegan 11, 12, 45, 47, 49–51, 58, 65, 73, 192
Mohican see *Last of the Mohicans*
Momaday, N. Scott 11, 28, 94, 104, 106, 114
Monacan 127, 128
Montauk 46–8, 50, 54
Moor's Charity School 73
Moore, David 150
Motecuhzoma 30
Mourning Dove 66, 93
Myers, Melissa 161

NAGPRA 146
Nahuatl 30, 31
NAISA 187
Nanabhozo (and variants) 29, 108, 162, 163, 172
Nanapush 108, 109, 158, 160–169, 171, 173–180
Native American Literary Renaissance 11, 88, 106, 108, 113, 141
Navajo 69, 105, 106, 146
Nesuton, Job 21
Nipmuc 21, 146
Norton, John 58

Oceti Sakowin 185, 189
Occom Circle Project 51
Occom, Samson 12, 41–43, 45–51, 53, 54, 58, 73, 78, 192
O'Connell, Barry 53, 192
Ojibway, 165, 180, 181; Ojibwe 37, 58, 59, 126, 158, 160, 162, 165, 167, 169, 172, 178, 180, 193

Okanagan 113
Oneida 46, 47
Onondaga 135, 191
Orange, Tommy 102, 156
Osage 56, 88, 94–101, 109, 141; *The Osage* 97
Osage Reign of Terror 96, 109,
Oskison, John Milton 93
Ortiz, Simon 11, 108, 113–120, 123, 128, 131, 136, 137, 155
Ousamequin 14
Owens, Louis 94, 104, 110, 147

Parker, Arthur 24–29, 33–35, 66, 84, 85, 136, 191
Parker, Eli 24
Parker, Robert Dale 58
Paul, Mihku 131
Paul, Moses 42, 47–50; *A Sermon Preached at the Execution* of 41, 50
Pauline Puyat 158, 161, 165–7, 169–173
Peacemaker 33, 136
Peterson, Nancy J. 159
Pequot 3, 11, 12, 34, 35, 51, 54, 55, 63, 186, 192; War 11, 34, 51
Perdue, Theda 60, 61, 190
Petroglyph 30, 167
Pillager 161, 164, 165, 167, 171, 175, 176
Pine Ridge 68, 77–80, 90, 91, 96, 114
Pocahontas 5–8, 15, 21, 73, 93, 191
Pokagan, Simon 66
post-Indian warrior 29, 120
Powhatan 5–7; confederacy 6, 15
Powless Jr., Irving 135, 136, 191
Pratt, Richard Henry 69, 73–75, 81, 84
Printer, James 21
Pueblo 104–106, 109, 114, 115, 136, 141
Pushing the Bear 61, 144

Quipu 30, 37

Raven 26, 28, 38, 149; *Tao of* 28
Red Power 103, 114, 141
Red Progressives 65, 66, 77, 78, 81, 84, 85, 90
Revard, Carter 114
Ridge, John 59, 60, 89
Ridge, John Rollin 66, 89, 90
Riding the Trail of Tears 61, 143, 144, 190, 193
Riggs, Lynn Rollie 101, 110
Rifkin, Mark 98
Rolfe, John 8, 73

Rose, Wendy 114, 119–123, 127, 189, 191
Ross, John 59–61, 90
The Round House 1, 2, 4, 158, 170, 176–181; structure 180

SAIL 187
Sand Creek 10, 117–119, 128
Satanta 186
Savageau, Cheryl 97, 127, 190, 193
Schoolcraft, Jane Johnston 58, 114
Schoolcraft, Henry Rowe 58
Selu 27, 192
Seminole 92, 116
Seneca 24, 34, 85, 191
Sequoyah 59, 188; state of 88, 92, 93
Shanley, Katherine 150
Shinnecock 46, 50
Silko, Leslie Marmon 11, 106, 107, 114, 115, 141, 156
Sioux 65, 72, 78, 82, 103, 150, 184, 187; *My People the Sioux* 76
Sitting Bull 72
Sky Woman 24, 25, 162
Smith, John 6
Smoke Signals 10, 155, 188
Snyder, Michael 97
Society of American Indians (S.A.I.) 24, 84, 85
Son of the Forest 52–55, 65, 90, 190, 192
Spokane 2, 10, 150, 152, 155
Standing Bear, Luther 66, 70, 74, 76–81, 94
Standing bear, Henry 84
Standing Rock 57, 72, 101, 184–190, 193, 194
Sundown 93–103, 107, 190, 193
Survivance 4, 13, 15, 29, 81, 99, 100, 102, 120, 139, 140, 145, 149, 159, 165, 189

Tamez, Margo 131
Tanner, John 160, 162, 174
Tapahonso, Lucy 114
Tayo 106, 107, 109, 115
Tenochtitlan 30, 31
Thoreau, Henry David 43, 57, 184, 185
Tlingit 28, 194
Tracks 108, 109, 124, 125, 158–177, 179, 180, 190, 193
Trail of Tears 10, 58–63, 143–145, 190, 193
Treaty of New Echota 61, 72, 89
Turner, Frederic Jackson 68
Turtle Island 9, 25, 93, 114, 162

Turtle Mountain Band, 158, 193; Reservation 125, 126, 152, 160, 174, 176, 181n.4

Underwater Panther *see* Mishepeshu

Van Camp, Richard 156
Vanishing Race 69
Vizenor, Gerald 11, 15, 29, 68, 92, 93, 107, 108, 120, 131, 139, 156, 162, 181
Vonnegut, Kurt 79

Wagamese, Richard 84, 156
Walters, Anna Lee 145, 146
Wampum 11, 14, 29, 30, 33, 34, 36, 37, 45, 51, 93, 190, 191
Warren, William 160, 165, 181
Warrior, Robert 11, 56, 63, 71, 80, 100, 136, 137, 139–141
Waterlily 104, 147, 149
water protectors 186
Weaver, Jace 15, 46, 53, 90, 136, 139
Welch, James 9, 108, 114, 130, 146–149, 156
Wet'suwet'en 187
Wheelock, Eleazar 46, 47, 50, 51, 73

Whereas 113, 129, 130, 134, 193
White Buffalo Woman 36
White, John 44, 45
Wildcat, Daniel 10
Windzer, Chal 95
Winnemucca, Sarah 66, 93, 94
winter counts 29, 30, 36, 38, 75, 160
Wood, Karenne 127–129, 155
Womack, Craig 11, 23, 91, 02, 110, 136, 137, 139, 192
Worcester, Samuel 59
Worcester vs. the State of Georgia 60
Wounded Knee 10, 68, 77, 79, 80, 91, 114, 193
Wovoka 79
Wynema 90, 91
Wyss, Hilary 30

x-mark 14, 77, 135, 176, 192

Yankton Sioux 65, 82, 103

Zitkala-Sa *see* Gertrude Simmons Bonnin
Zobel, Melissa Tantiquidgeon 50, 51

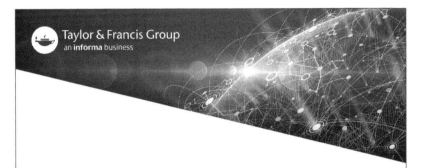

Printed in Poland
by Amazon Fulfillment
Poland Sp. z o.o., Wrocław